11+ Non-Verbal Reasoning
Spatial
For GL Assessment

Spatial Reasoning questions are a seriously tricky part of the GL 11+, so we've made a whole book of 10-Minute Tests to help children master them!

Each test is packed with GL-style practice at the perfect level for ages 10-11, all with detailed answers included. Nobody does 11+ prep better than CGP.

10-Minute Tests

Ages 10-11

How to access your free Online Edition

This book includes a free Online Edition to read on your PC, Mac or tablet.
You'll just need to go to **cgpbooks.co.uk/extras** and enter this code:

2296 4263 3054 5054

By the way, this code only works for one person. If somebody else has used this book before you, they might have already claimed the Online Edition.

How to use this book

This book is made up of 10-minute tests and puzzle pages.
There are answers and detailed explanations at the back of the book.

10-Minute Tests

- There are 33 tests in this book, each containing 13 or 14 questions.

- Each test is designed to focus on spatial questions that your child could come across in their 11+ test. They cover a variety of skills and techniques at the right difficulty levels.

- Your child should aim to score at least 11 in each 10-minute test.
If they score less than this, use their results to work out the areas they need more practice on.

- If your child hasn't managed to finish the test in time, they need to work on increasing their speed, whereas if they have made a lot of mistakes, they need to work more carefully.

- Keep track of your child's scores using the progress chart on the inside back cover of the book.

Puzzle Pages

- There are 10 puzzle pages in this book, which are a great break from test-style questions.
They encourage children to practise the same skills that they will need in the test, but in a fun way.

Published by CGP

Editors:
Emma Clayton, Katherine Faudemer, Emily Sheraton.

With thanks to Amanda MacNaughton and Glenn Rogers for the proofreading.

ISBN: 978 1 78908 210 4
Printed by Elanders Ltd, Newcastle upon Tyne
Clipart from Corel®

Based on the classic CGP style created by Richard Parsons.

Text, design, layout and original illustrations © Coordination Group Publications Ltd. (CGP) 2018
All rights reserved.

Photocopying this book is not permitted, even if you have a CLA licence.
Extra copies are available from CGP with next day delivery • 0800 1712 712 • www.cgpbooks.co.uk

Contents

Question Type Examples 2

Test 1 9
Test 2 12
Test 3 15

Puzzles 1 18

Test 4 19
Test 5 22
Test 6 25

Puzzles 2 28

Test 7 29
Test 8 32
Test 9 35

Puzzles 3 38

Test 10 39
Test 11 42
Test 12 45

Puzzles 4 48

Test 13 49
Test 14 52
Test 15 55

Puzzles 5 58

Test 16 59
Test 17 62
Test 18 65

Puzzles 6 68

Test 19 69
Test 20 72
Test 21 75

Puzzles 7 78

Test 22 79
Test 23 82
Test 24 85
Test 25 88

Puzzles 8 91

Test 26 92
Test 27 95
Test 28 98
Test 29 101

Puzzles 9 104

Test 30 105
Test 31 108
Test 32 111
Test 33 114

Puzzles 10 117

Glossary 118

Answers 119

Question Type Examples

These pages contain a completed example question for each question type that appears in this book. Have a look through them to familiarise yourself with the question types before you do the tests.

Building Blocks

Work out which set of blocks can be put together to make the 3D figure on the left.

Example:

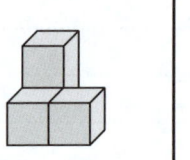 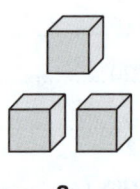 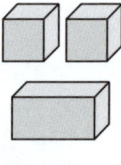  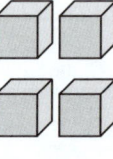

                                   a   b   c   d

Answer: b

The block at the bottom of B rotates to become the block at the back of the figure. The two cubes move to the front.

Complete the Shape

Without rotating the figure on the left, work out which option fits onto it to make the 3D shape in the grey box.

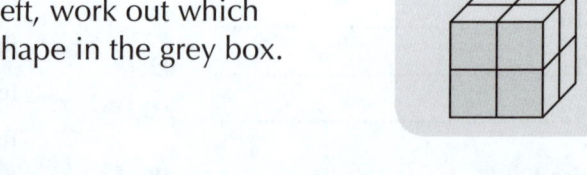

Example:

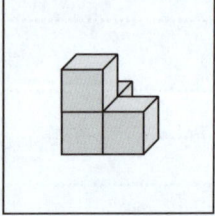 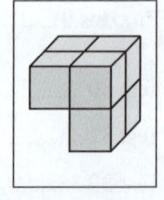 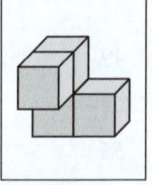 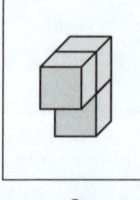 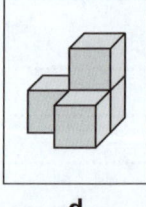

                                   a   b   c   d

Answer: d

D rotates 90 degrees anticlockwise in the plane of the page (see the glossary on page 118) to fit with the figure on the left.

3D Rotation

Work out which 3D figure in the grey box has been rotated to make the new 3D figure.

Example:

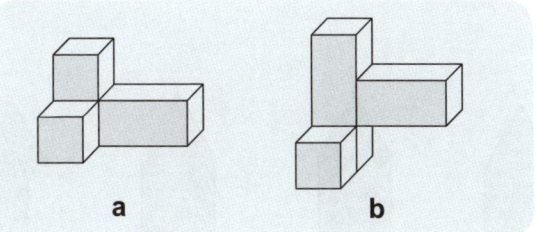 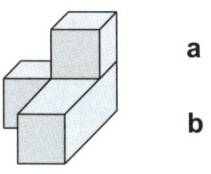

Answer: a

Figure A has been rotated 90 degrees right-to-left (see the glossary on page 118).

Fold along the Line

Work out which option shows the figure on the left when folded along the dotted line.

Example:

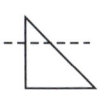 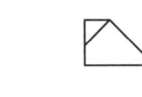  

a b c d

Answer: a

The small triangle above the dotted line folds down.

Fold and Punch

A square is folded and then a hole is punched, as shown on the left.
Work out which option shows the square when unfolded.

Example:

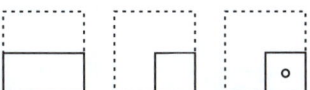 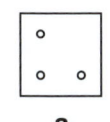 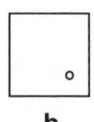 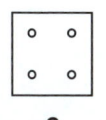 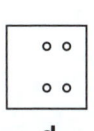

a b c d

Answer: c

Connecting Shapes

Work out which option shows how the three shapes will look when they are joined by matching the sides with the same letter.

Example:

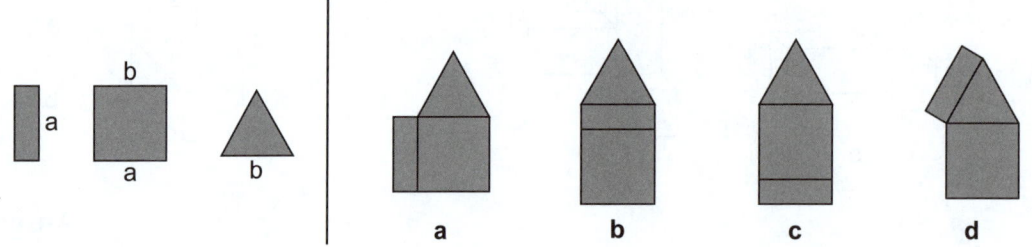

Answer: c

In options B and D, the square is only connected to one of the other shapes. In option A, the rectangle is connected to the wrong side of the square.

Hidden Shape

Work out which option contains the hidden shape shown. It should be the same size and orientation.

Example:

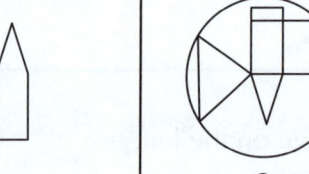 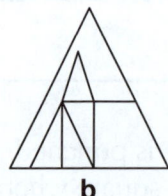 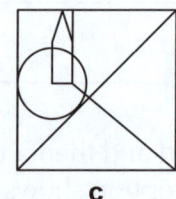 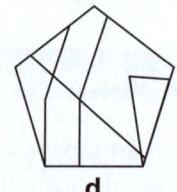

Answer: b

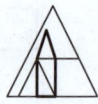

For the 2D Views of 3D Shapes questions, you could be asked to pick out the view from the **left**, **right**, **back** or from **above** the 3D figure. Make sure you read the question carefully.

2D Views of 3D Shapes

Work out which option is a 2D view from **above** the 3D figure shown.

Example:

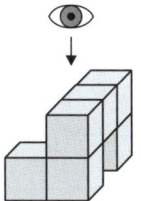  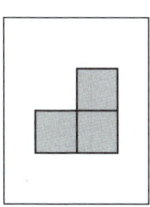 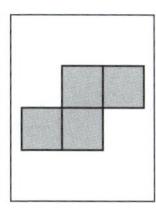 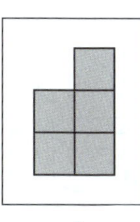

a　　　　b　　　　c　　　　d

Answer: a

There are four blocks visible from above, which rules out B and D.
There is a line of three blocks on the right-hand side of the shape, which rules out C.

Work out which option is a 2D view from the **left** of the 3D figure shown.

Example:

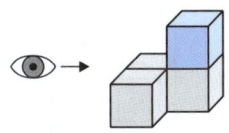 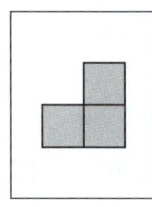 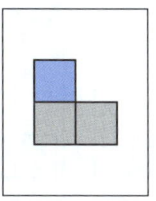 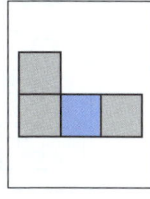 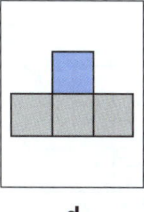

a　　　　b　　　　c　　　　d

Answer: b

There are three blocks visible from the left, which rules out C and D.
There is a blue block at the top of the figure, which rules out A.

For the Different Views of 3D Shapes questions, you could be asked to find the view from the **left**, **right**, **back** or from **above** the 3D figure. Make sure you read the question carefully.

Different Views of 3D Shapes

Work out which option is the 3D figure viewed from the **right**.

Example:

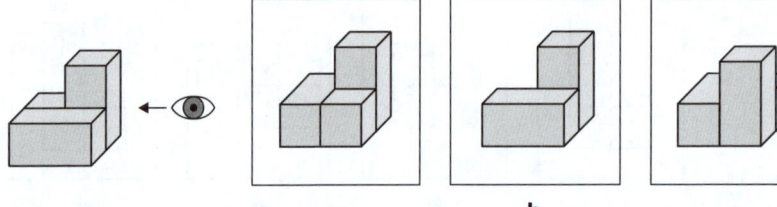

a   b   c   d

Answer: c

There is a vertical block two cubes high visible at the front when viewed from the right, which rules out A, B and D.

Work out which option is the 3D figure viewed from the **back**.

Example:

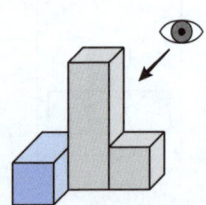 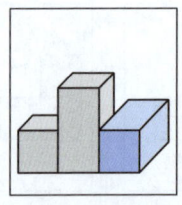 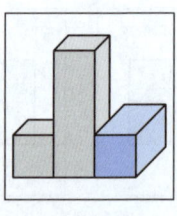 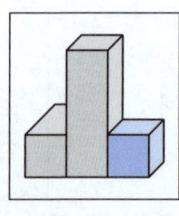 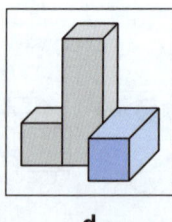

a   b   c   d

Answer: b

In option A, the middle block is the wrong size. The cube is grey, which rules out C. When viewed from the back, the blue block should go away from you, which rules out D.

For questions involving nets, the net must be folded **into** the page —
see the glossary on page 118.

Cubes and Nets

Work out which of the four cubes can be made from the net.

Example:

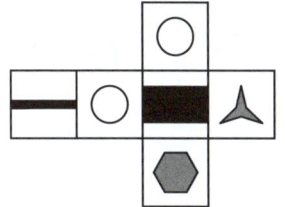            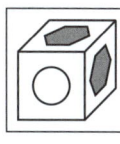

                                             a   b   c   d

Answer: c

There is no black circle, which rules out A. The thick black line and the thin black line must be on opposite sides, which rules out B. There is only one grey hexagon, which rules out D.

Partial Nets

Work out which of the four partial nets can be folded to make the cube on the left.

Example:

   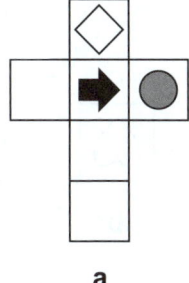   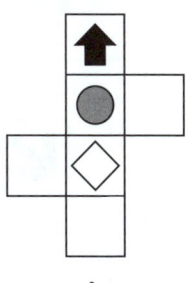   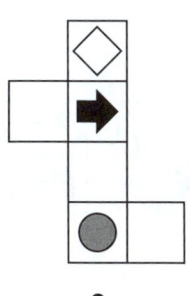   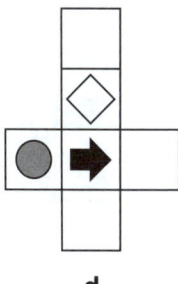

                                           a   b   c   d

Answer: d

The arrow points away from the circle, which rules out A.
None of the shapes can be on opposite sides, which rules out B and C.

Shaded Nets

Work out which of the 3D shapes can be made from the net.

Example:

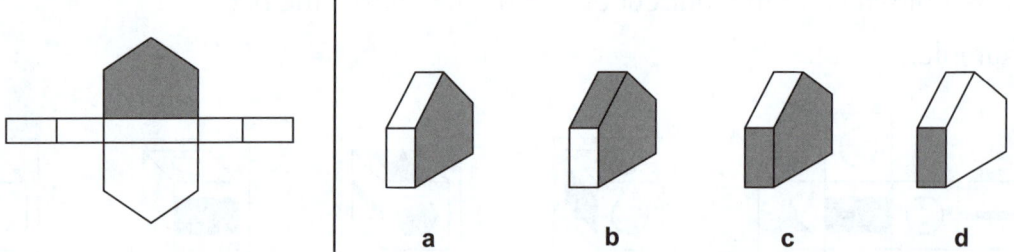

Answer: a

In the net, all the rectangular faces are white, which rules out B, C and D.

Cube Views

The figures on the left show different views of the same cube. All the cube faces are different. Work out which of the options should replace the blue cube face.

Example:

                                                            a   b   c   d

Answer: b

In the first two figures, the grey triangle points to the white heart. So in the third figure, the grey triangle must also point to the white heart.

Test 1

You have **10 minutes** to do this test. Circle the letter for each correct answer.

> Work out which option shows how the three shapes will look when they are joined by matching the sides with the same letter.

1.

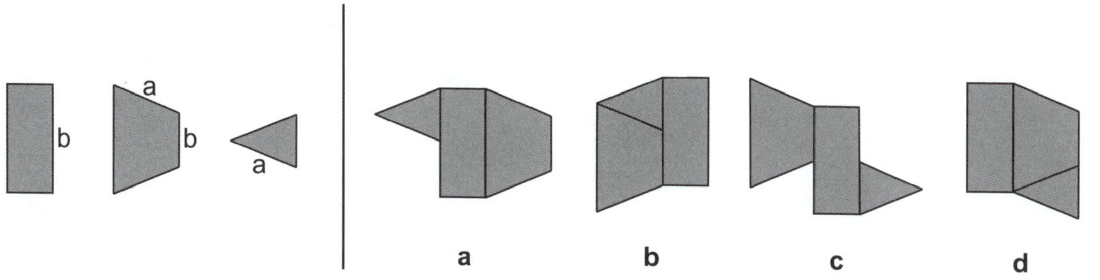

2.

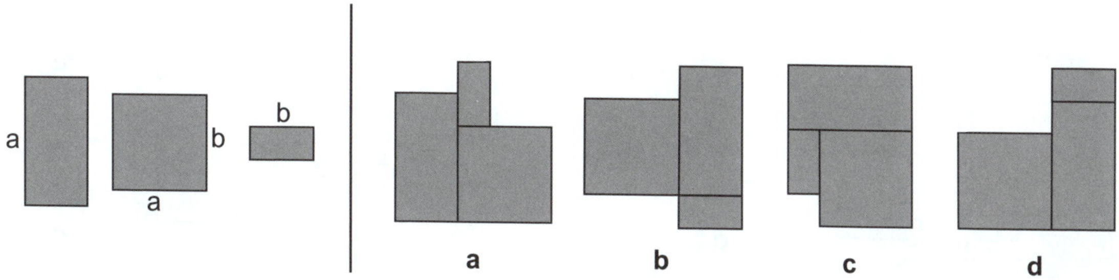

3.

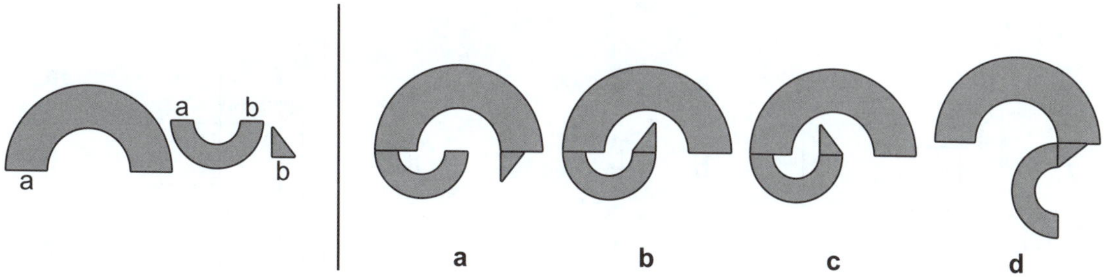

4.

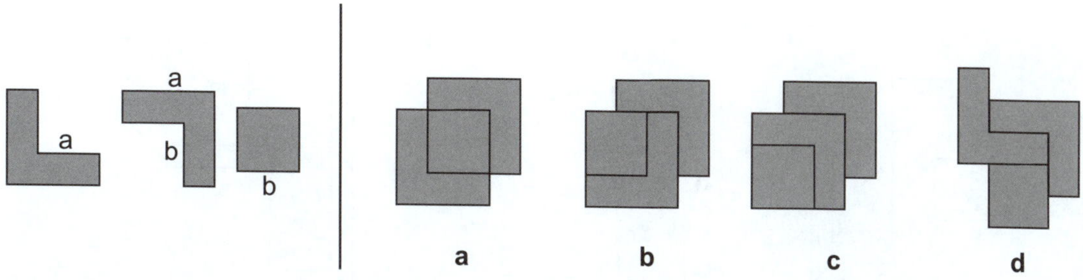

Work out which 3D figure in the grey box has been rotated to make the new 3D figure.

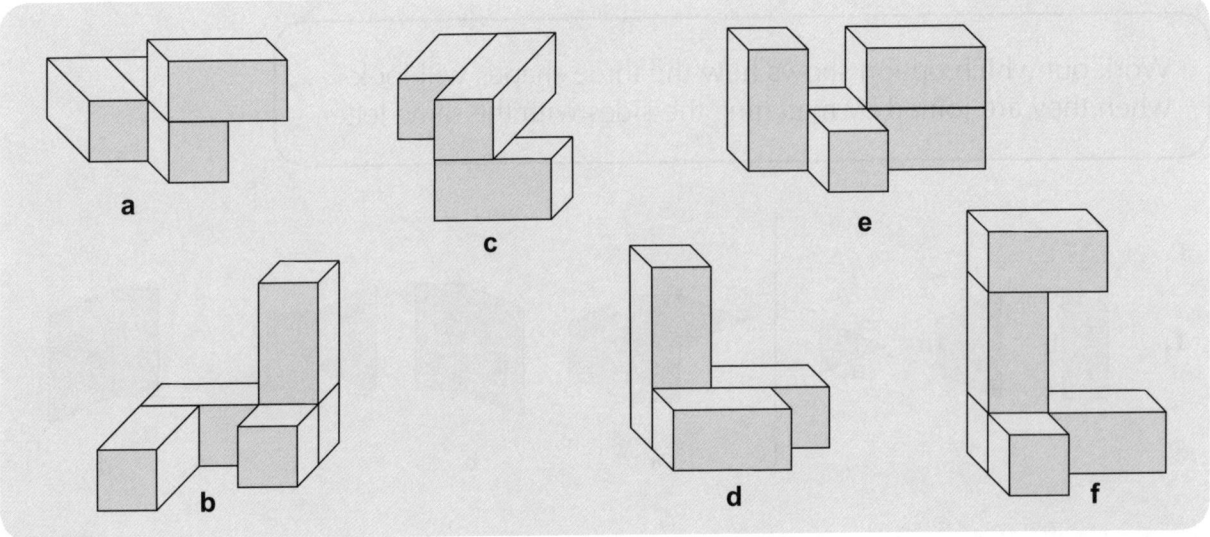

5.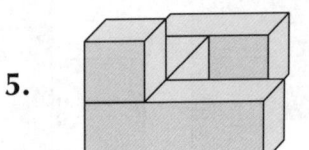

a   d
b   e
c   f

6.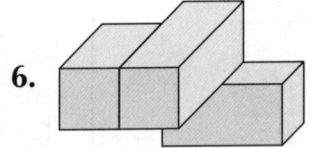

a   d
b   e
c   f

7.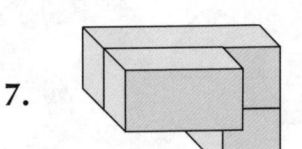

a   d
b   e
c   f

8.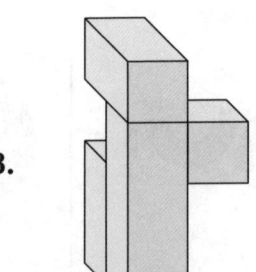

a   d
b   e
c   f

9.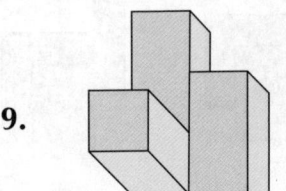

a   d
b   e
c   f

10.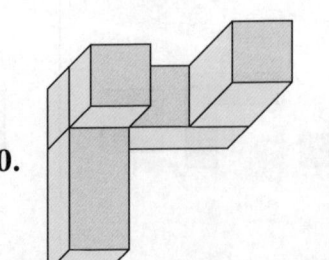

a   d
b   e
c   f

Work out which of the four cubes can be made from the net.

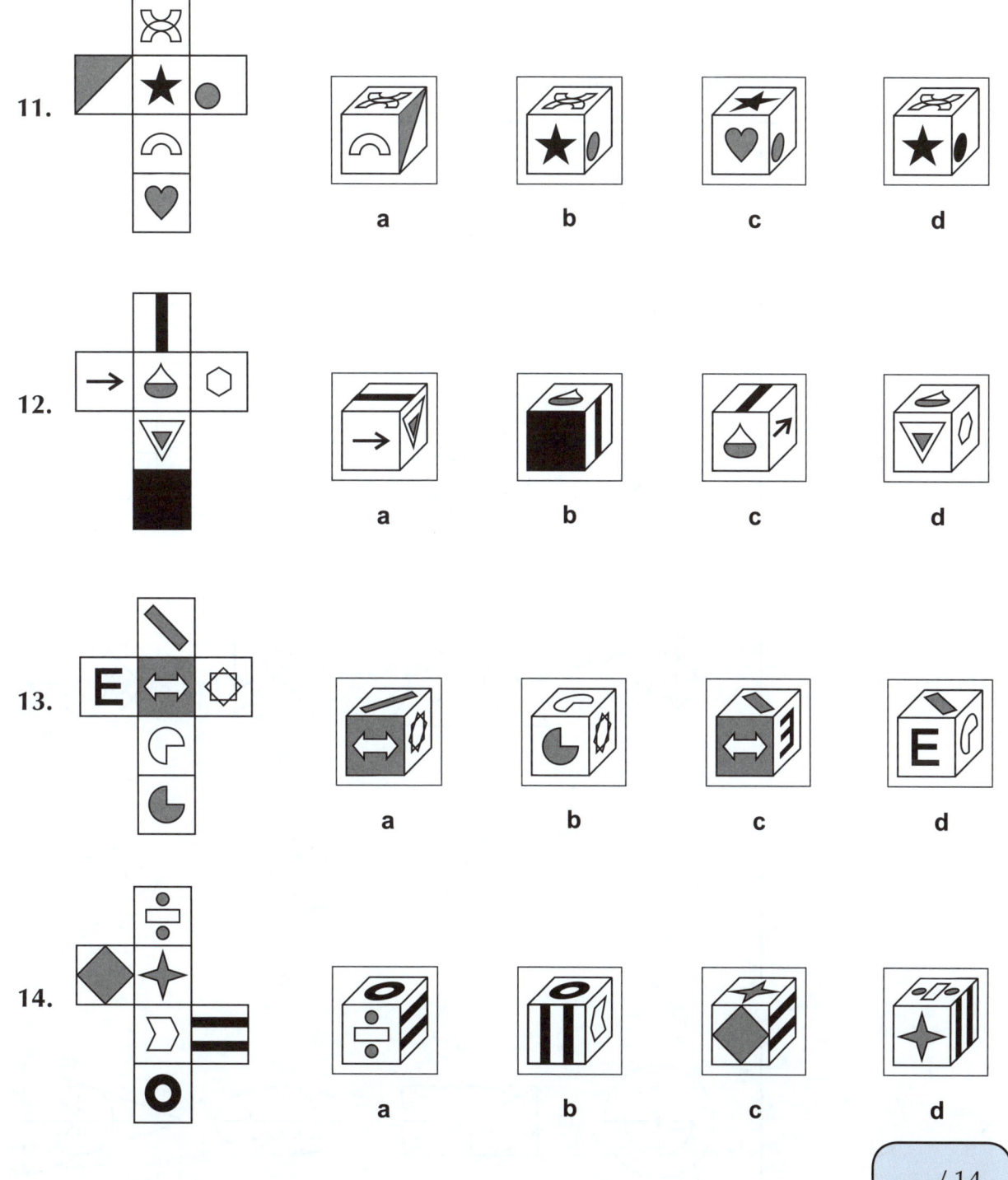

Test 2

You have **10 minutes** to do this test. Circle the letter for each correct answer.

Work out which option contains the hidden shape shown.
It should be the same size and orientation.

1. |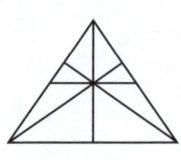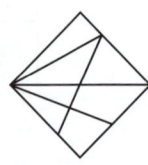
                           a   b   c   d

2.  |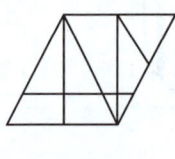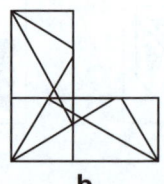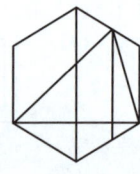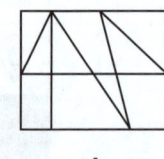
                           a   b   c   d

3. |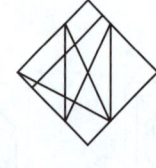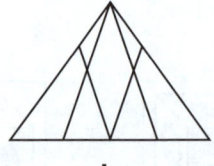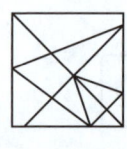
                           a   b   c   d

4. |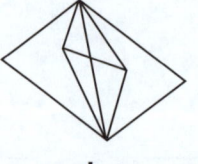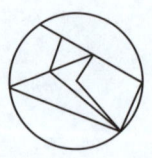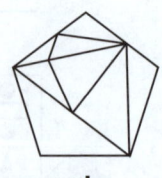
                           a   b   c   d

5. |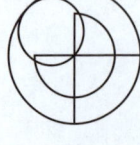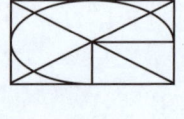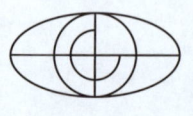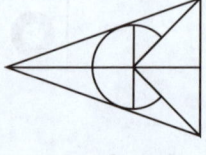
                           a   b   c   d

Work out which option is the 3D figure viewed from the **right**.

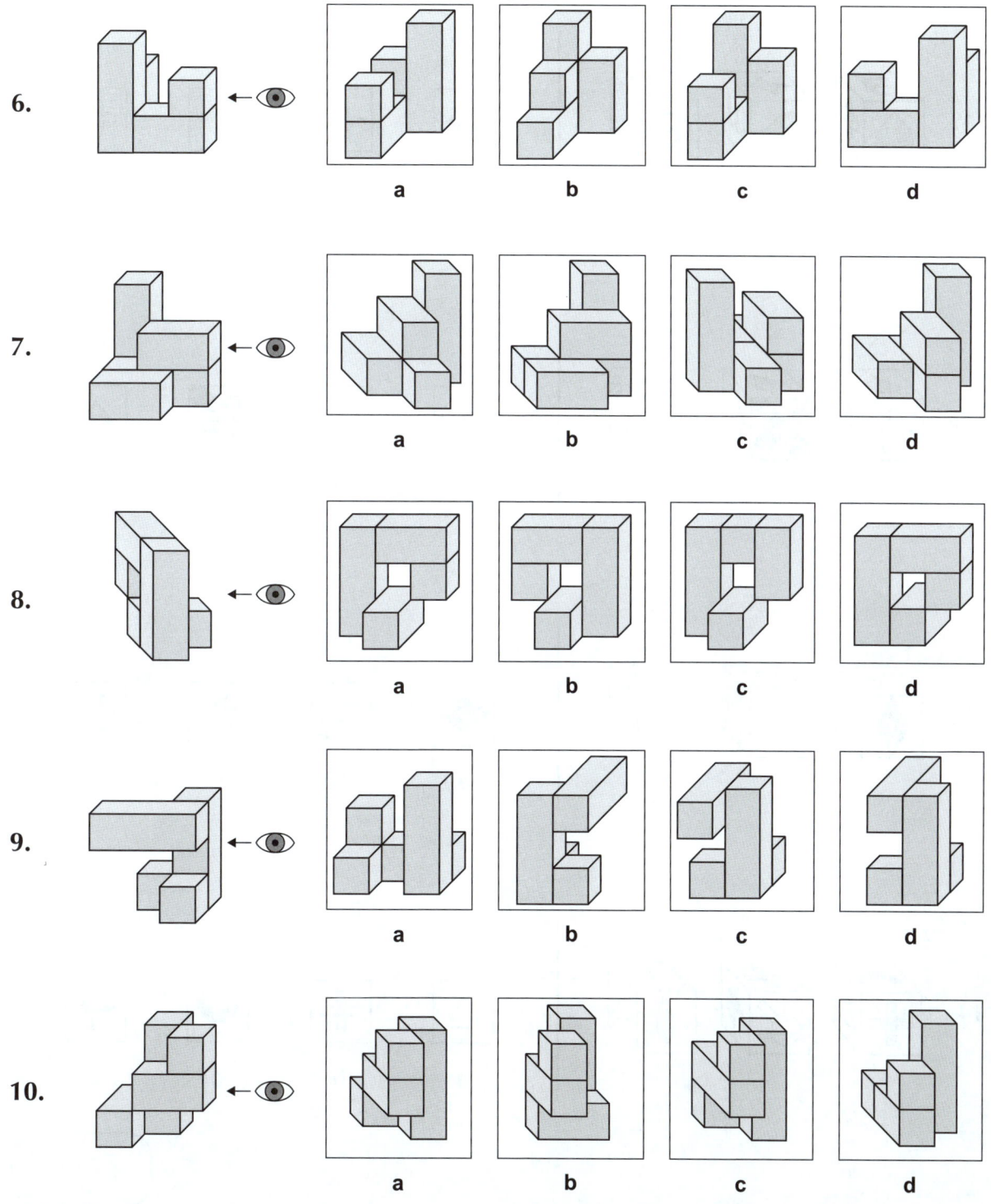

The figures on the left show different views of the same cube. All the cube faces are different. Work out which of the options should replace the blue cube face.

11.

12.

13.

14.

/ 14

Test 3

You have **10 minutes** to do this test. Circle the letter for each correct answer.

Work out which option shows the figure on the left when folded along the dotted line.

1. 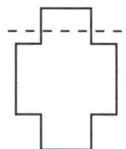   a   b   c   d

2.   a   b   c   d

3. 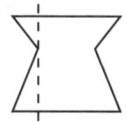    a    b    c    d

4. 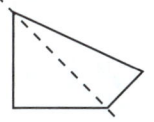    a   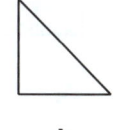 b    c   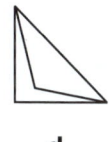 d

5. 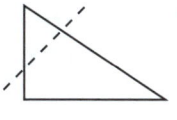   a   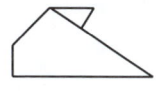 b   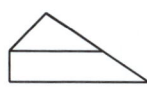 c   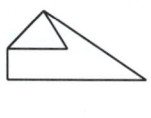 d

© CGP — not to be photocopied

Work out which option is a 2D view from the **back** of the 3D figure shown.

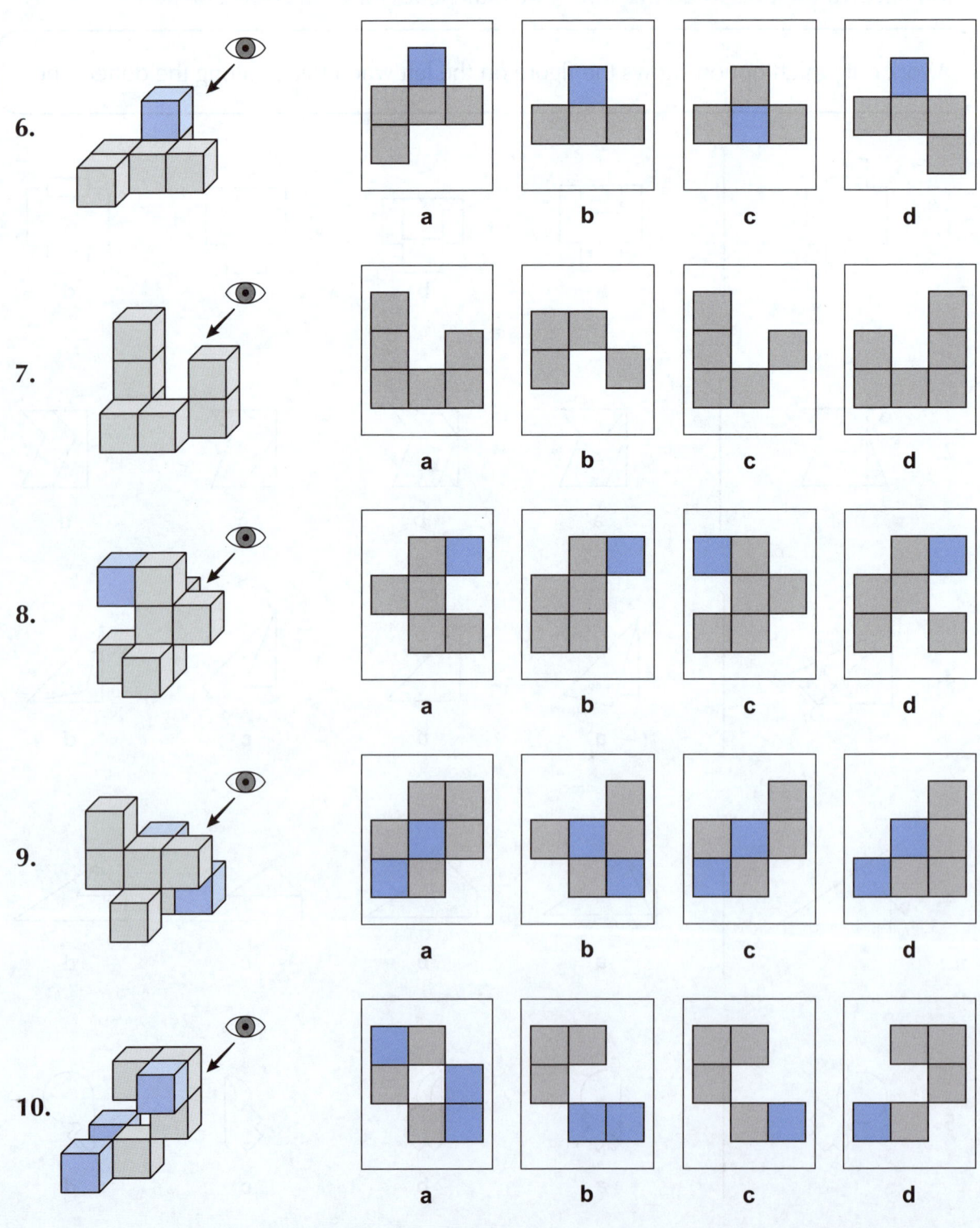

Work out which option shows how the three shapes will look when they are joined by matching the sides with the same letter.

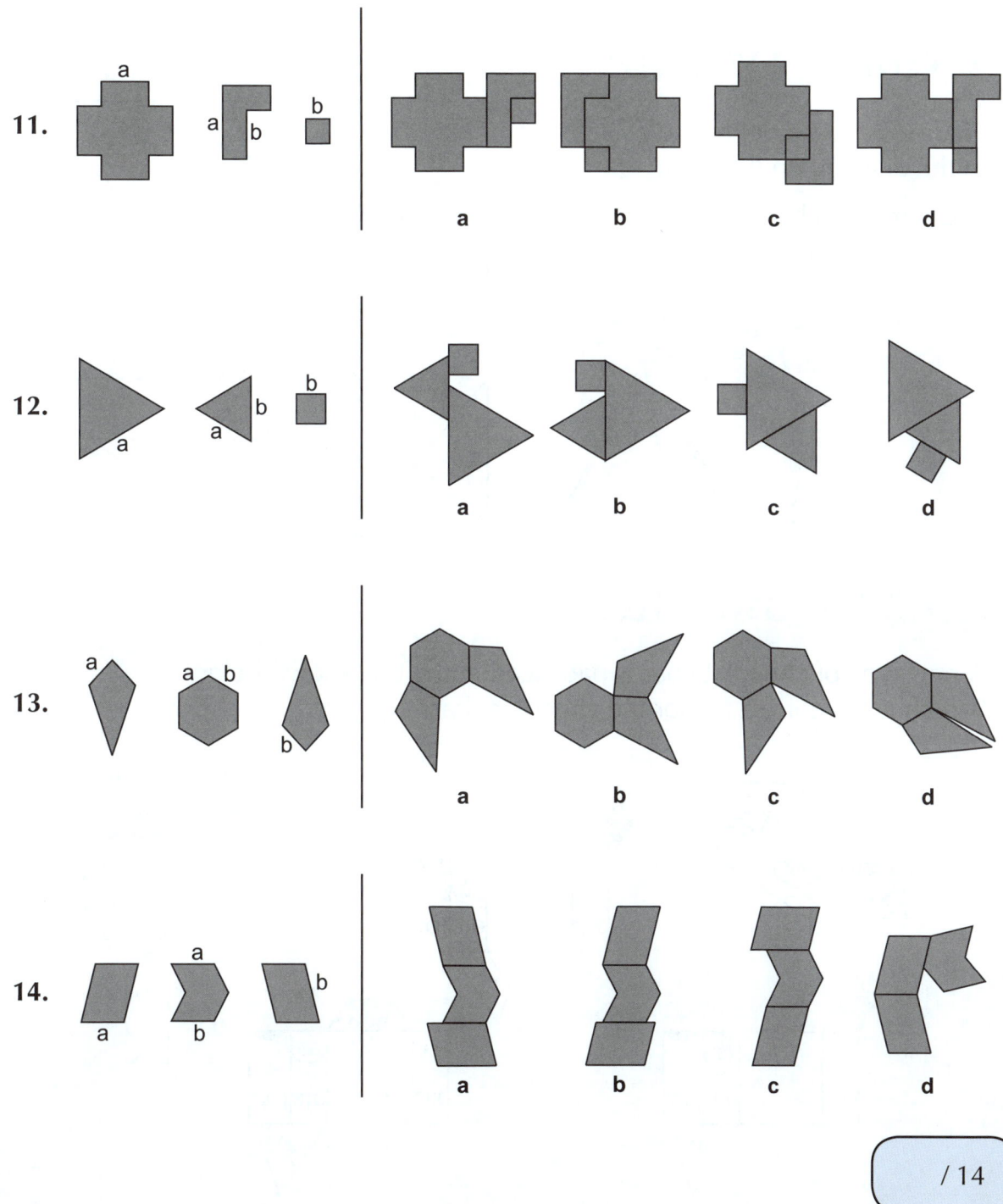

Puzzles 1

Try these puzzles to practise your skills with **hidden shapes** and **nets**.

Twinkle Twinkle...

Find **two** five-pointed stars in the diagram on the right.

The stars must both have five lines of symmetry.

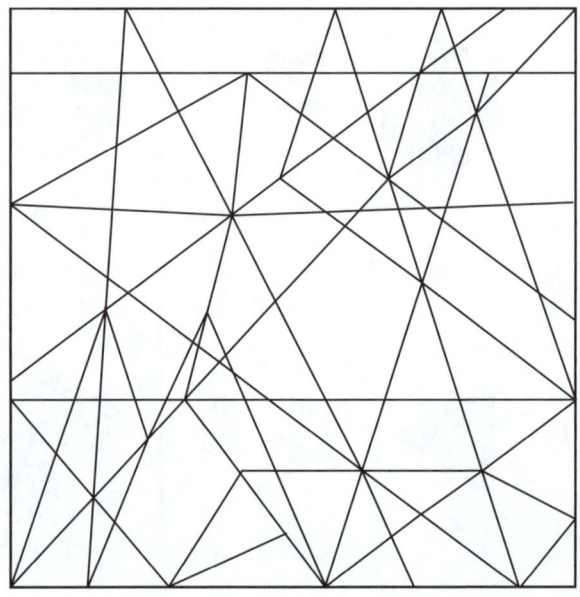

...Chocolate Baa

A new type of chocolate bar is packaged in the box shown below. Which is the correct net for the chocolate bar?

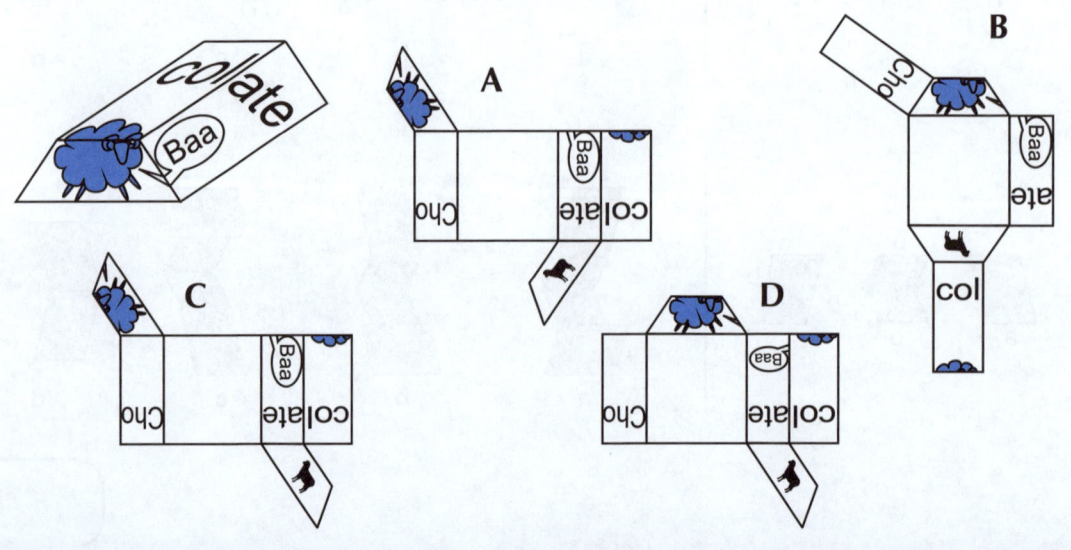

Test 4

You have **10 minutes** to do this test. Circle the letter for each correct answer.

Work out which option shows how the three shapes will look when they are joined by matching the sides with the same letter.

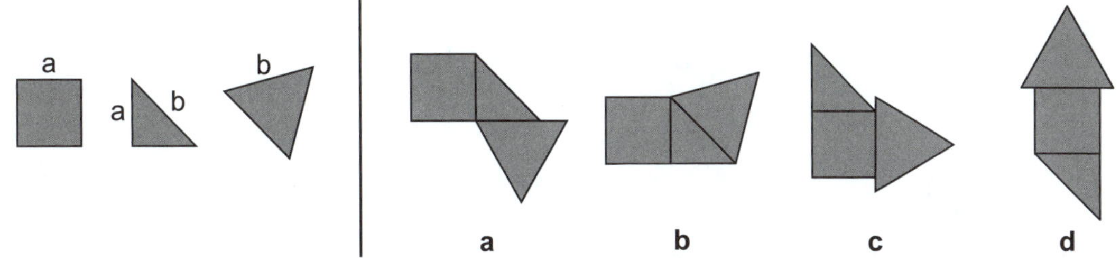

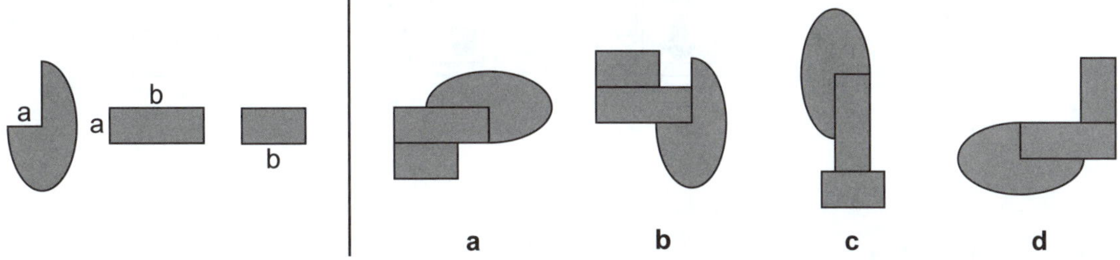

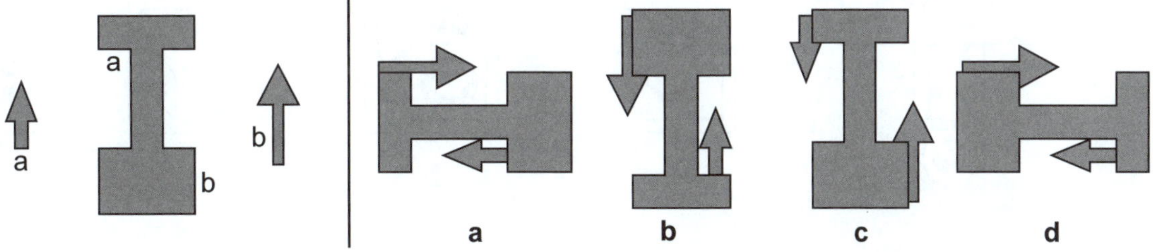

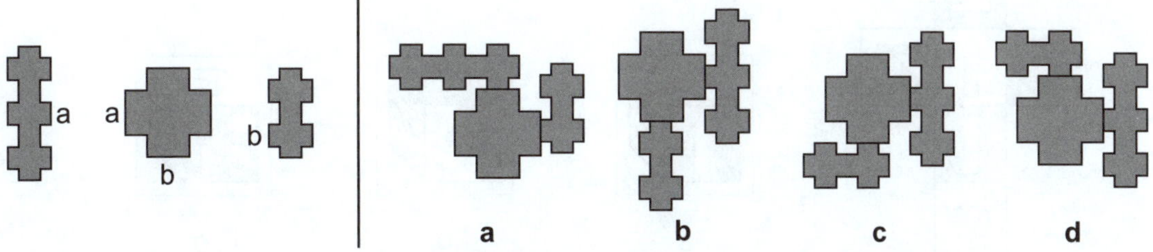

Work out which of the four cubes can be made from the net.

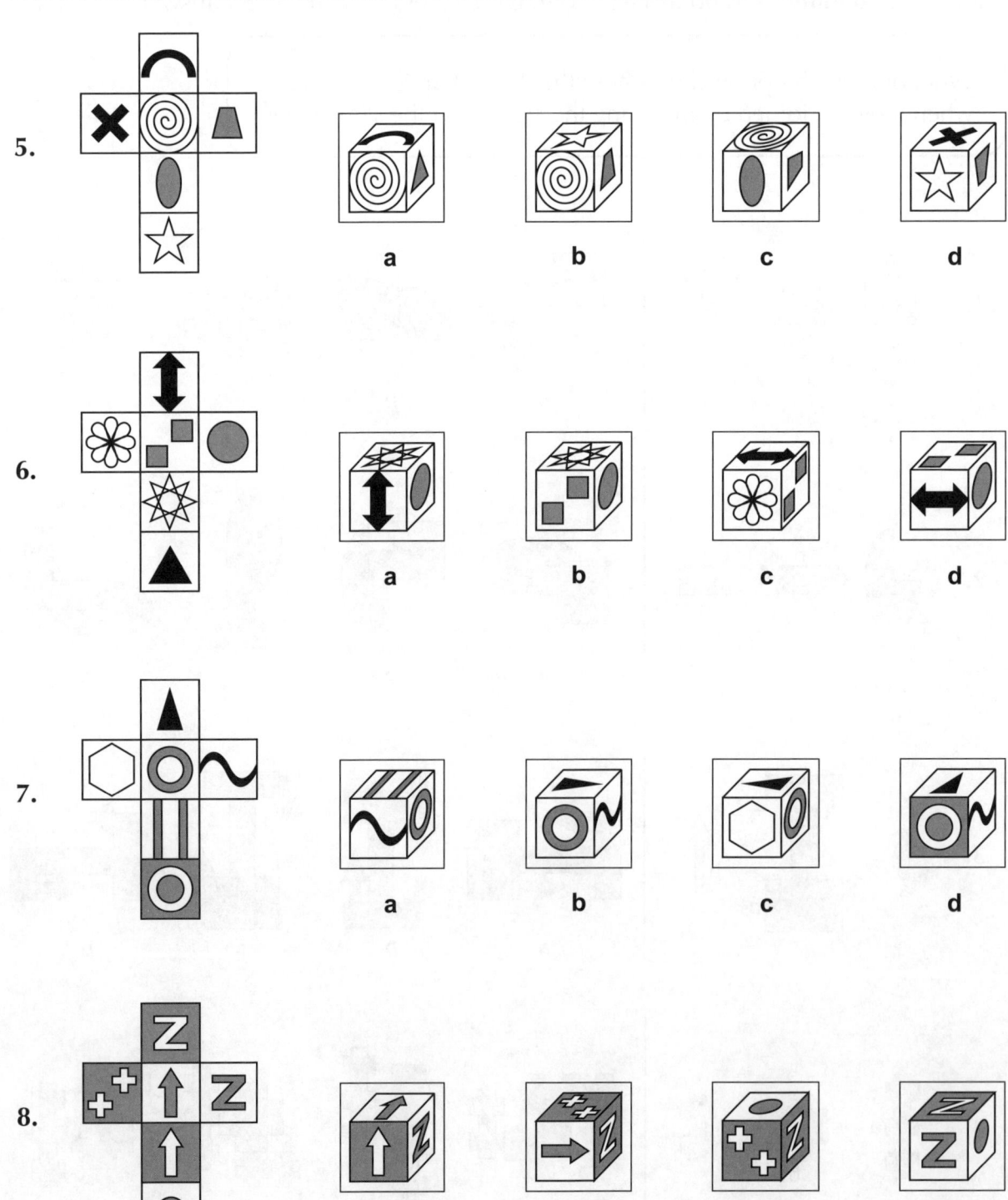

A square is folded and then a hole is punched, as shown on the left. Work out which option shows the square when unfolded.

Test 5

You have **10 minutes** to do this test. Circle the letter for each correct answer.

Work out which set of blocks can be put together to make the 3D figure on the left.

1.

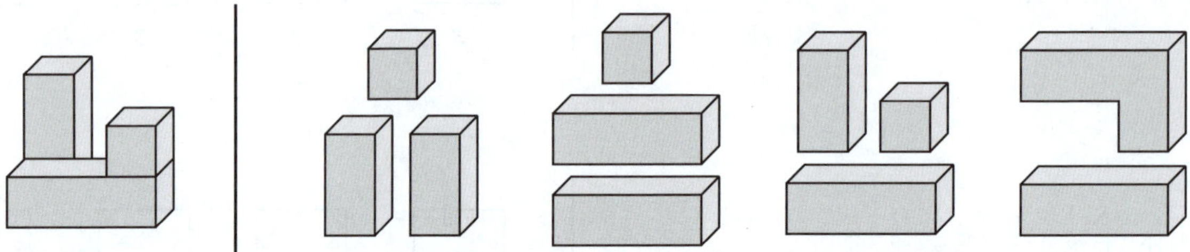

a   b   c   d

2.

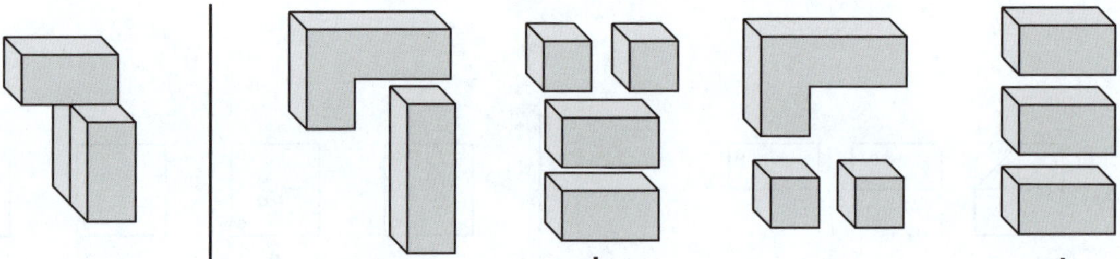

a   b   c   d

3.

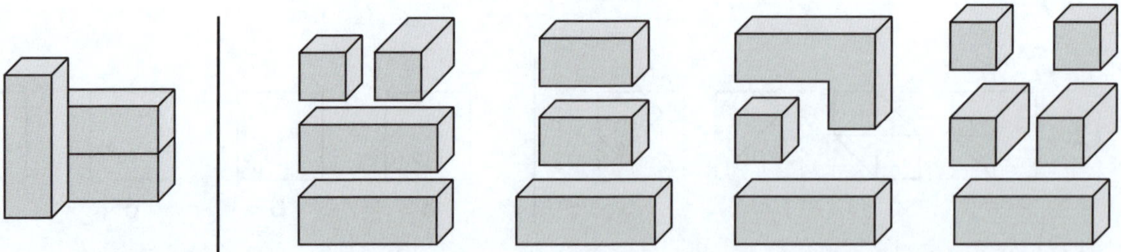

a   b   c   d

4.

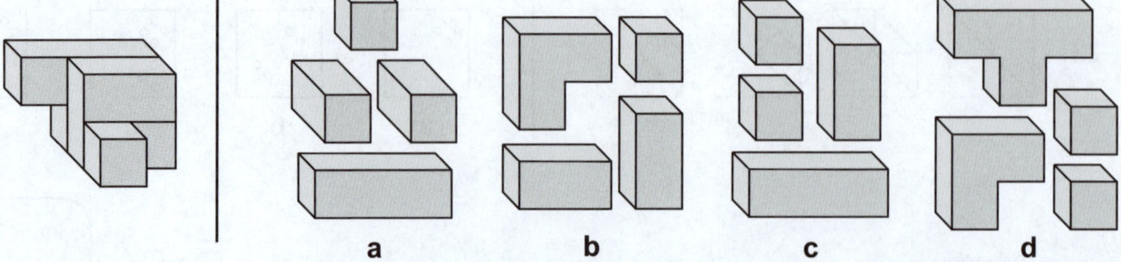

a   b   c   d

Test 5

Work out which option is a 2D view from **above** the 3D figure shown.

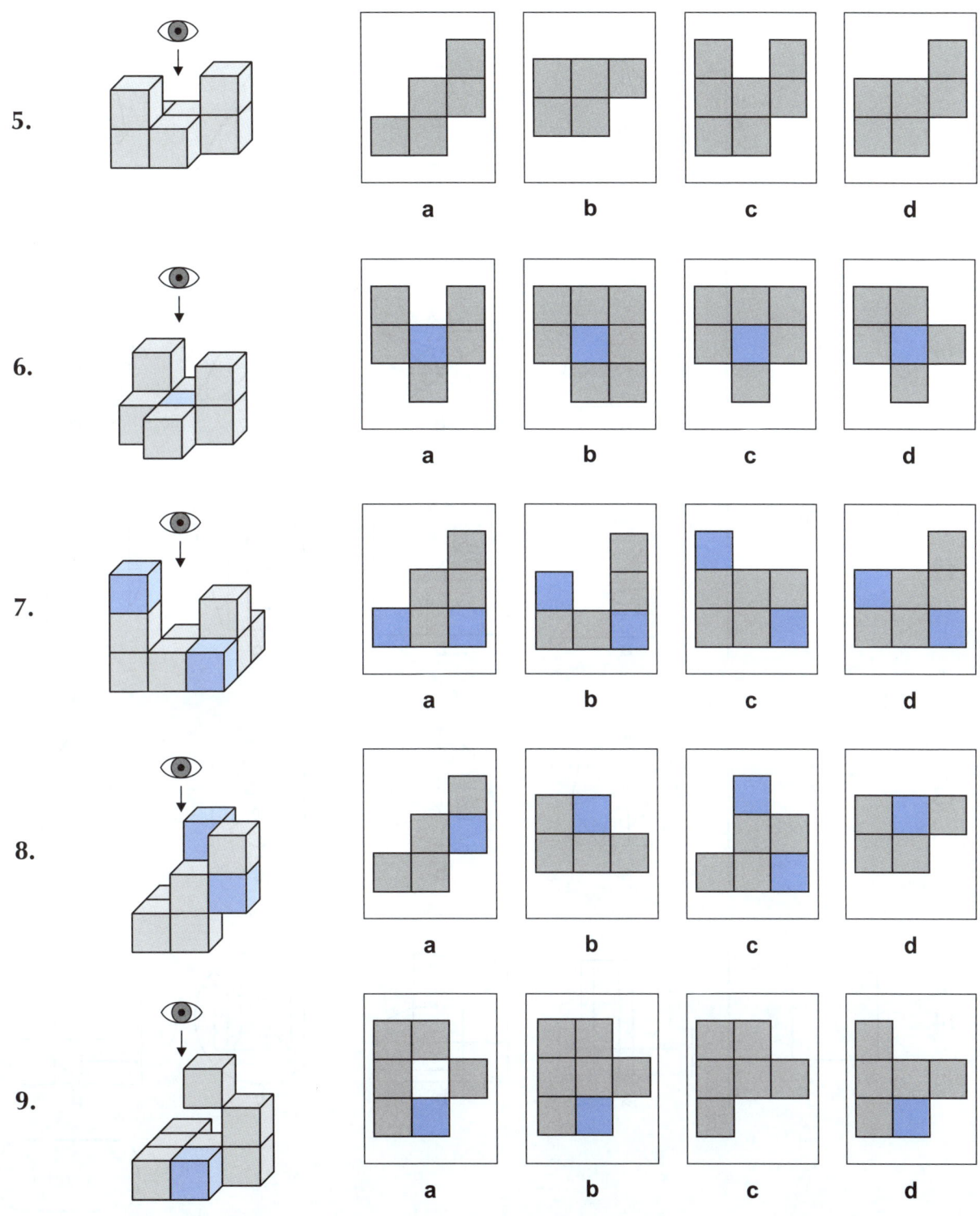

Work out which option contains the hidden shape shown. It should be the same size and orientation.

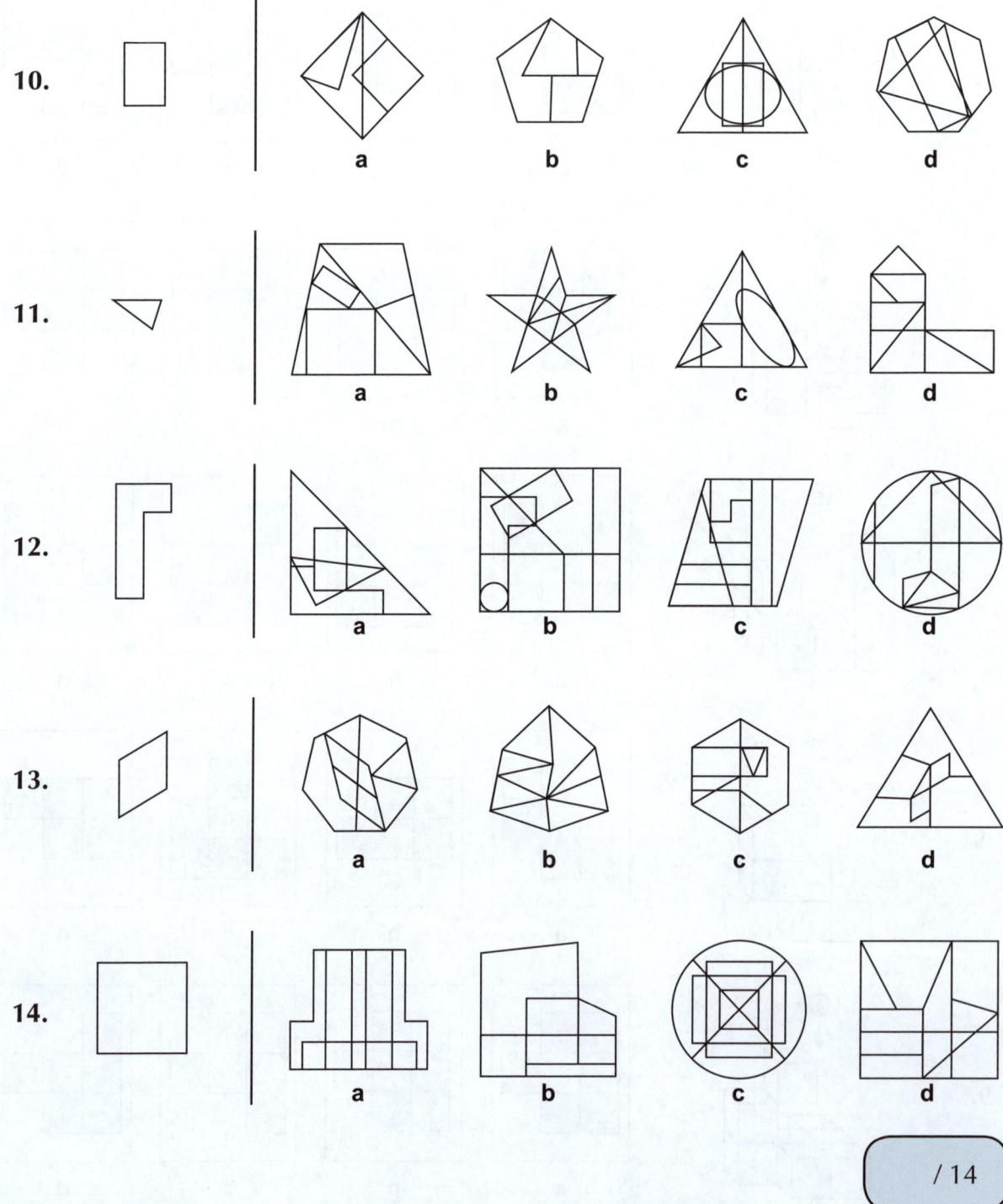

Test 6

You have **10 minutes** to do this test. Circle the letter for each correct answer.

Work out which option shows the figure on the left when folded along the dotted line.

1. 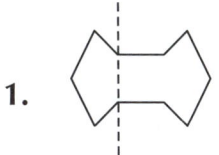 |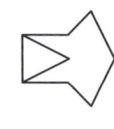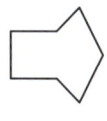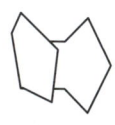

                                 a   b   c   d

2. 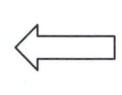 |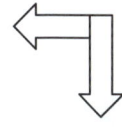

3.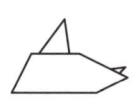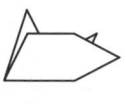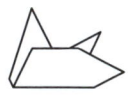

4.

5.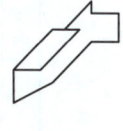

Without rotating the figure on the left, work out which option fits onto it to make the 3D shape in the grey box.

6.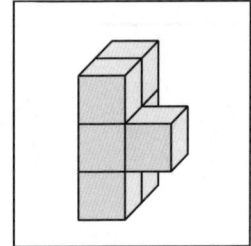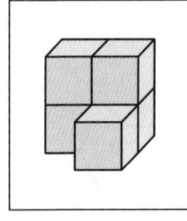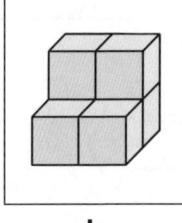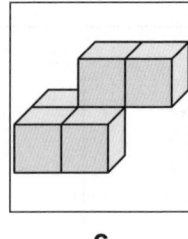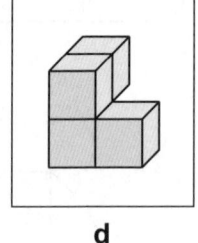
                             a   b   c   d

7.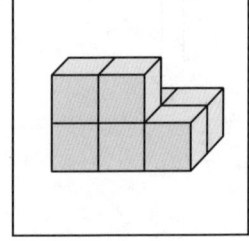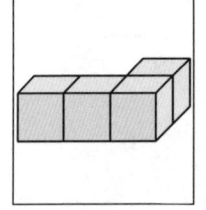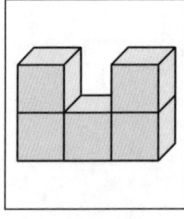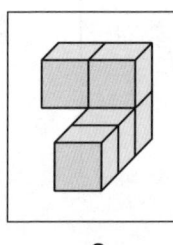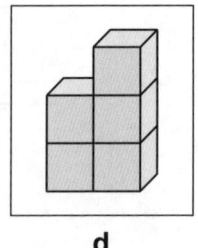
                             a   b   c   d

8.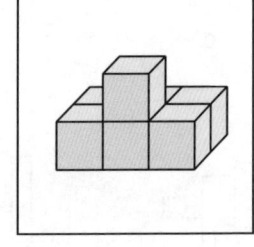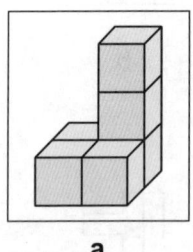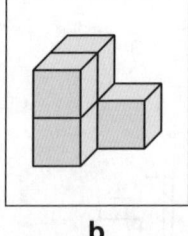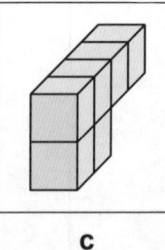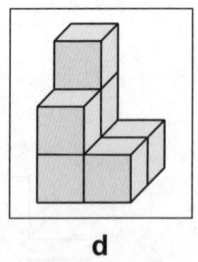
                             a   b   c   d

9.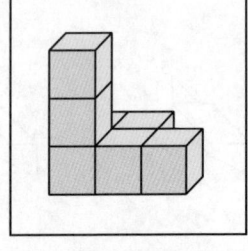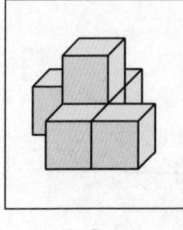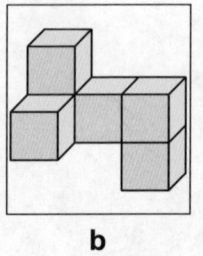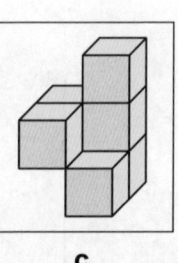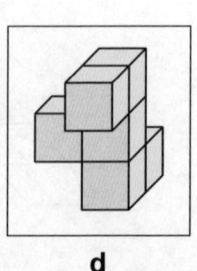
                             a   b   c   d

Work out which option shows how the three shapes will look when they are joined by matching the sides with the same letter.

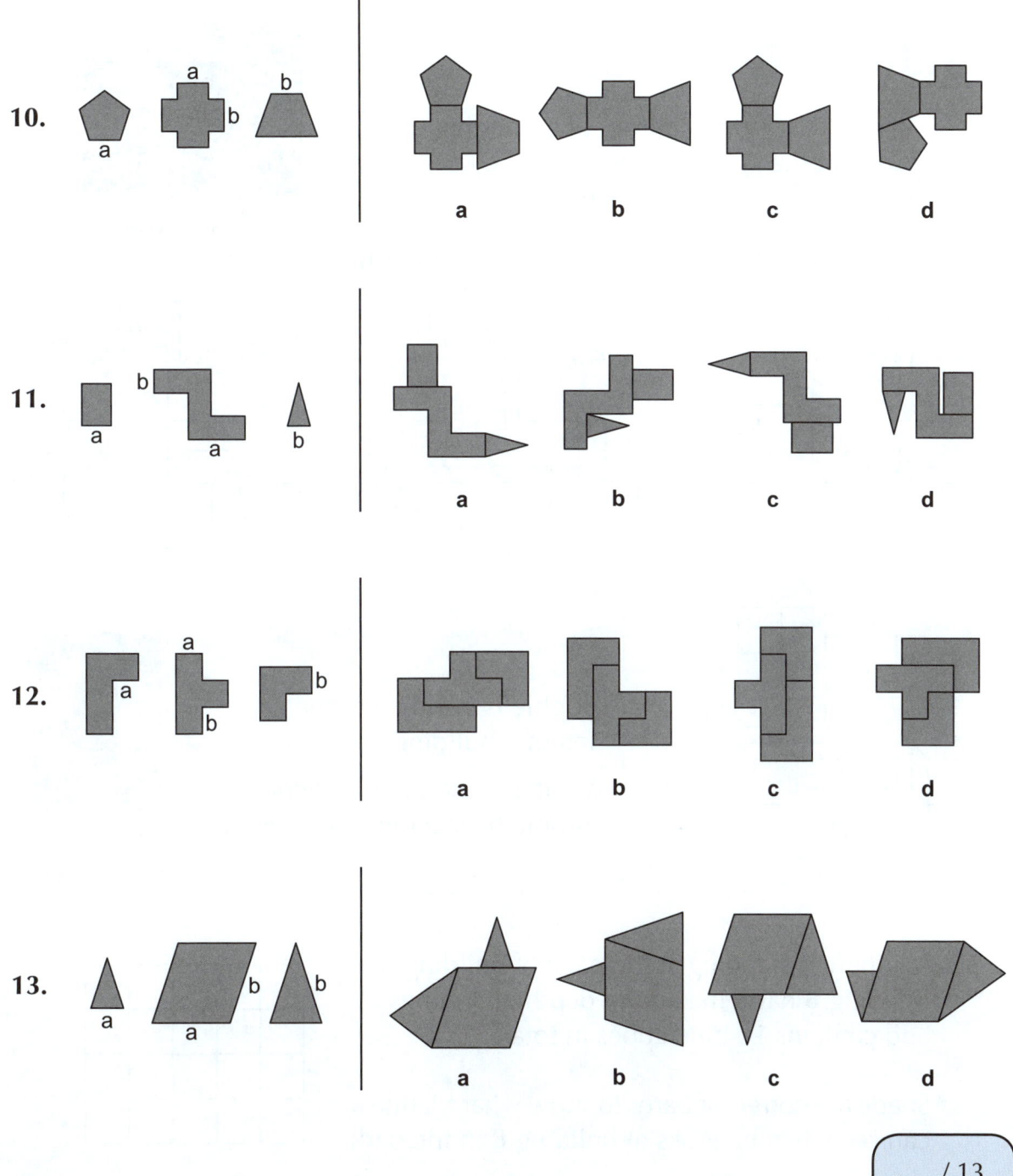

Puzzles 2

That's another three tests done. Now try this page of puzzles to practise **2D views**.

Night Lights

1. Michael is standing in front of a building made of blue and grey cubes. In the dark, only the blue cubes are visible.

   Which building is Michael standing in front of?

This is what Michael sees.

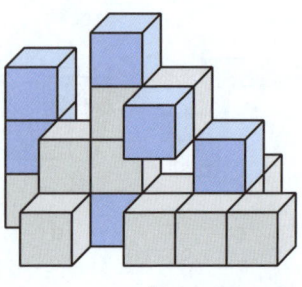
A

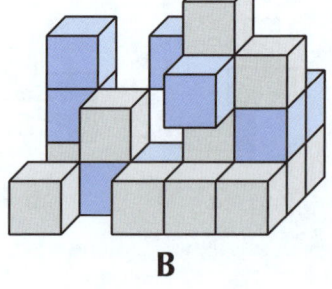
B

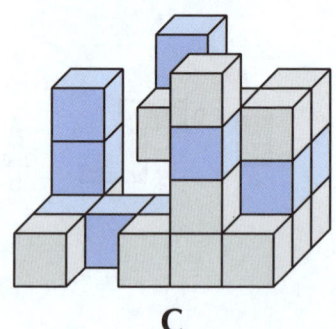
C

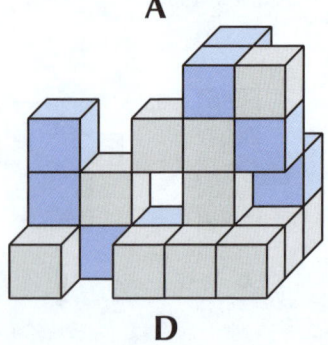
D

2. Sophie is standing to the left of a building.

   Which of the buildings could Sophie be standing to the left of?

This is what Sophie sees.

3. Matthew is standing at the back of building **B**. Building **B** has a maximum depth of 3 cubes and contains 10 blue cubes in total.

   Shade the correct squares to show what Matthew can see when he looks at building **B** in the dark.

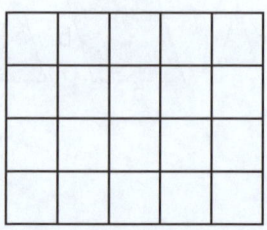

Test 7

You have **10 minutes** to do this test. Circle the letter for each correct answer.

Work out which 3D figure in the grey box has been rotated to make the new 3D figure.

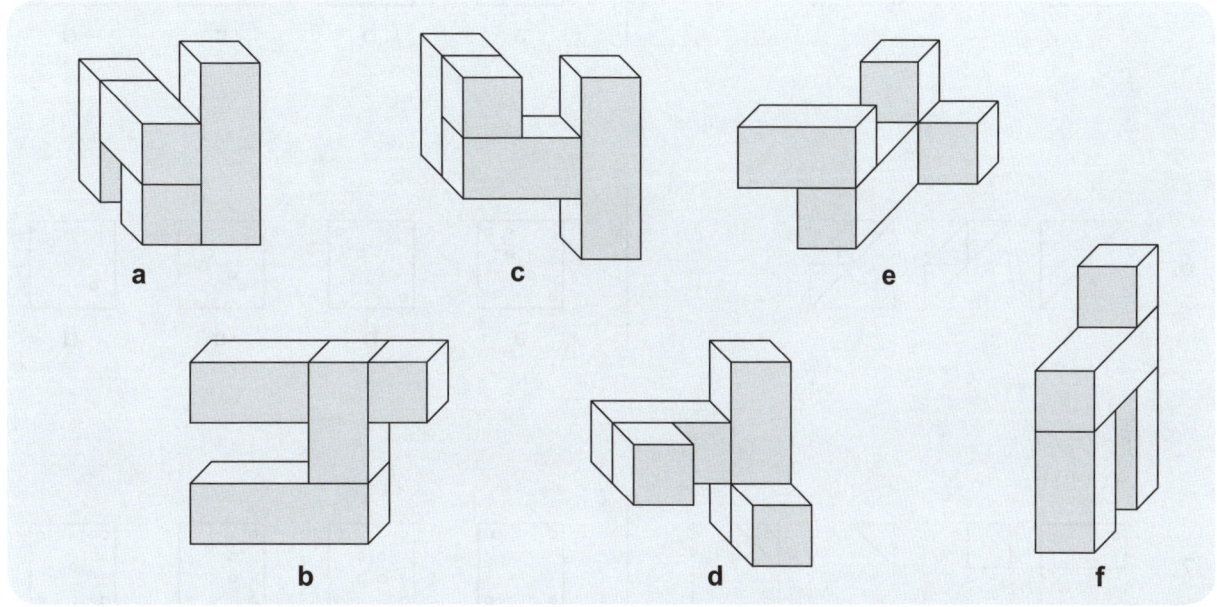

1.   a   d
               b   e
               c   f

2. 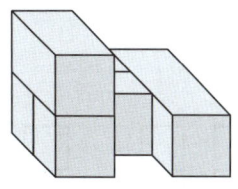   a   d
               b   e
               c   f

3.   a   d
      b   e
      c   f

4. 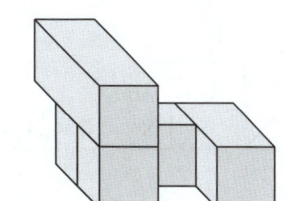   a   d
               b   e
               c   f

A square is folded and then a hole is punched, as shown on the left. Work out which option shows the square when unfolded.

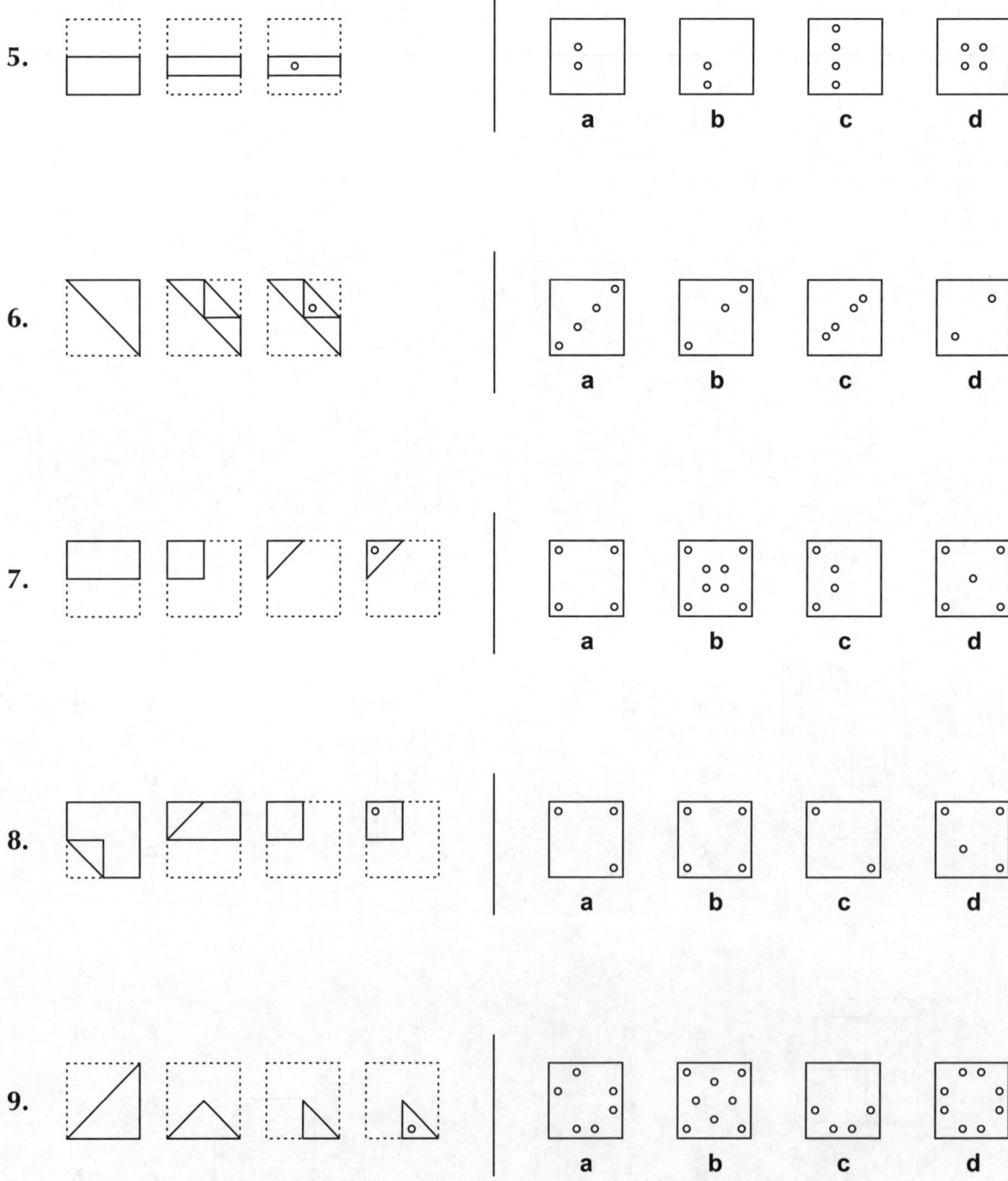

Work out which of the 3D shapes can be made from the net.

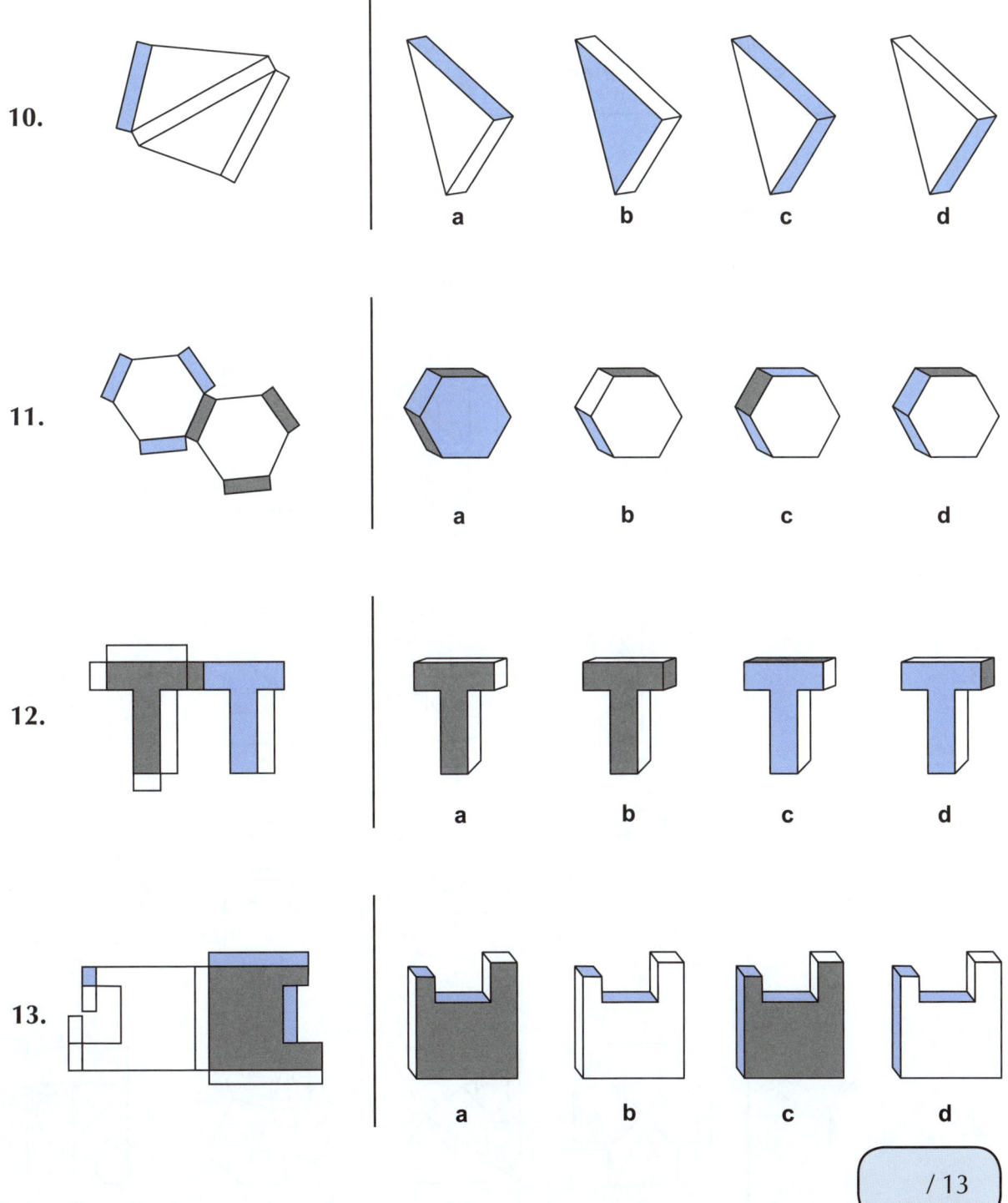

Test 8

You have **10 minutes** to do this test. Circle the letter for each correct answer.

Work out which option contains the hidden shape shown. It should be the same size and orientation.

1. 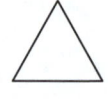 |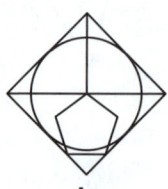
   a   b    c    d

2.  |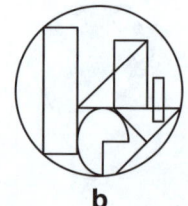
   a   b   c   d

3. | 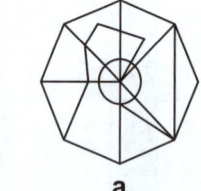      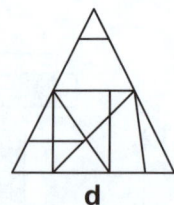
   a   b   c   d

4.  |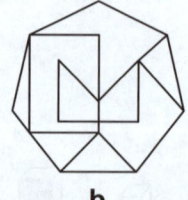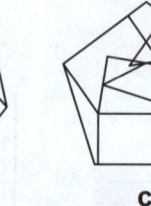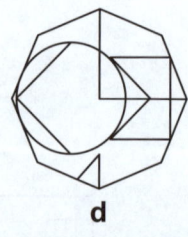
   a   b   c   d

5.  |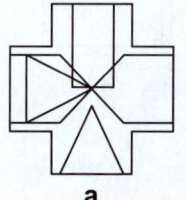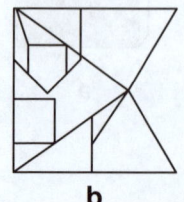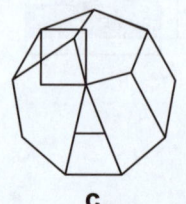
   a   b   c   d

Work out which of the four partial nets can be folded to make the cube on the left.

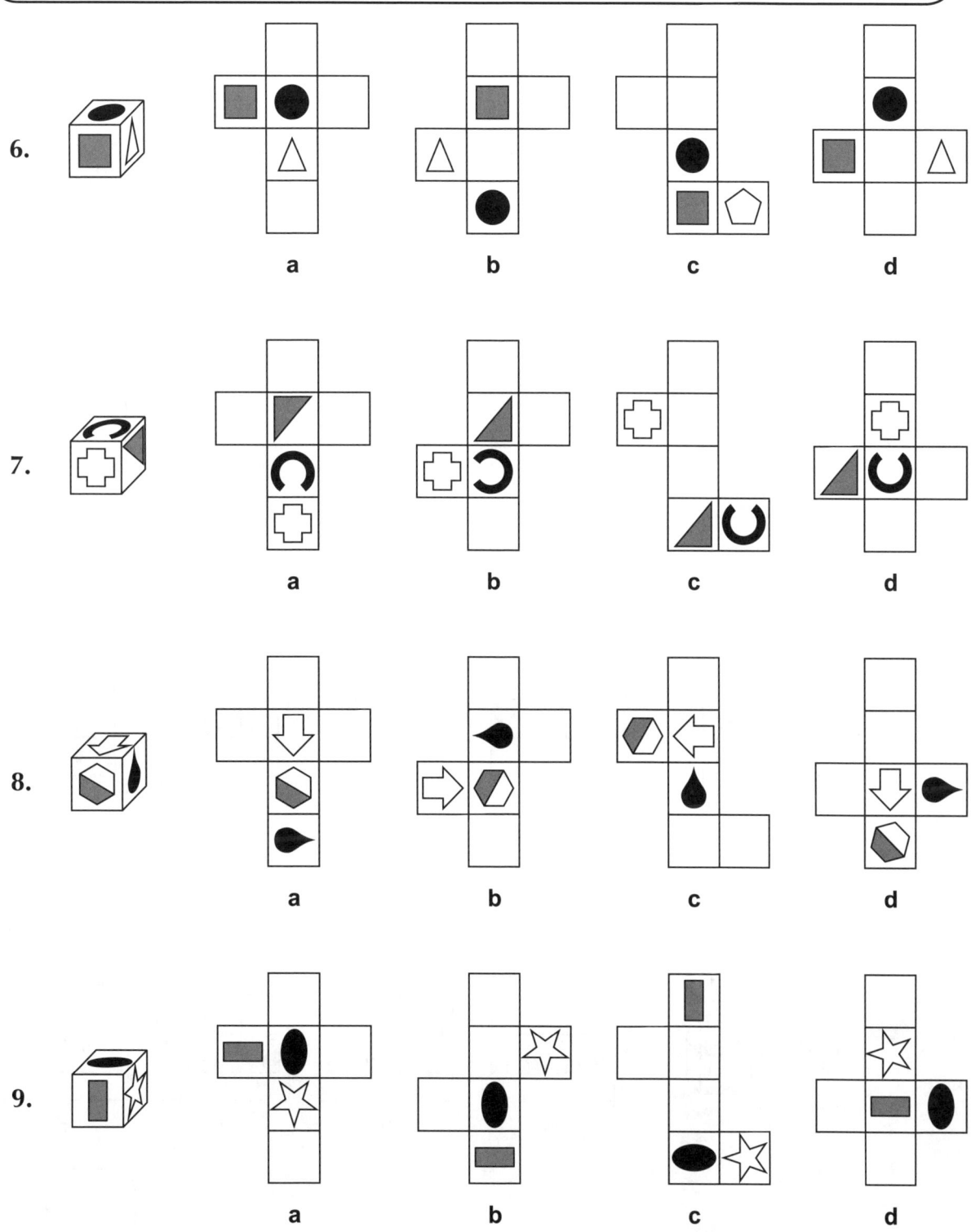

Work out which option is a 2D view from the **left** of the 3D figure shown.

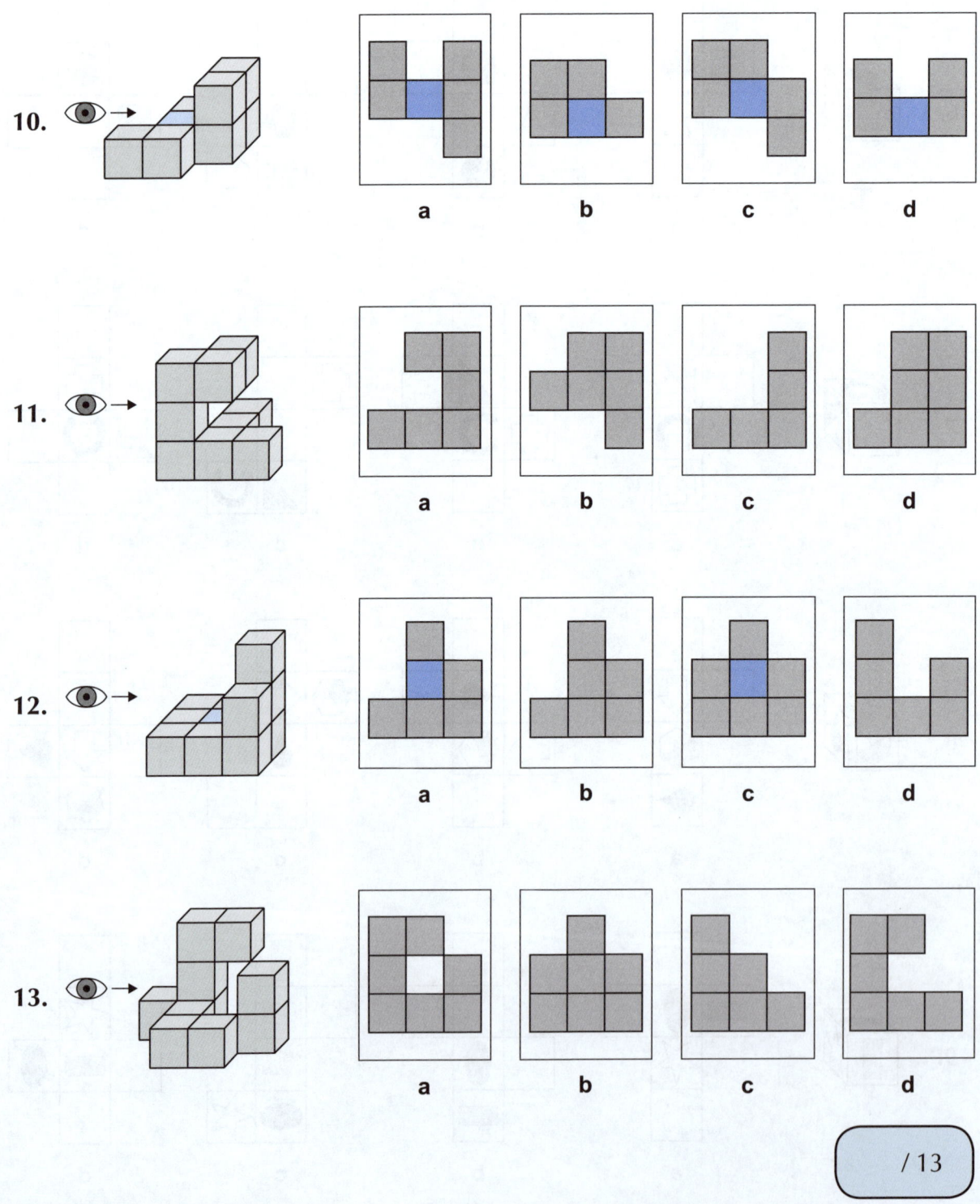

Test 9

You have **10 minutes** to do this test. Circle the letter for each correct answer.

> Work out which option shows the figure on the left when folded along the dotted line.

1.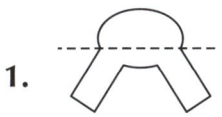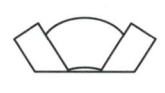
                        a   b   c   d

2.
                        a   b   c   d

3.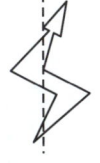
                        a   b   c   d

4.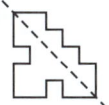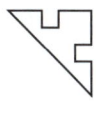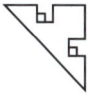
                        a   b   c   d

5.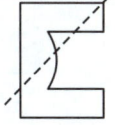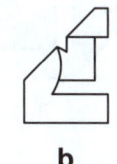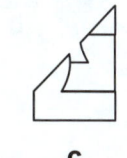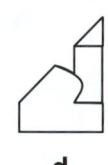
                        a   b   c   d

Work out which option shows how the three shapes will look when they are joined by matching the sides with the same letter.

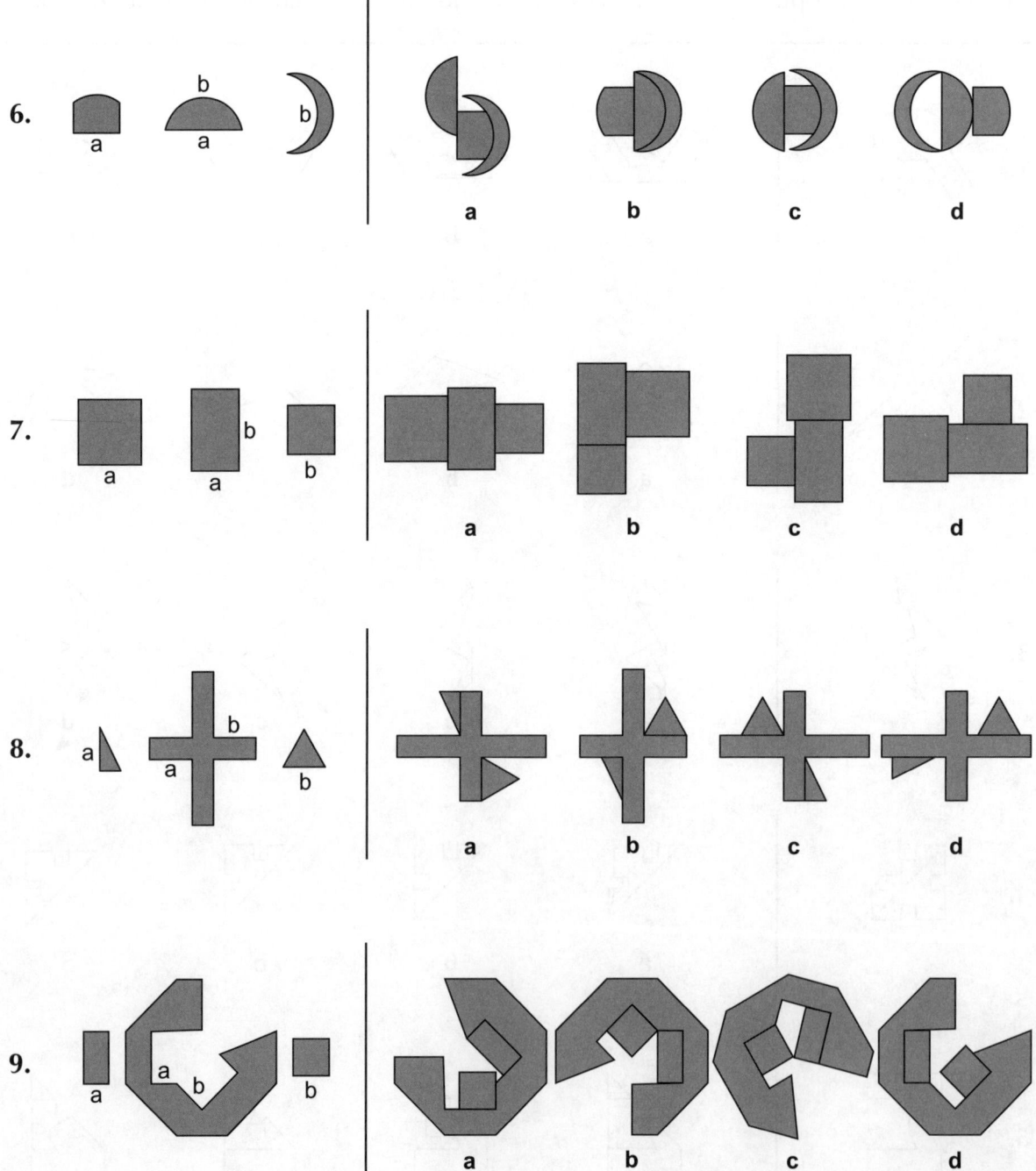

Work out which of the four cubes can be made from the net.

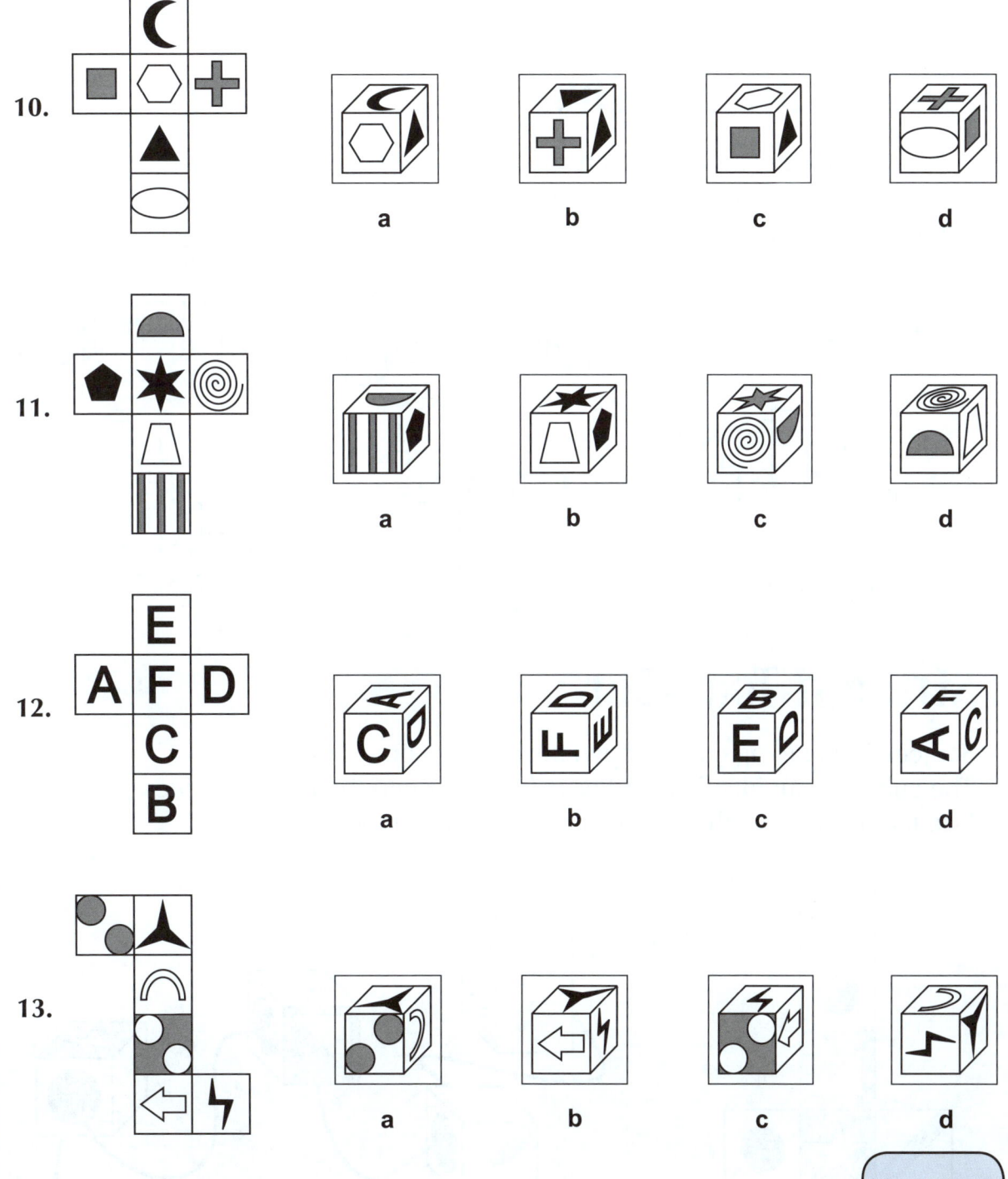

10. a b c d

11. a b c d

12. a b c d

13. a b c d

/ 13

Puzzles 3

Perfect your **3D rotation** and **net** skills all in a single puzzle break.

Disorganised Dinos

Disaster! Megan and her sisters made some dinosaurs from building blocks, but they have been mixed up. Work out which dinosaur belongs to Megan.

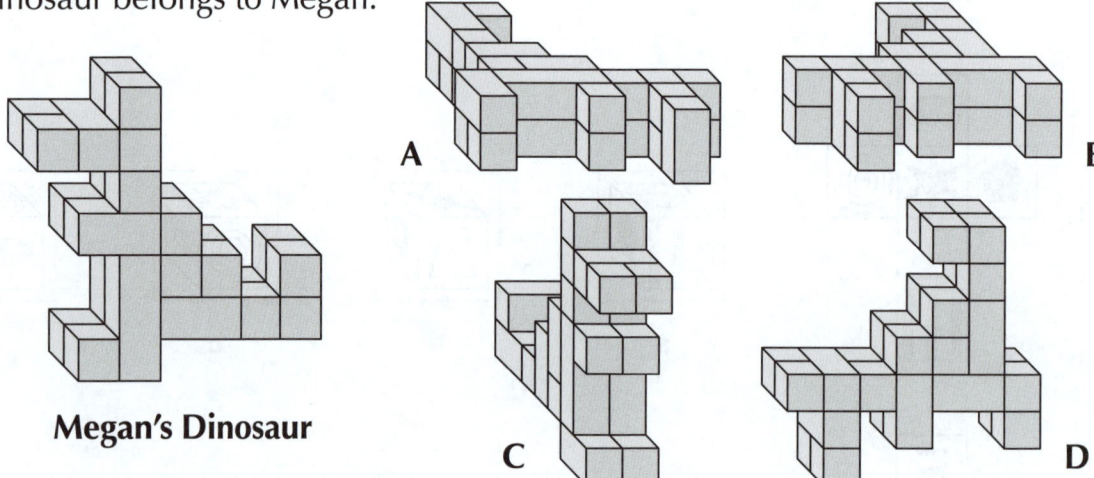

String It Together

Sanjeev is threading cube-shaped beads onto some string.
The cubes are all identical and have holes cut into them on two sides.
Use the net to fill in the missing faces on each of the cubes.

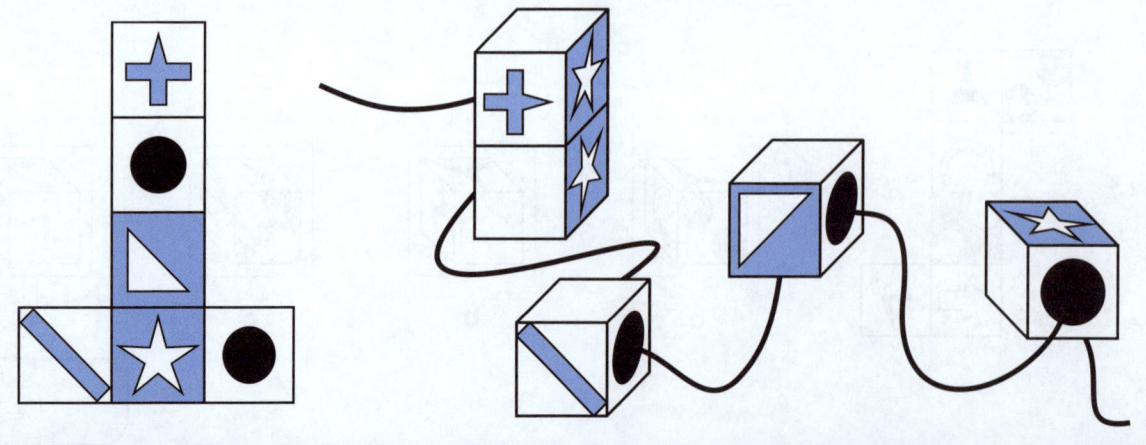

Test 10

You have **10 minutes** to do this test. Circle the letter for each correct answer.

The figures on the left show different views of the same cube. All the cube faces are different. Work out which of the options should replace the blue cube face.

1.
                                                                                                a   b   c   d

2.
                                                                                                a   b   c   d

3.
                                                                                                a   b   c   d

4.
                                                                                                a   b   c   d

Work out which option contains the hidden shape shown. It should be the same size and orientation.

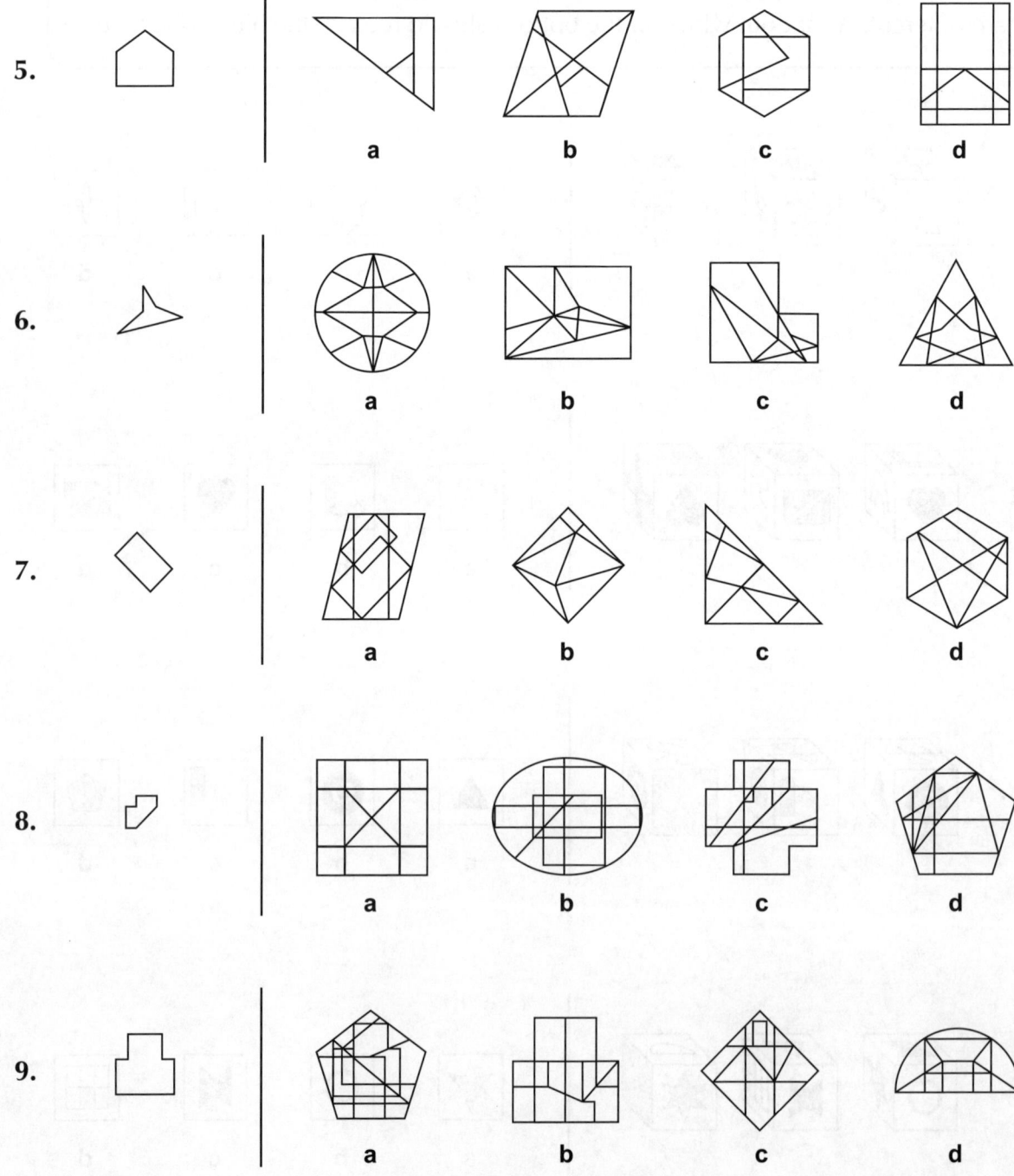

Without rotating the figure on the left, work out which option fits onto it to make the 3D shape in the grey box.

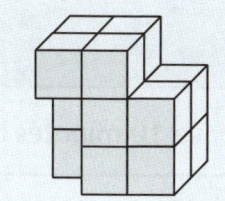

10.  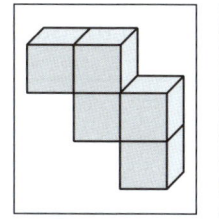 a 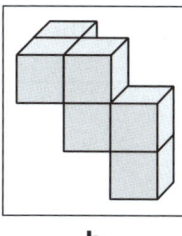 b 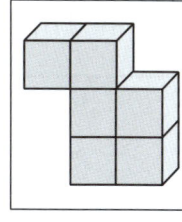 c 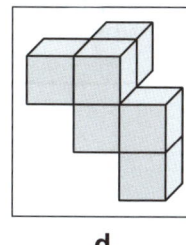 d

11.  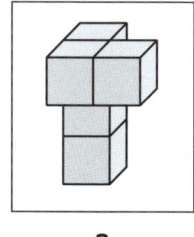 a 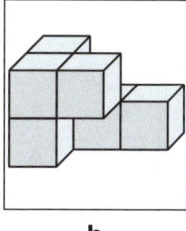 b 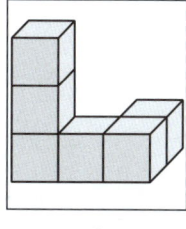 c 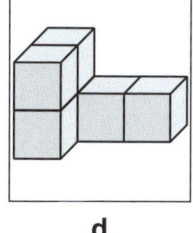 d

12.  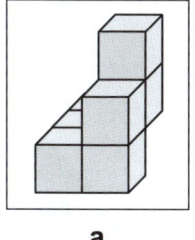 a 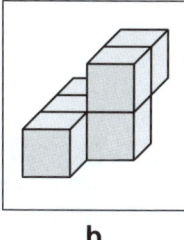 b 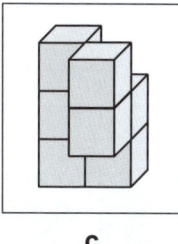 c 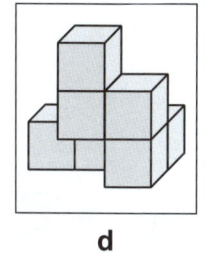 d

13. 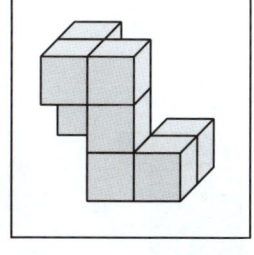 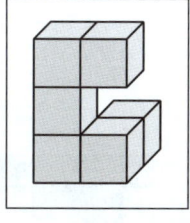 a 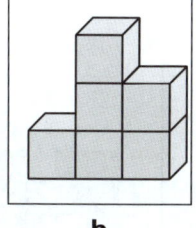 b 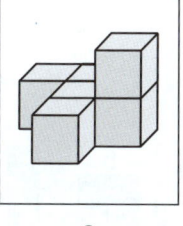 c 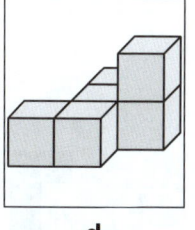 d

/ 13

© CGP — not to be photocopied   41   Test 10

Test 11

You have **10 minutes** to do this test. Circle the letter for each correct answer.

> Work out which option shows how the three shapes will look when they are joined by matching the sides with the same letter.

1.

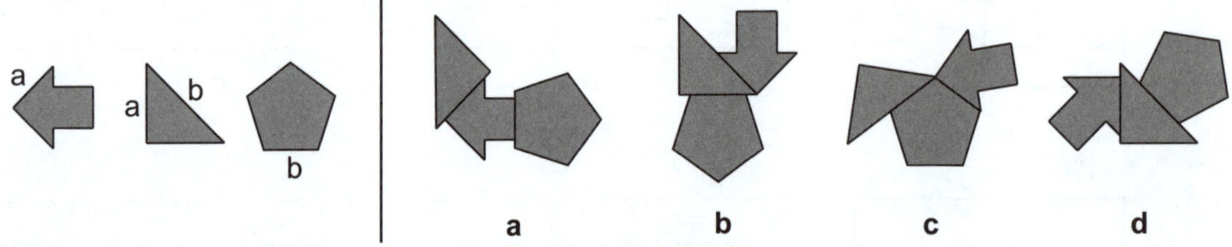

2.

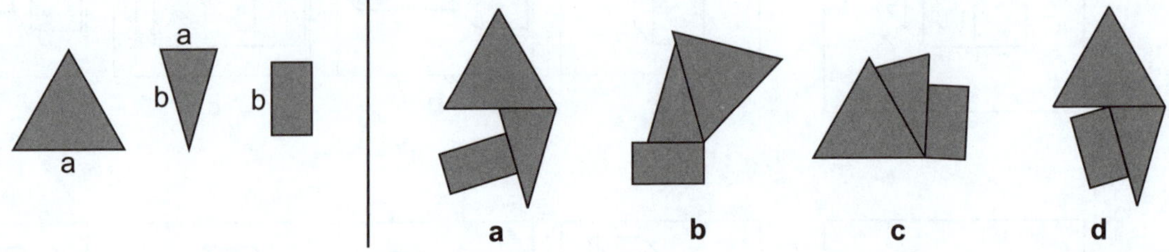

3.

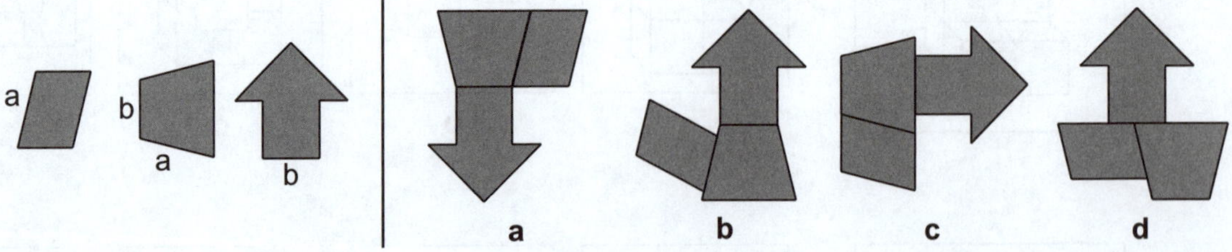

4.

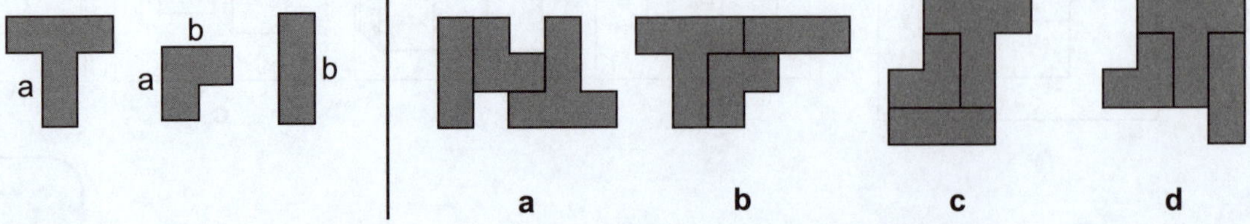

Test 11
42
© CGP — not to be photocopied

Work out which option is the 3D figure viewed from **above**.

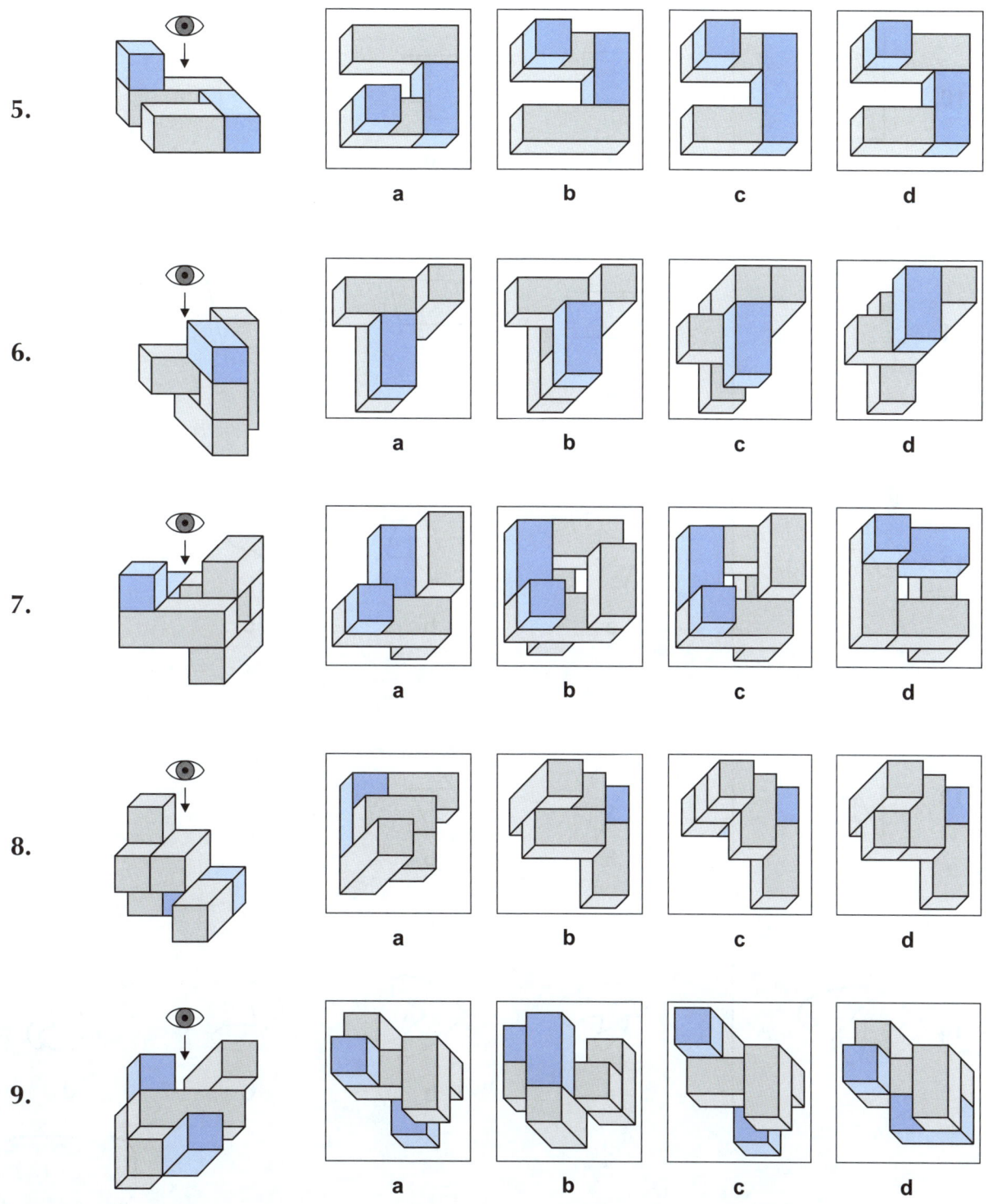

Work out which option shows the figure on the left when folded along the dotted line.

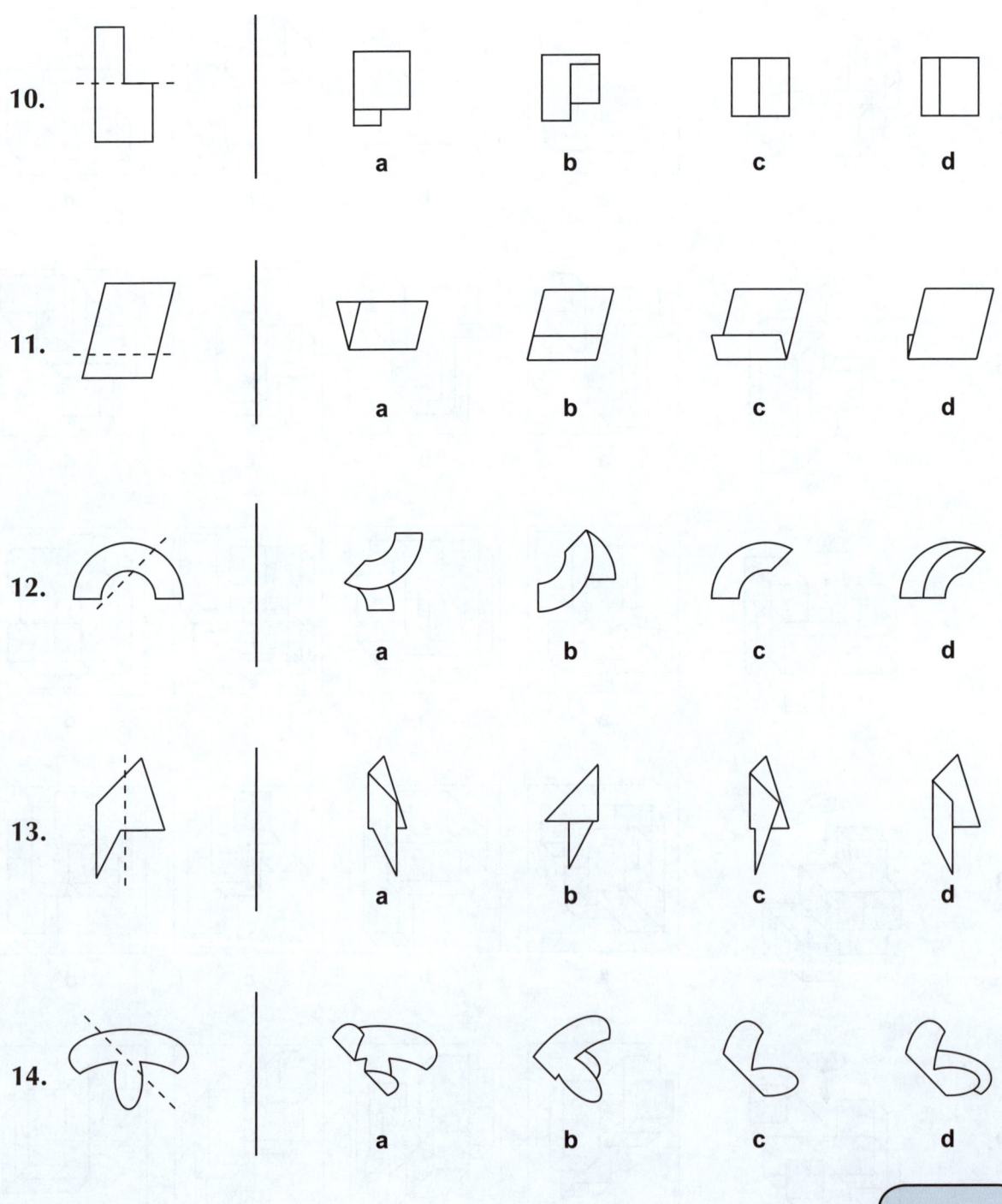

Test 12

You have **10 minutes** to do this test. Circle the letter for each correct answer.

Work out which 3D figure in the grey box has been rotated to make the new 3D figure.

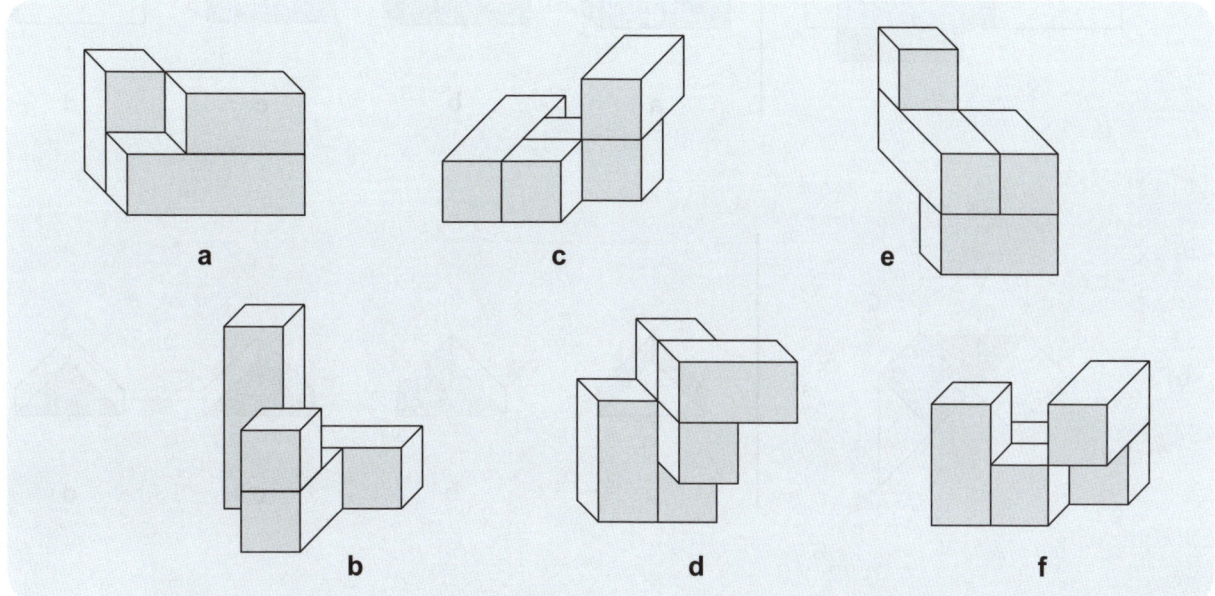

1. a   d
    b   e
    c   f

2. 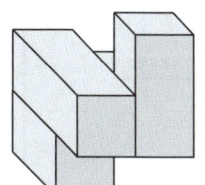   a   d
                          b   e
                          c   f

3. 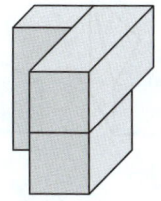   a   d
                          b   e
                          c   f

4. 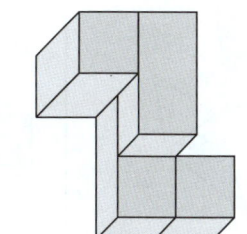   a   d
                          b   e
                          c   f

© CGP — not to be photocopied

Work out which of the 3D shapes can be made from the net.

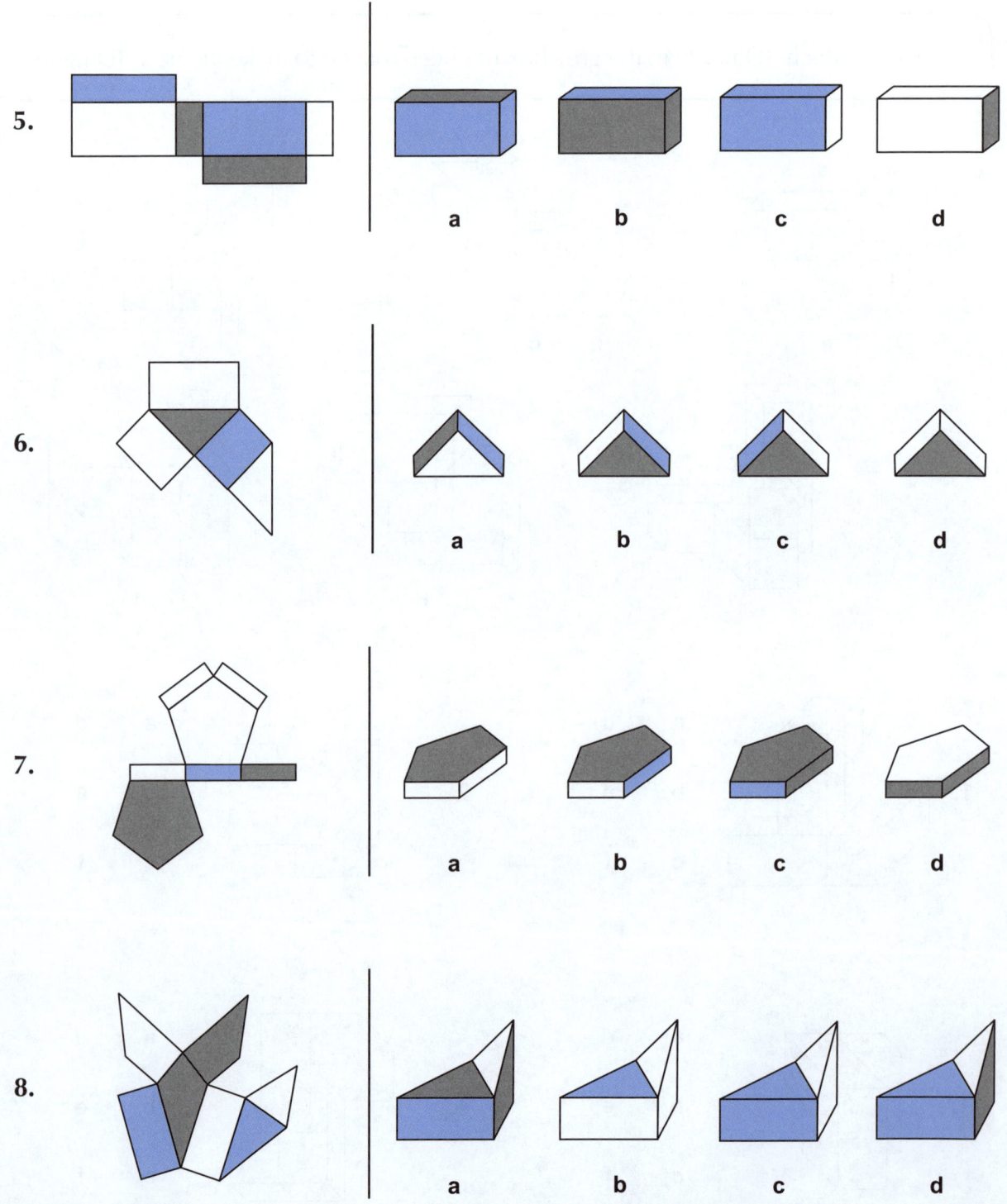

Work out which option contains the hidden shape shown. It should be the same size and orientation.

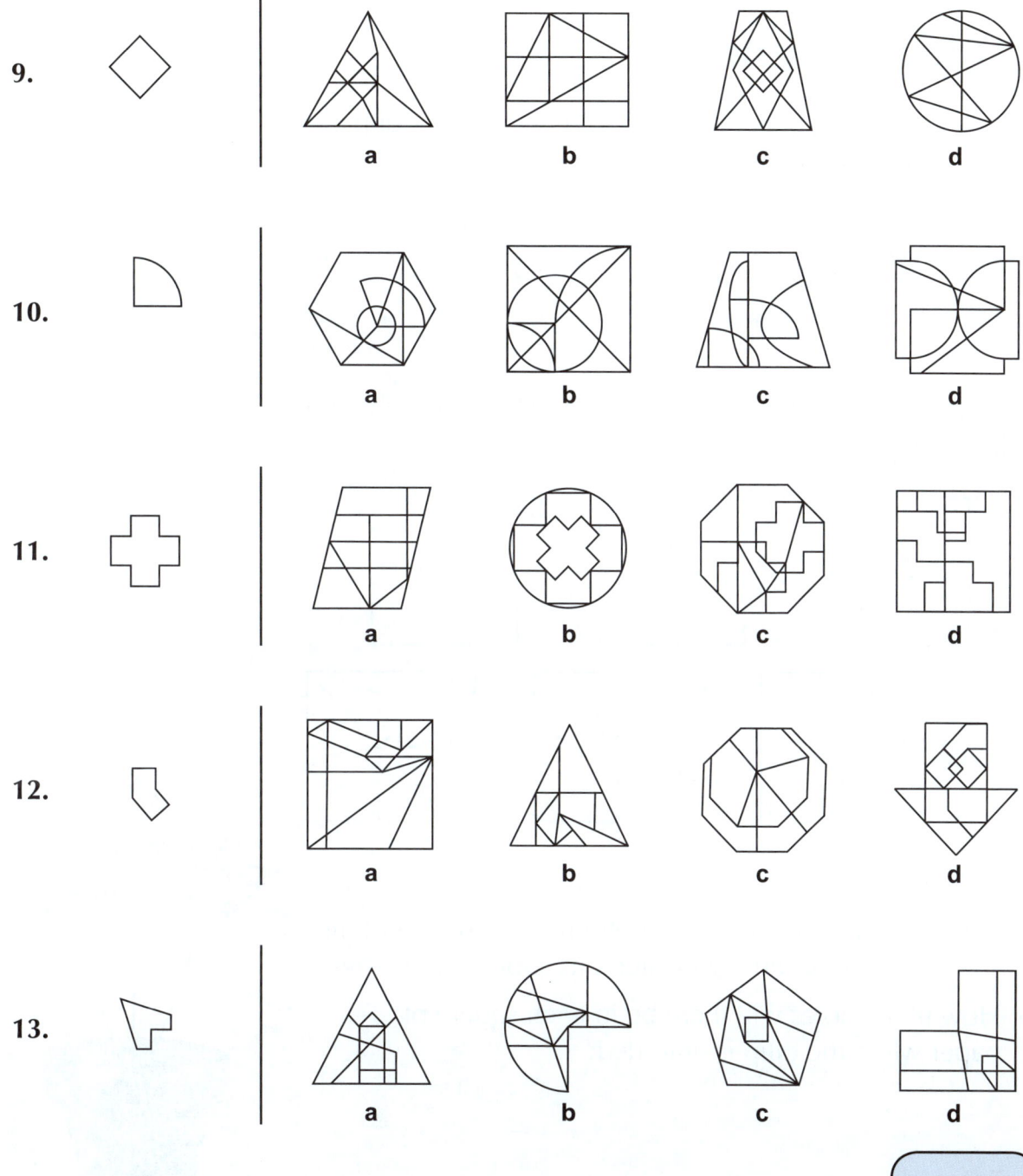

Puzzles 4

Time for a break. These puzzles will help you practise your **folding** skills.

Folding Flowers

Kevin is making paper tulips by folding a square of paper. The instructions he is following are shown below.

1.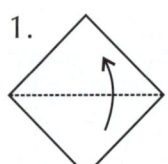
2.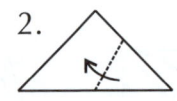
3.
4.
5.

If Kevin unfolds the tulip, which of the following shows the creases in the paper?

A 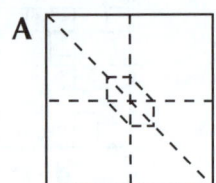 **B** 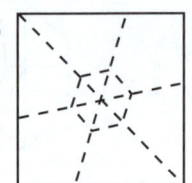 **C**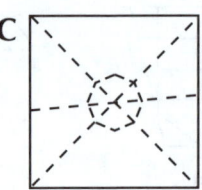

D 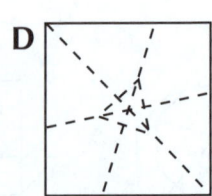 **E** 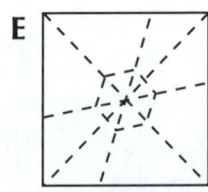 **F**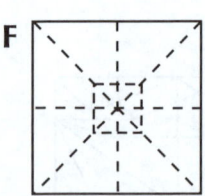

Kevin punches a hole in the bottom of each paper tulip so that he can insert a wire stem, as shown on the right.

How many holes will there be in each square of paper when the tulip is unfolded?

Test 13

You have **10 minutes** to do this test. Circle the letter for each correct answer.

A square is folded and then a hole is punched, as shown on the left. Work out which option shows the square when unfolded.

1.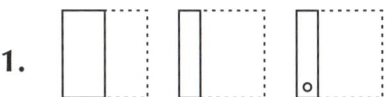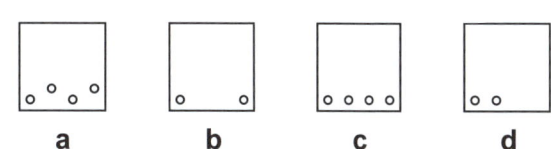

2.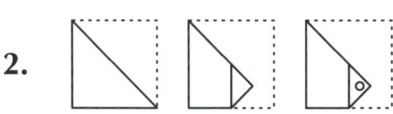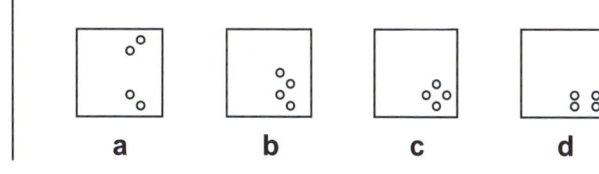

3.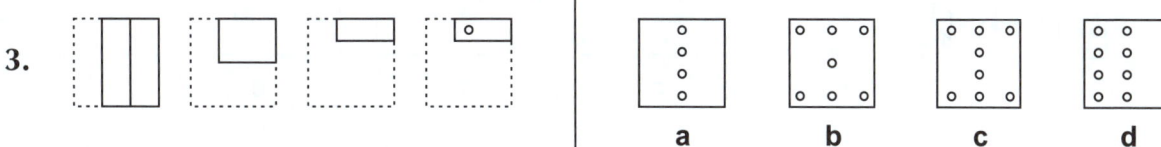

4.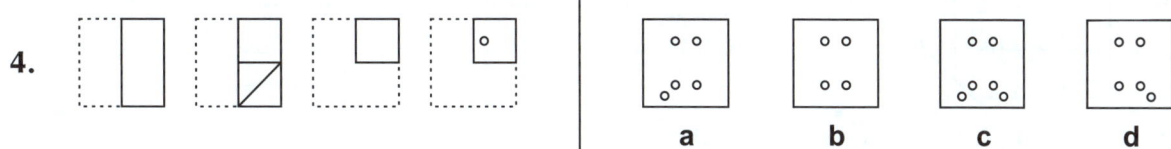

5.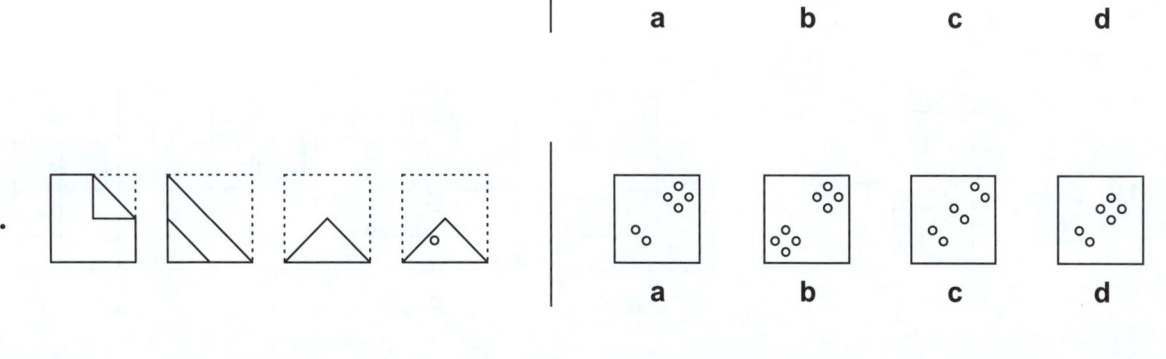

Work out which option is a 2D view from the **right** of the 3D figure shown.

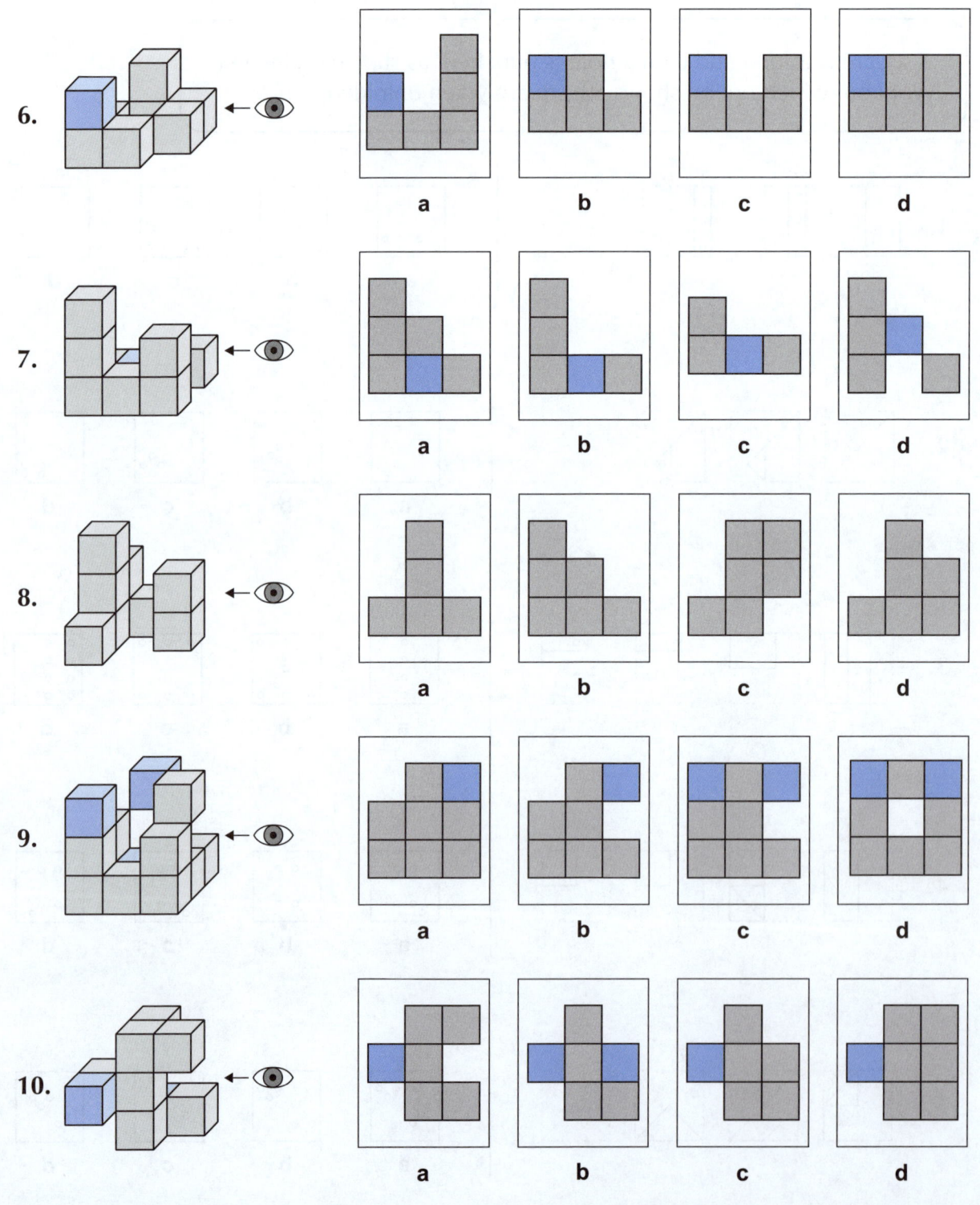

Work out which option shows how the three shapes will look when they are joined by matching the sides with the same letter.

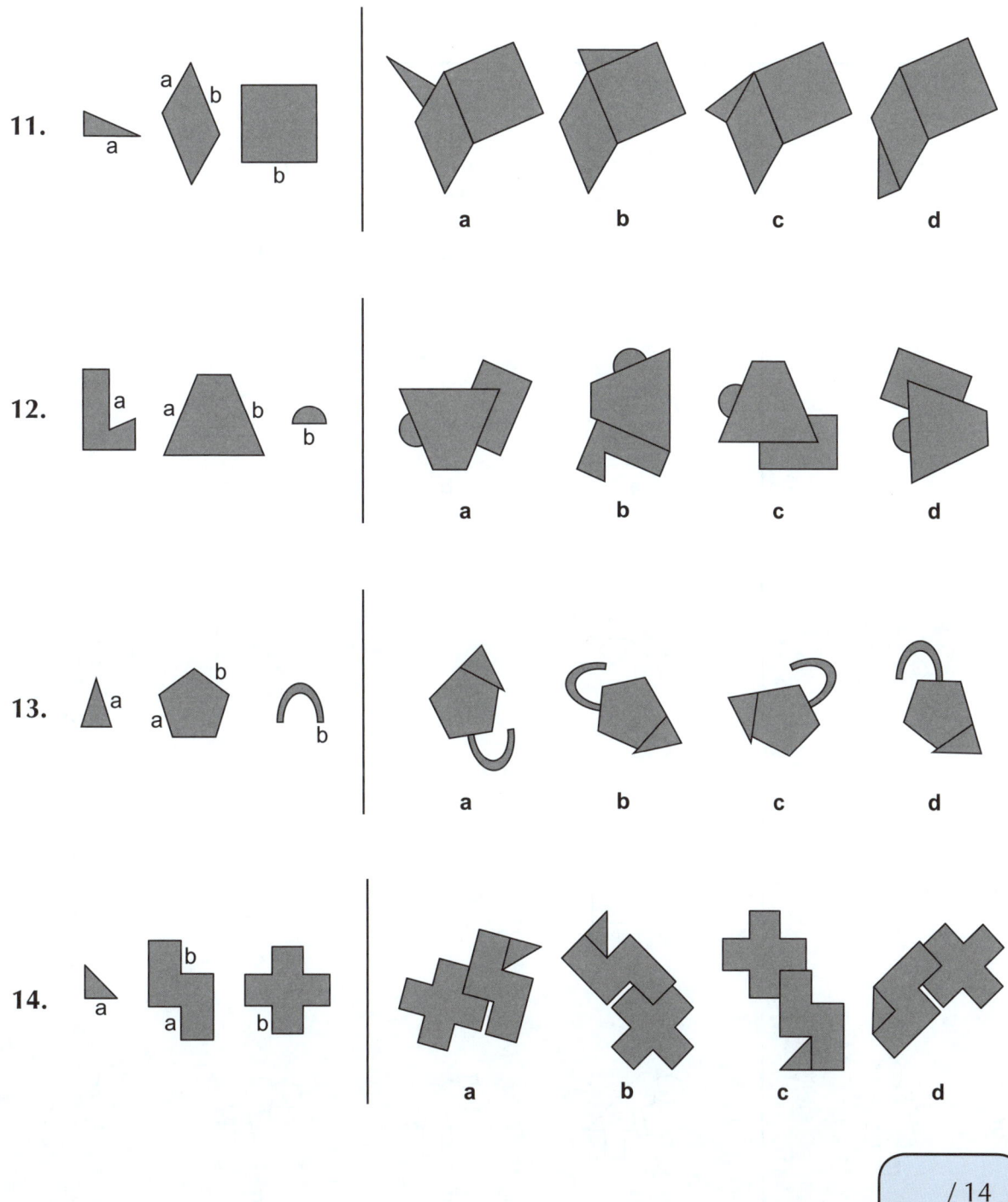

Test 14

You have **10 minutes** to do this test. Circle the letter for each correct answer.

Work out which option shows the figure on the left when folded along the dotted line.

1.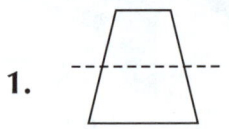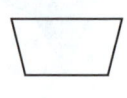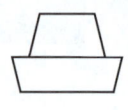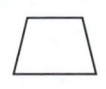
                                         a   b   c   d

2.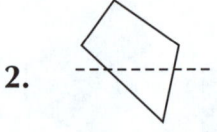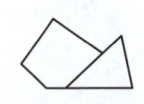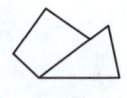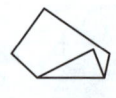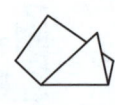

                                         a   b   c   d

3.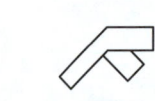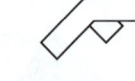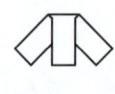

                                         a   b   c   d

4.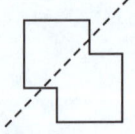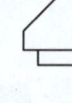

                                         a   b   c   d

5.

                                         a   b   c   d

Work out which set of blocks can be put together to make the 3D figure on the left.

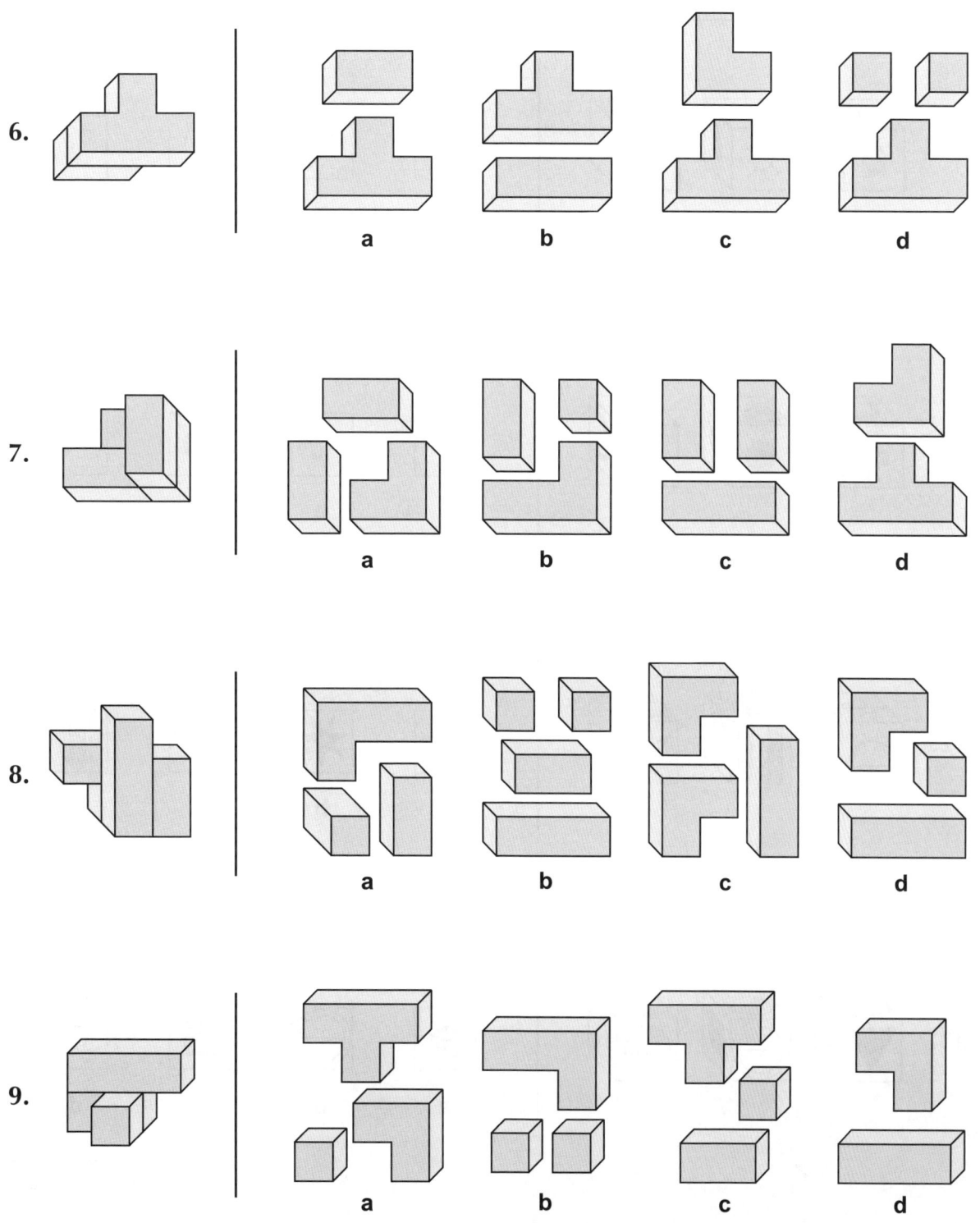

The figures on the left show different views of the same cube. All the cube faces are different. Work out which of the options should replace the blue cube face.

10.

a b c d

11.

a b c d

12.

a b c d

13.

a b c d

/ 13

Test 15

You have **10 minutes** to do this test. Circle the letter for each correct answer.

Work out which option contains the hidden shape shown. It should be the same size and orientation.

1.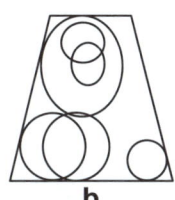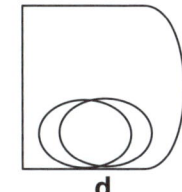
                       a   b   c   d

2.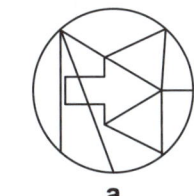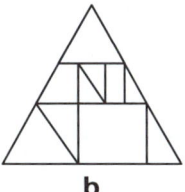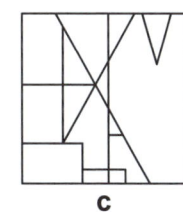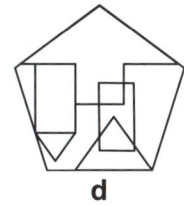
                       a   b   c   d

3.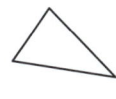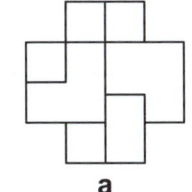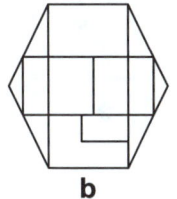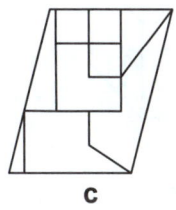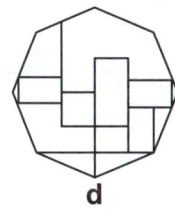
                       a   b   c   d

4.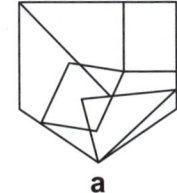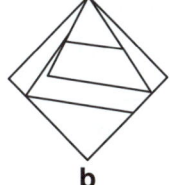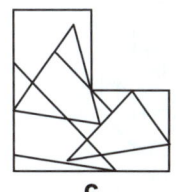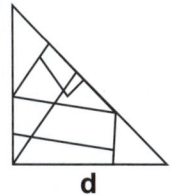
                       a   b   c   d

5.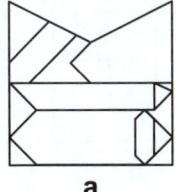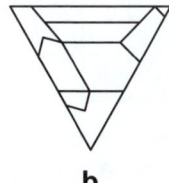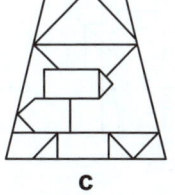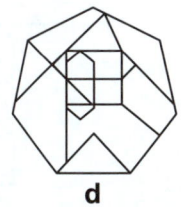
                       a   b   c   d

Work out which option is a 2D view from **above** the 3D figure shown.

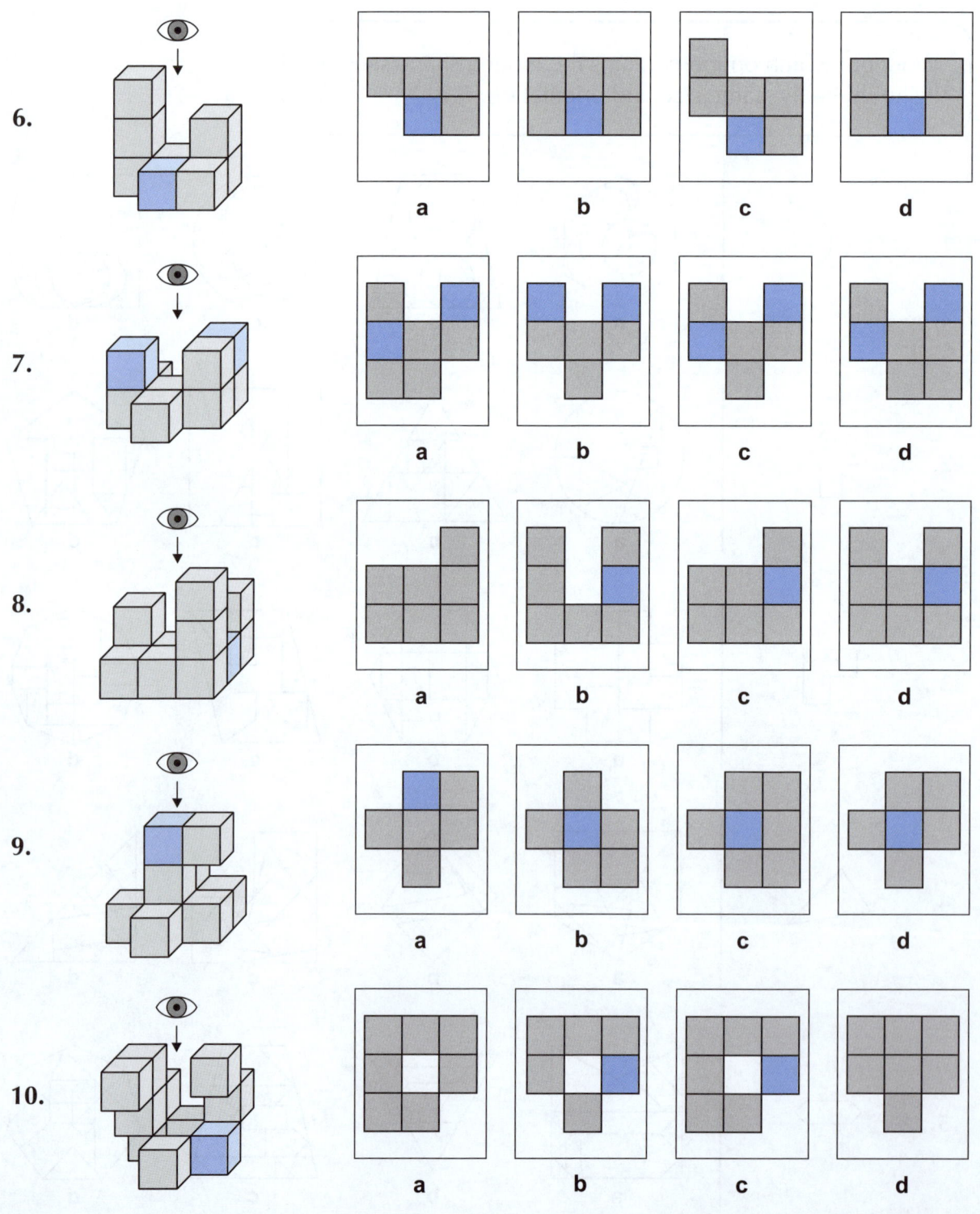

Work out which of the 3D shapes can be made from the net.

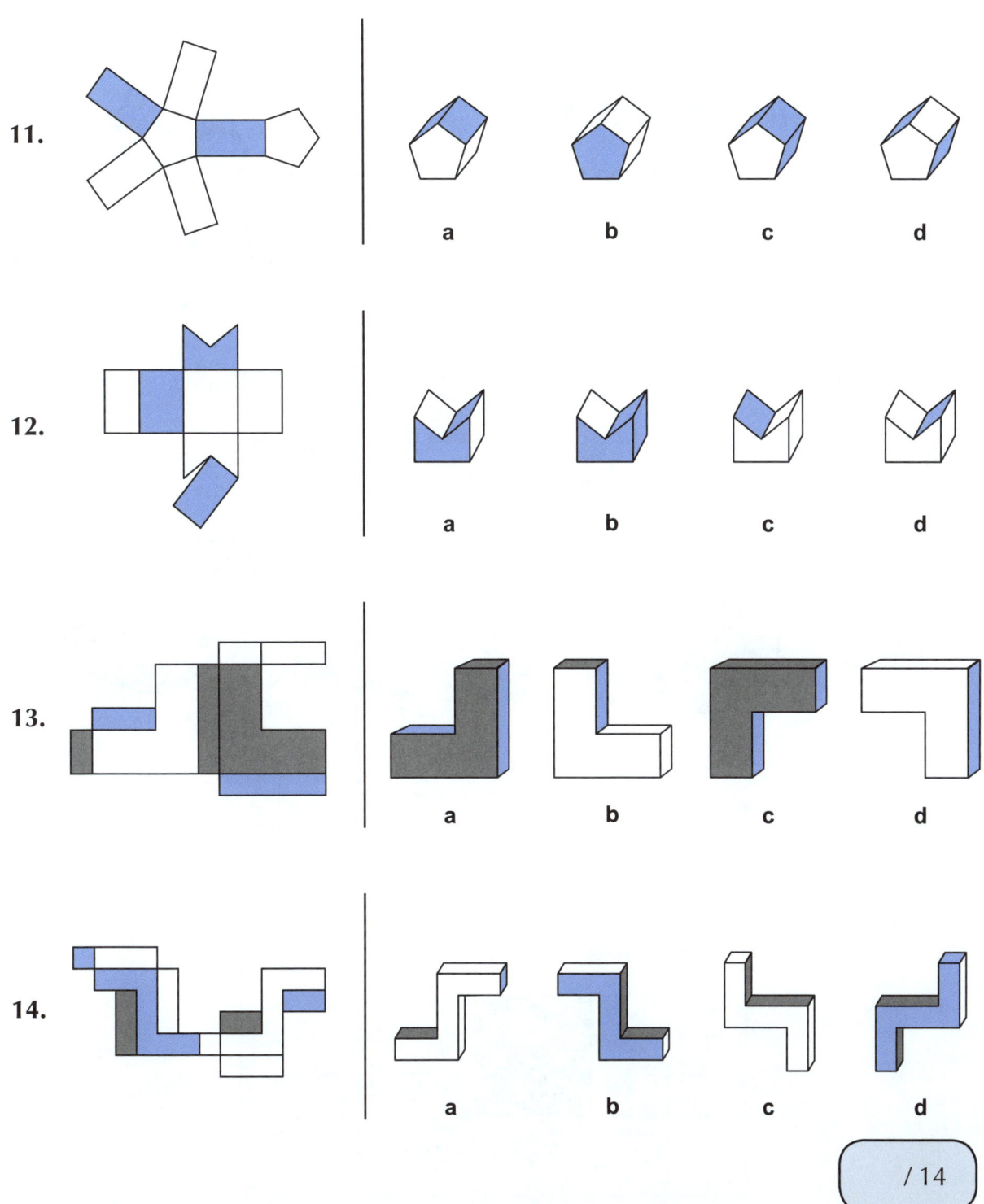

Puzzles 5

Here's another puzzle page. Use this one to practise your **connecting shapes** skills.

Daylight Robbery

Someone has stolen Winston the wise owl's prize acorn. Help Winston catch the woodland thief by connecting the shapes below to reveal the culprit.

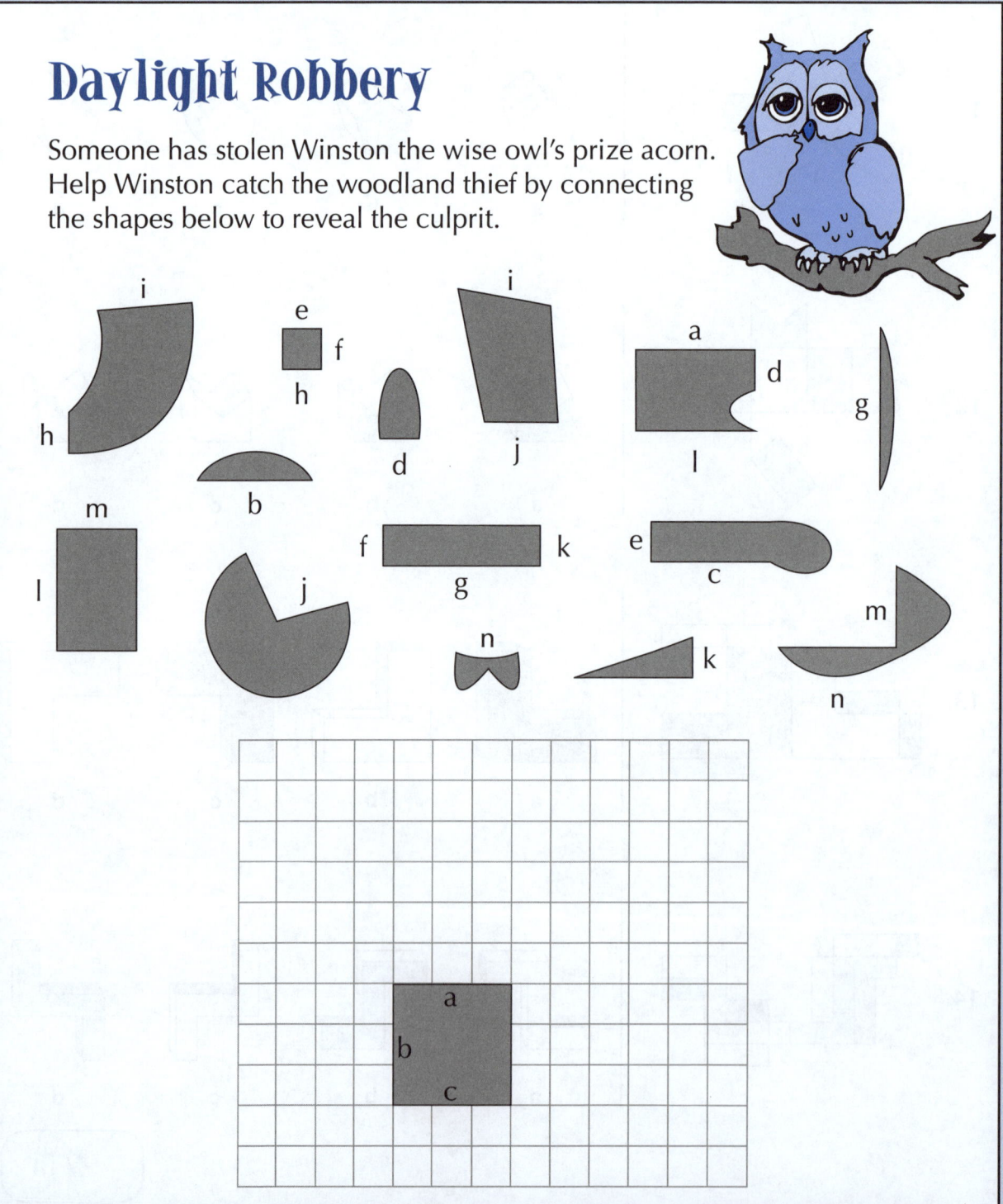

Test 16

You have **10 minutes** to do this test. Circle the letter for each correct answer.

Work out which option shows the figure on the left when folded along the dotted line.

1.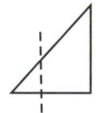
                     a   b   c   d

2.
                     a   b   c   d

3.
                     a   b   c   d

4.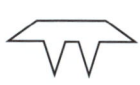
                     a   b   c   d

5.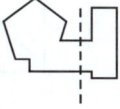
                     a   b   c   d

© CGP — not to be photocopied

The figures on the left show different views of the same cube. All the cube faces are different. Work out which of the options should replace the blue cube face.

6.
                                                     a   b   c   d

7.
                                                     a   b   c   d

8.
                                                     a   b   c   d

9.
                                                     a   b   c   d

Test 16

Work out which 3D figure in the grey box has been rotated to make the new 3D figure.

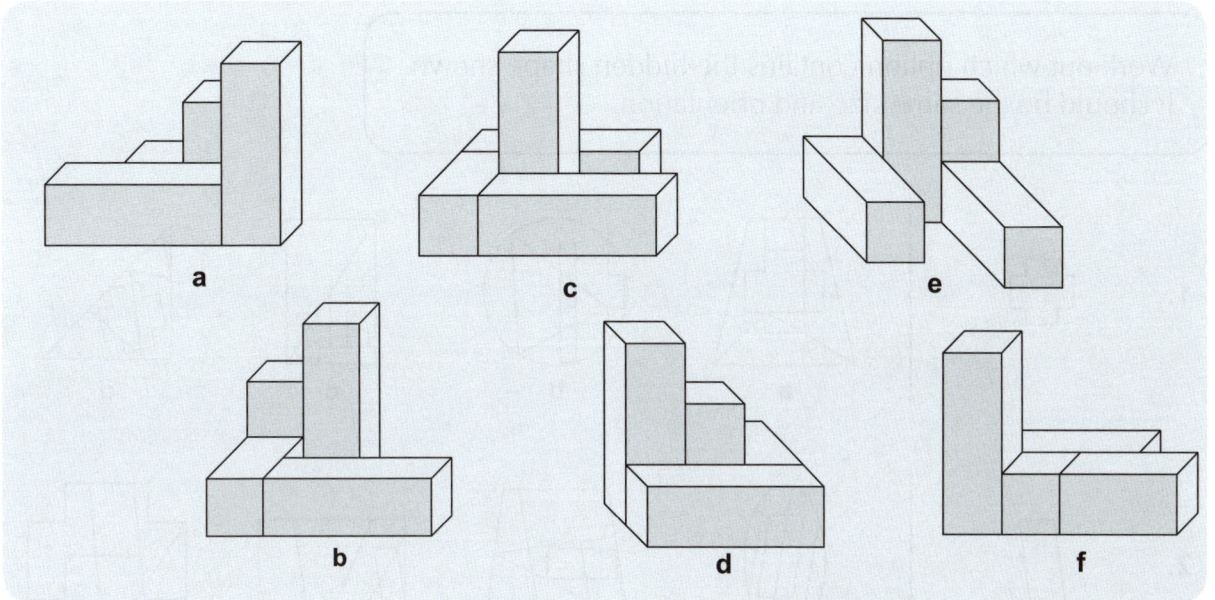

10. 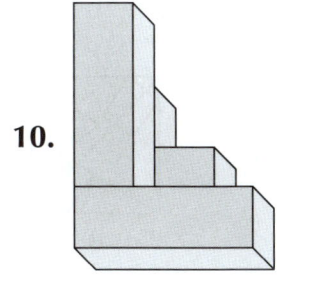   a   d
                            b   e
                            c   f

11.    a   d
                            b   e
                            c   f

12. 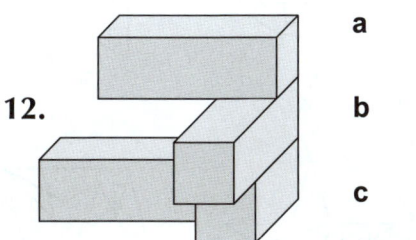   a   d
                            b   e
                            c   f

13. 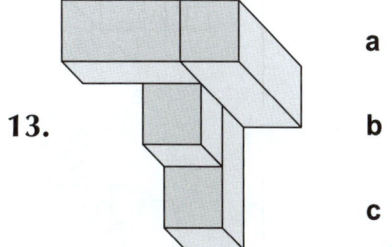   a   d
                            b   e
                            c   f

Test 17

You have **10 minutes** to do this test. Circle the letter for each correct answer.

> Work out which option contains the hidden shape shown. It should be the same size and orientation.

1.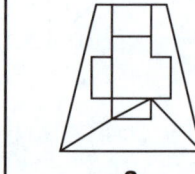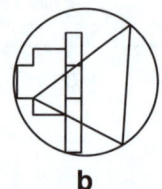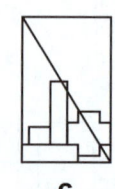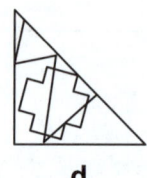
                 a   b   c   d

2.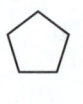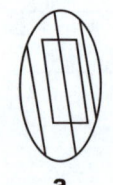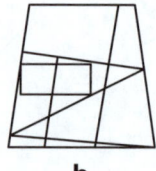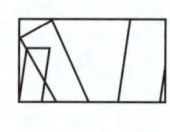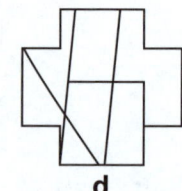
                 a   b   c   d

3.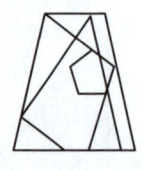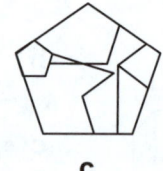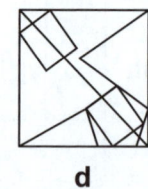
                 a   b   c   d

4.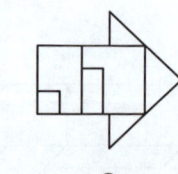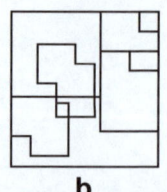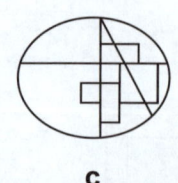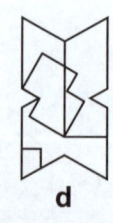
                 a   b   c   d

5.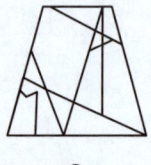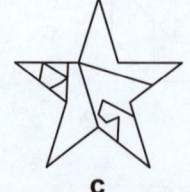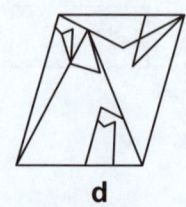
                 a   b   c   d

Work out which of the four cubes can be made from the net.

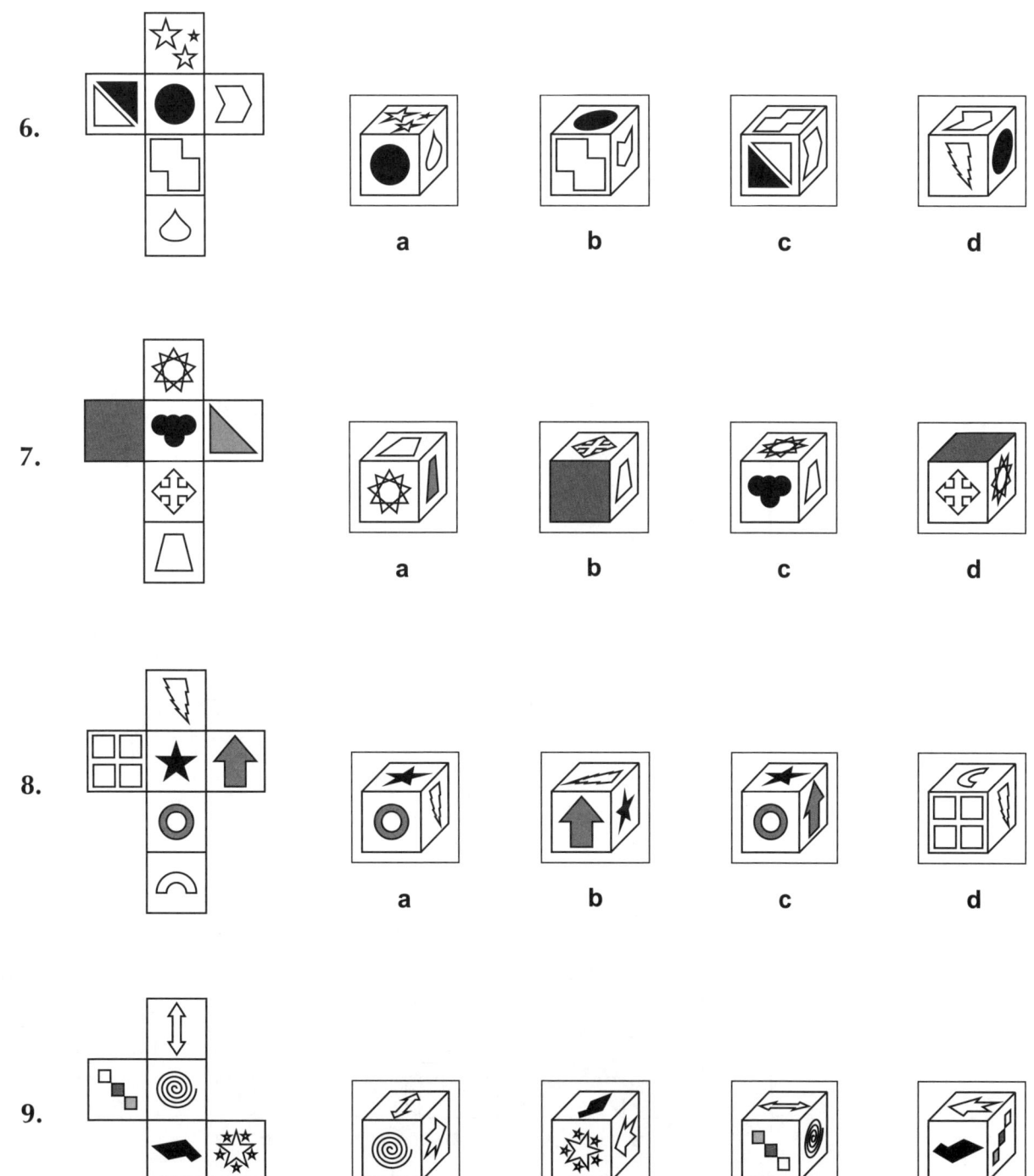

Work out which set of blocks can be put together to make the 3D figure on the left.

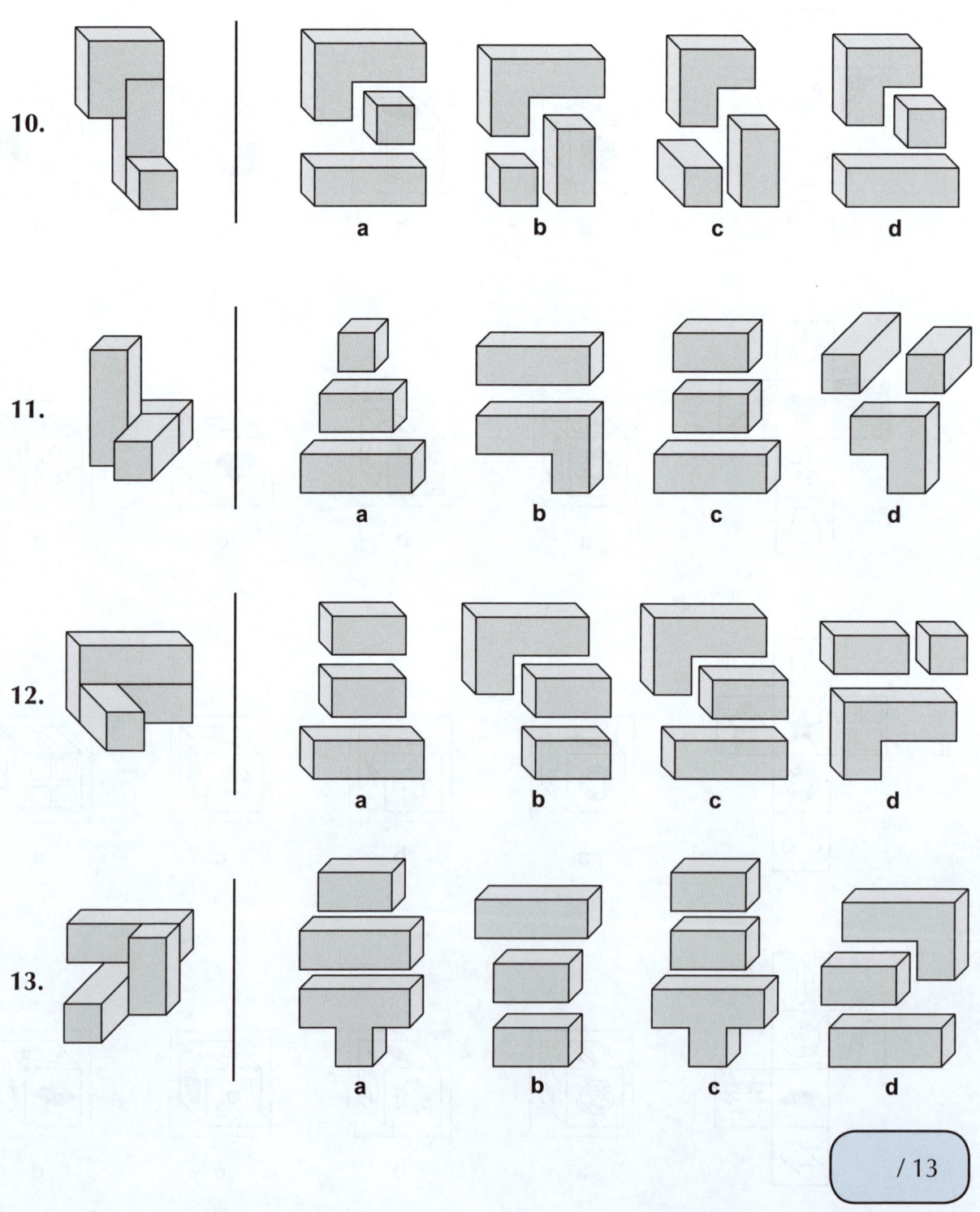

10.

11.

12.

13.

/ 13

Test 17

Test 18

You have **10 minutes** to do this test. Circle the letter for each correct answer.

A square is folded and then a hole is punched, as shown on the left. Work out which option shows the square when unfolded.

1.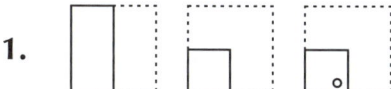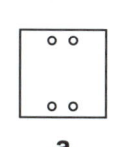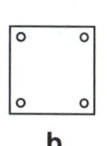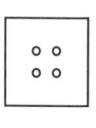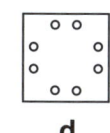
                                         a   b   c   d

2.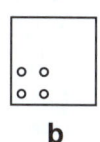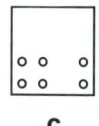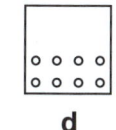
                                         a   b   c   d

3.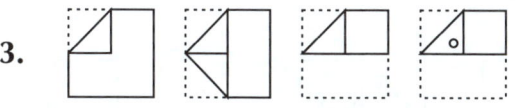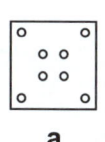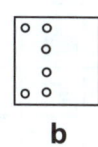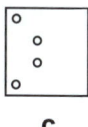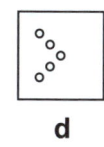
                                       a   b   c   d

4.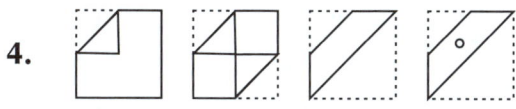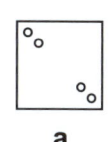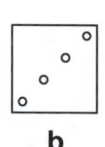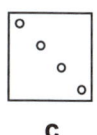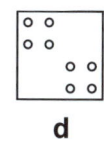
                                         a   b   c   d

5.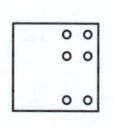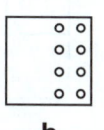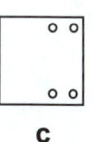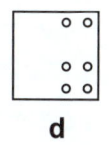
                                         a   b   c   d

Work out which of the four partial nets can be folded to make the cube on the left.

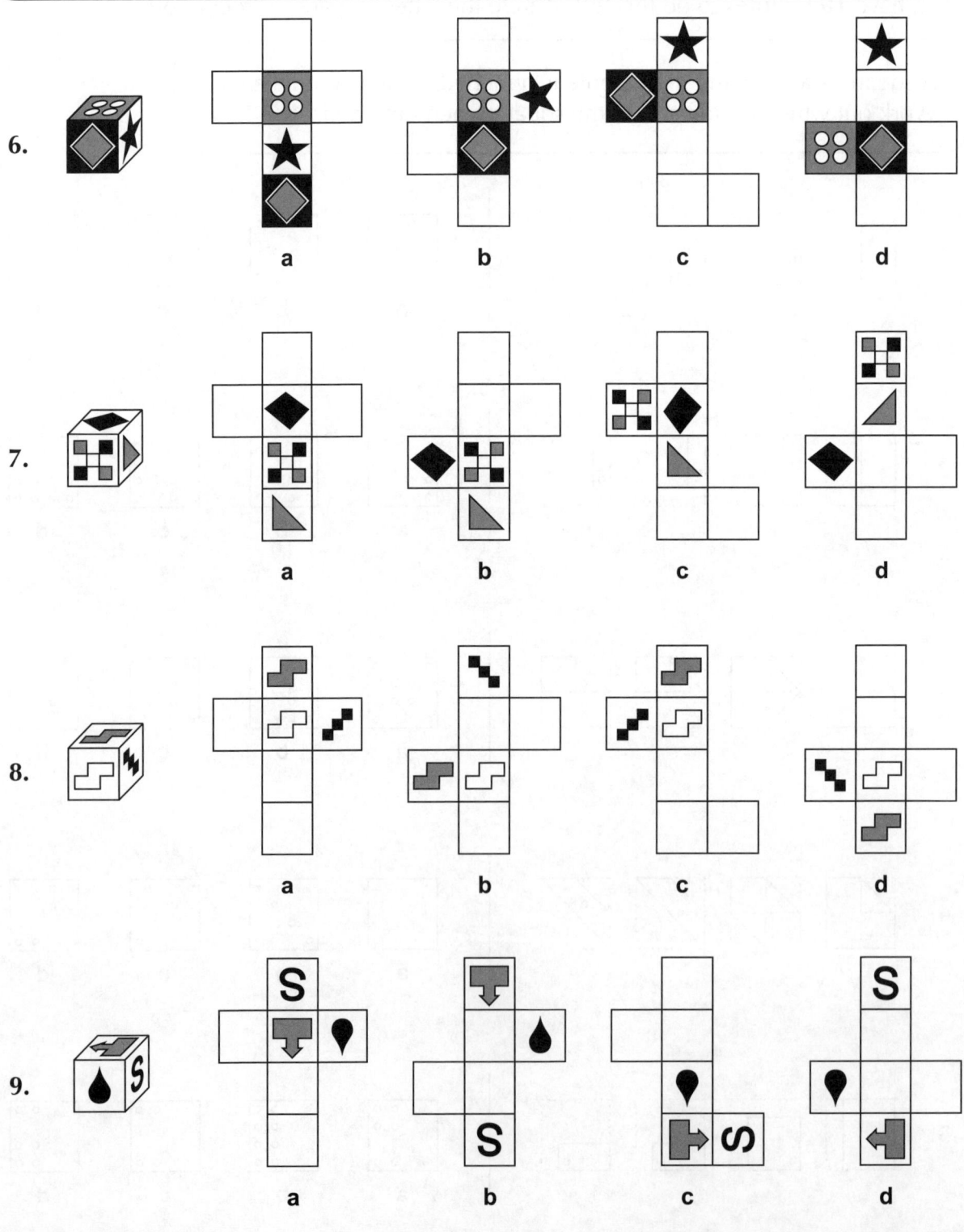

Work out which option shows how the three shapes will look when they are joined by matching the sides with the same letter.

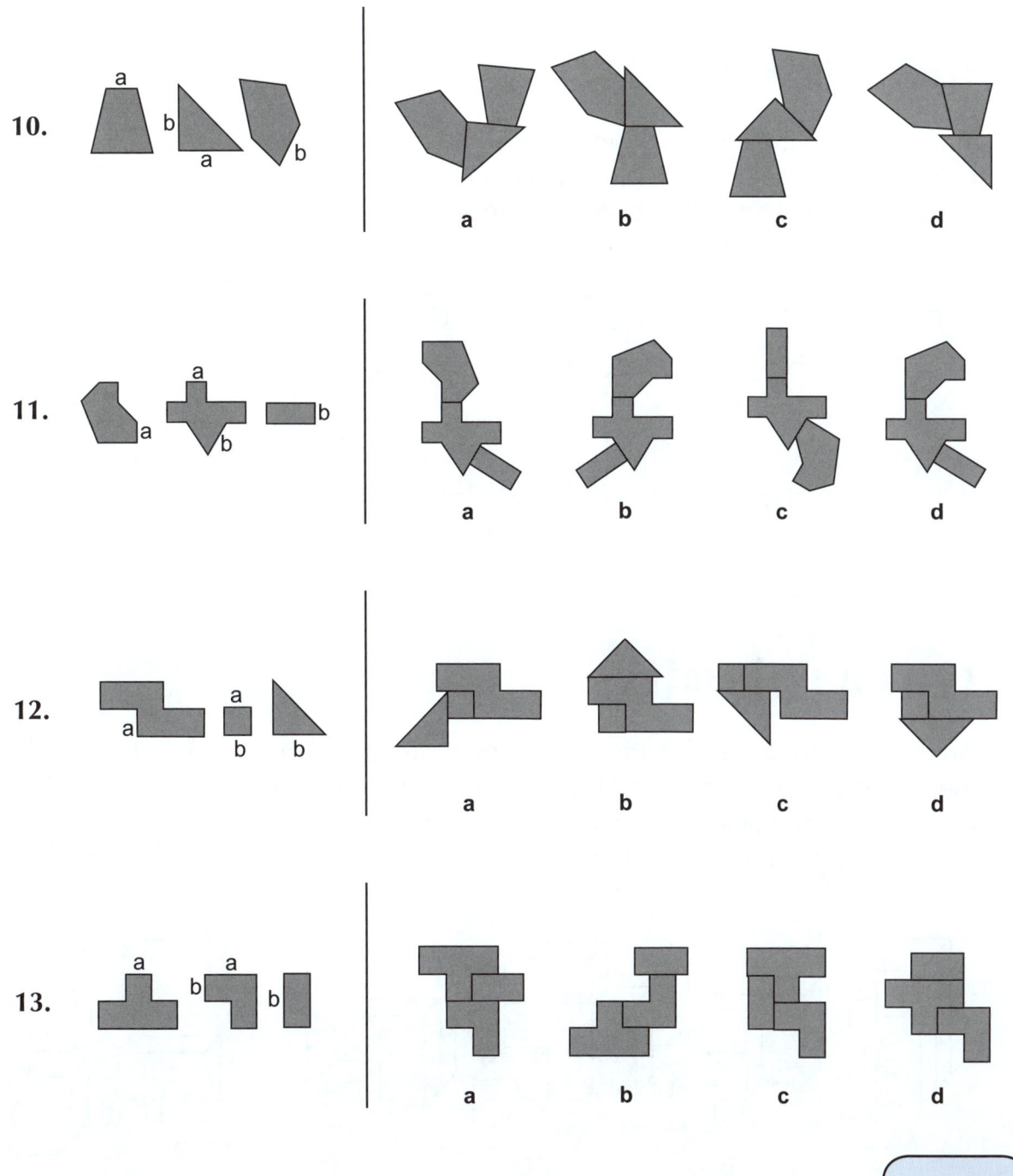

Puzzles 6

Here's a page of puzzles to help you practise **3D views** and **building blocks**.

Hear Me Roar...

Tim is exploring the cuboid jungle when he catches a glimpse of a rare block tiger. He only sees it from the back. What does Tim see?

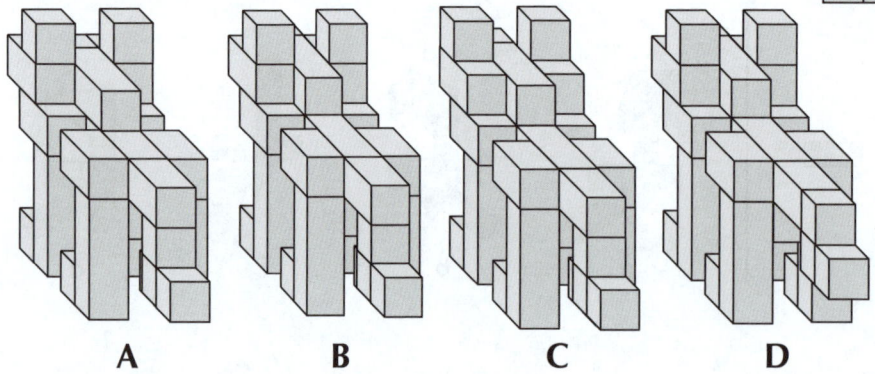

A   B   C   D

Crown Calamity

An evil sorcerer has stolen the king's crown. To get it back, the king must solve a puzzle. He must work out which of these shapes he could **not** make from the blocks he is given. Help the king get his crown back.

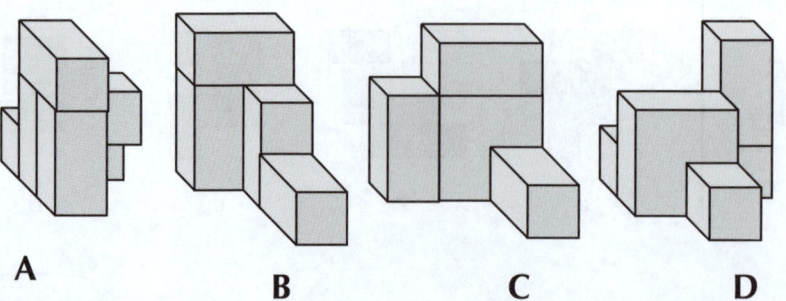

A   B   C   D

Test 19

You have **10 minutes** to do this test. Circle the letter for each correct answer.

Work out which set of blocks can be put together to make the 3D figure on the left.

1. 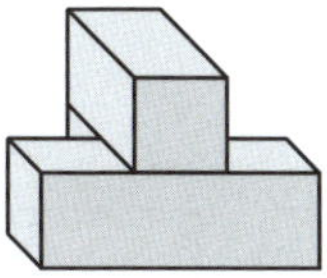

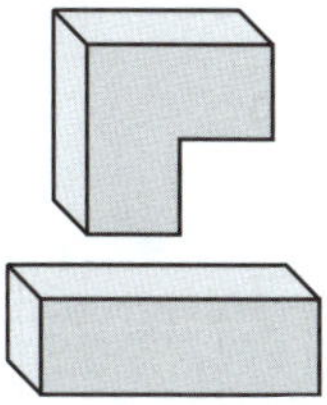
a

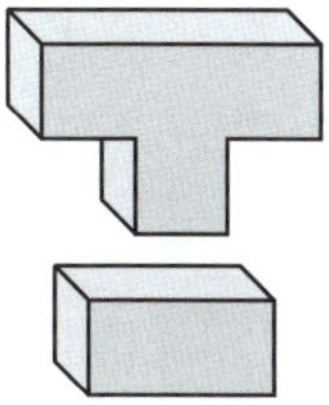
b

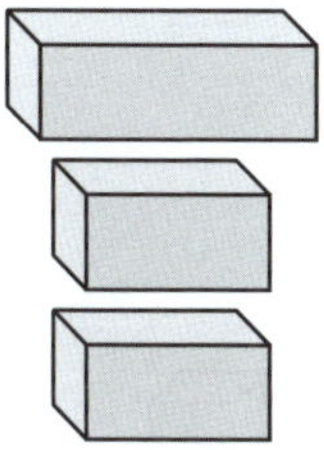
c

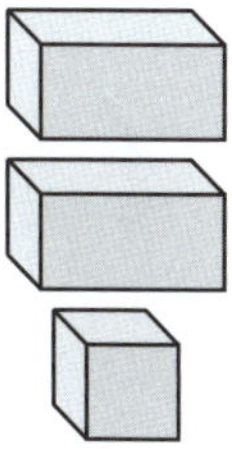
d

2. 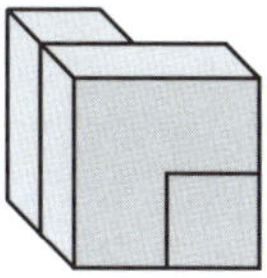

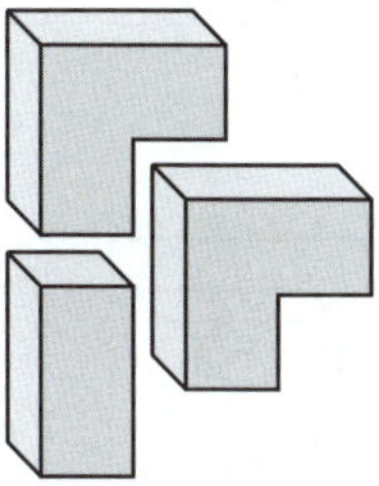
a

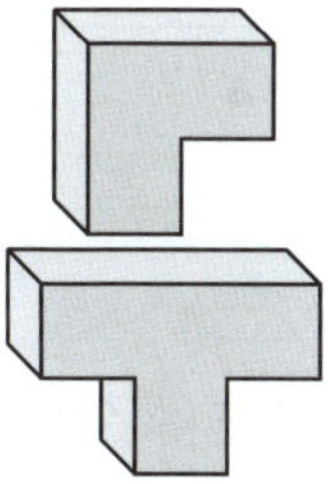
b

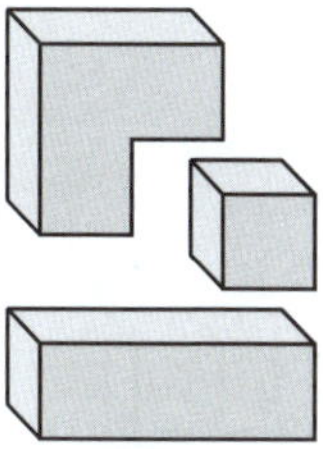
c

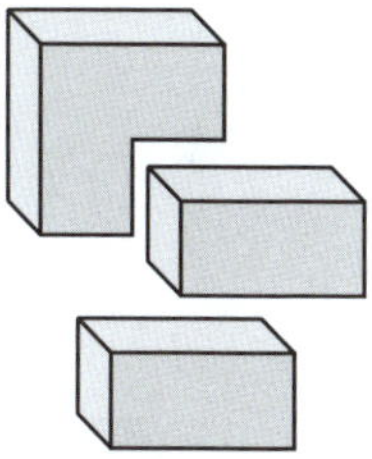
d

3. 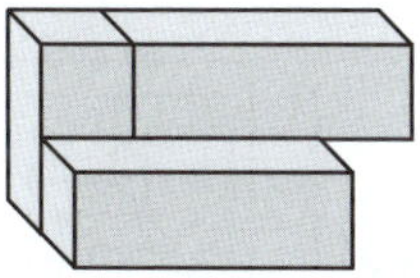

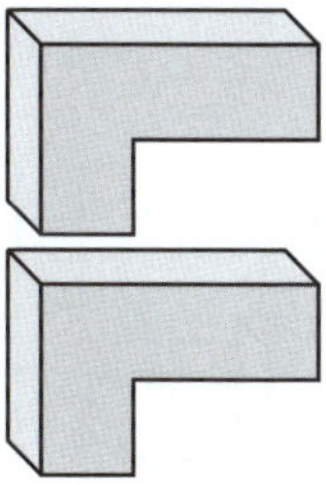
a

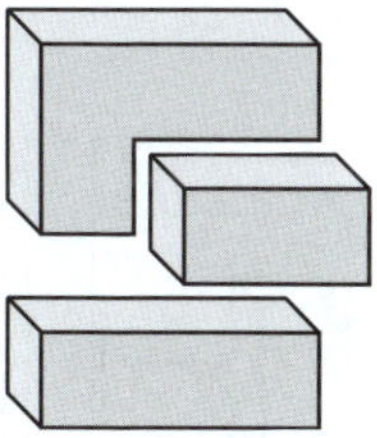
b

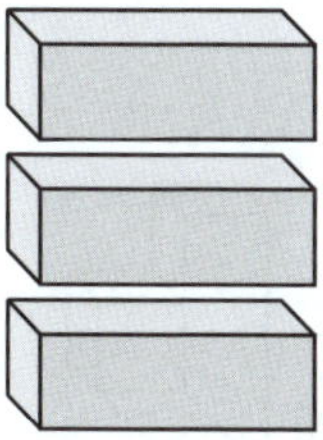
c

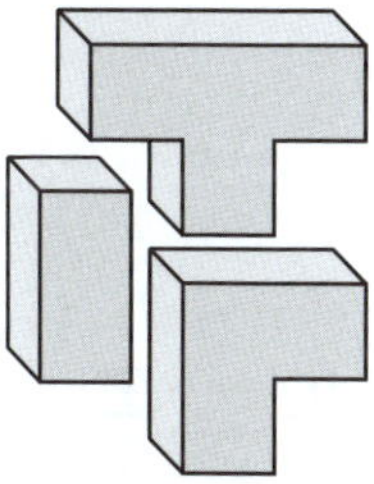
d

4. 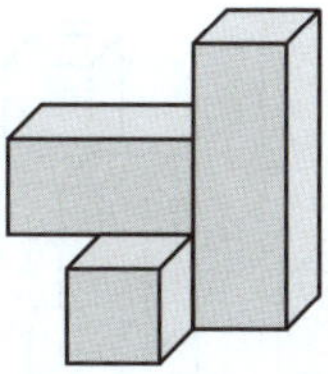

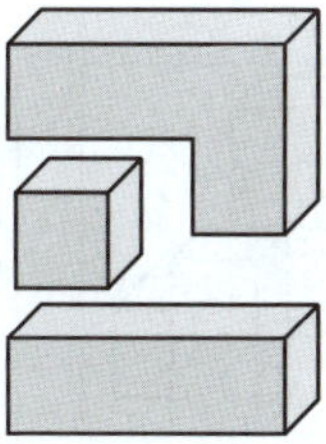
a

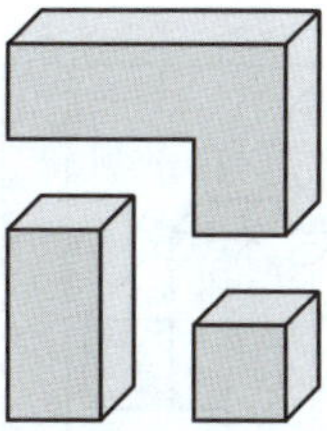
b

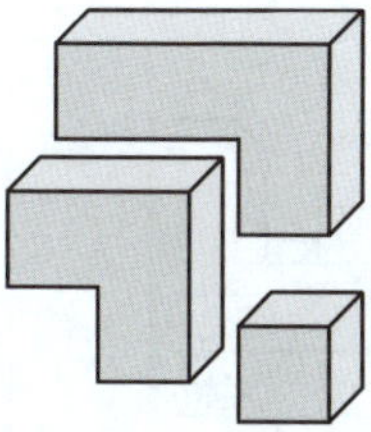
c

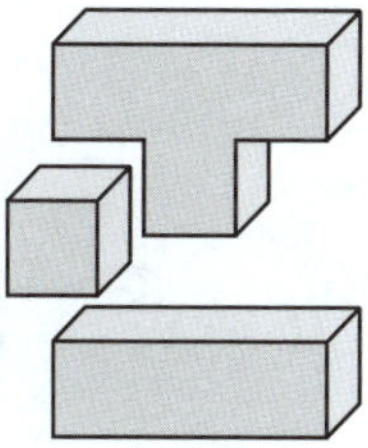
d

Work out which option is the 3D figure viewed from the **left**.

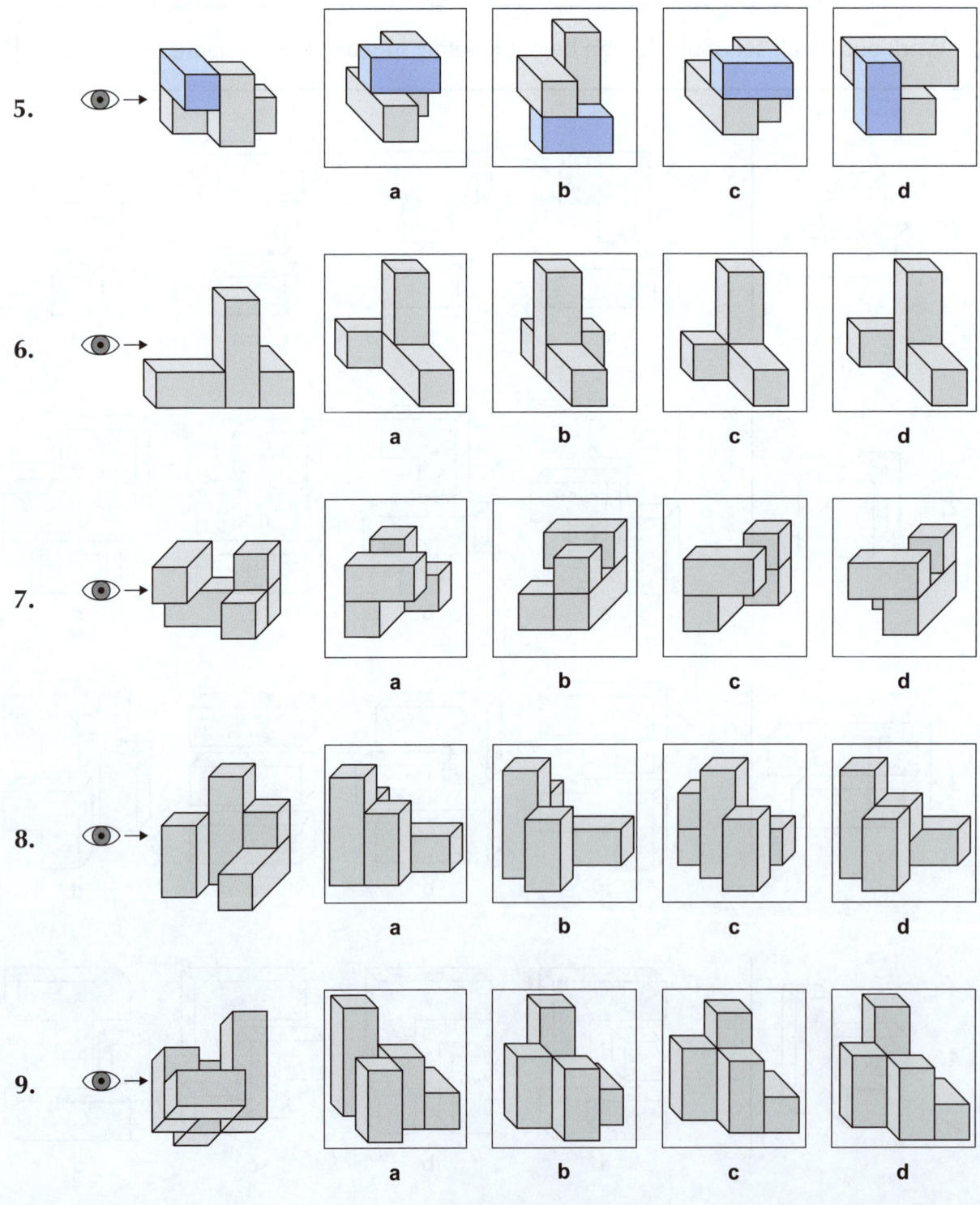

A square is folded and then a hole is punched, as shown on the left. Work out which option shows the square when unfolded.

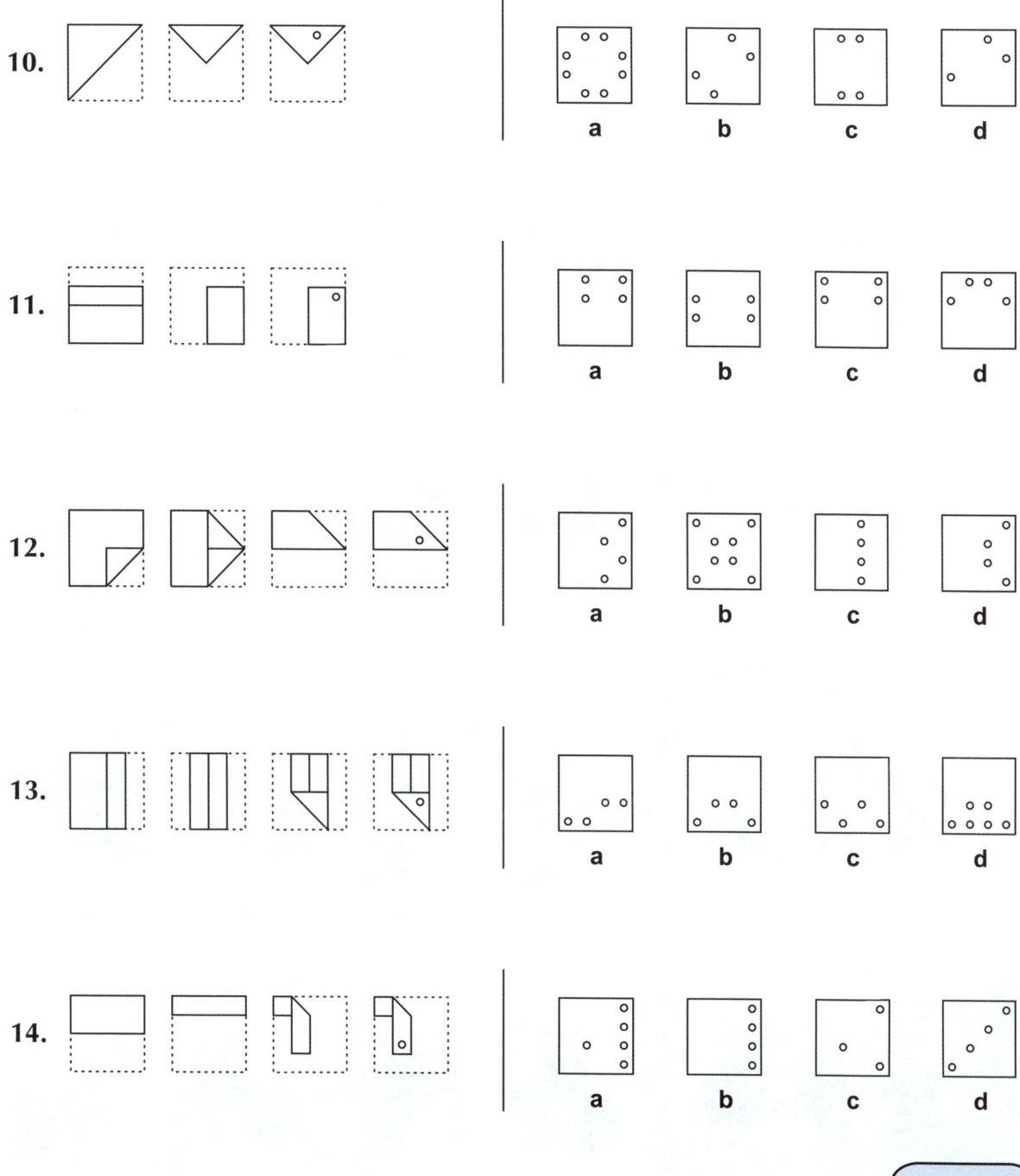

/ 14

Test 20

10

You have **10 minutes** to do this test. Circle the letter for each correct answer.

Work out which option shows how the three shapes will look when they are joined by matching the sides with the same letter.

1.

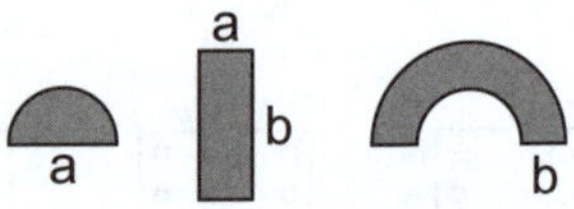

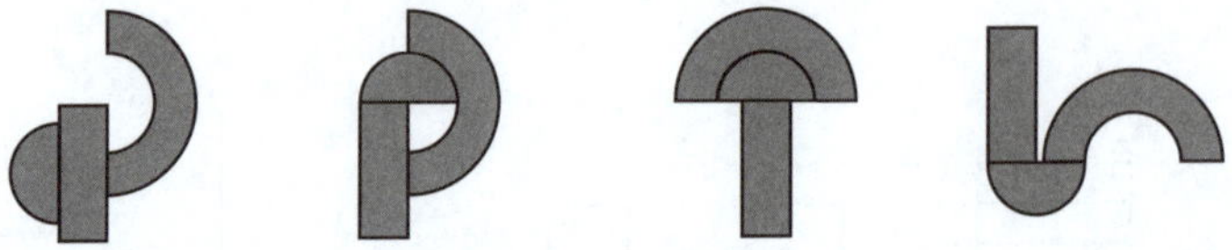

a b c d

2.

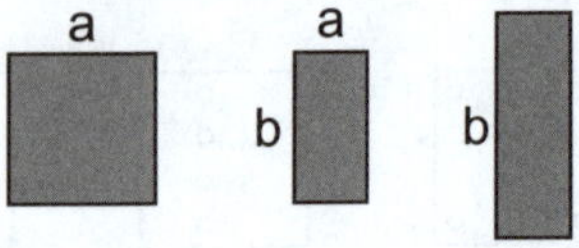

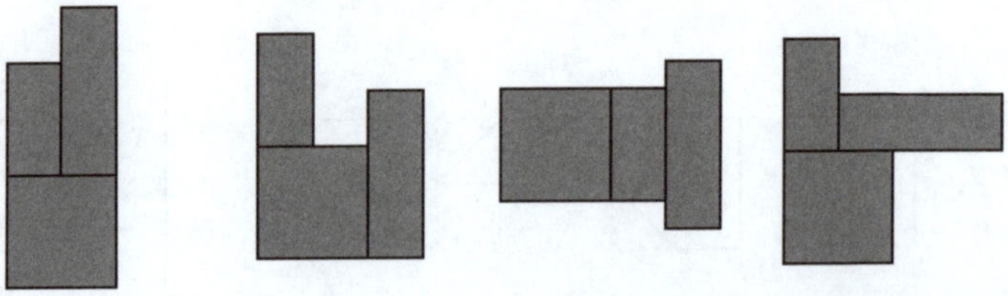

a b c d

3.

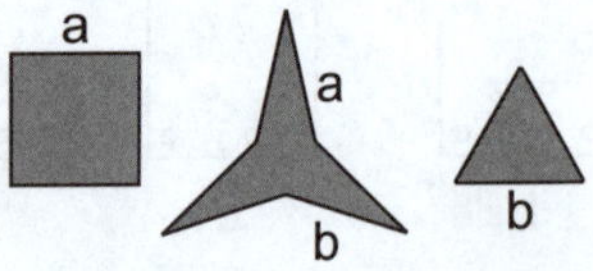

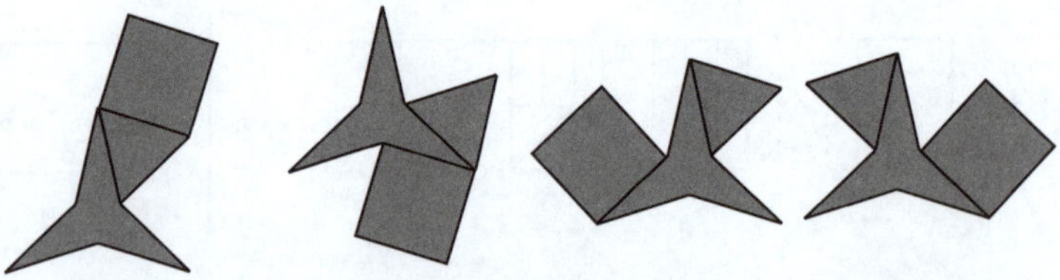

a b c d

4.

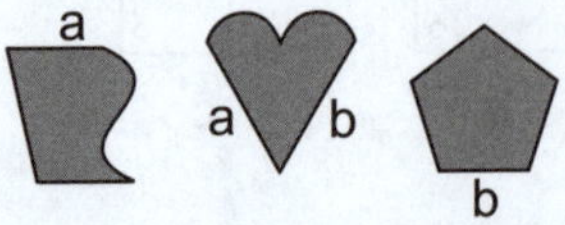

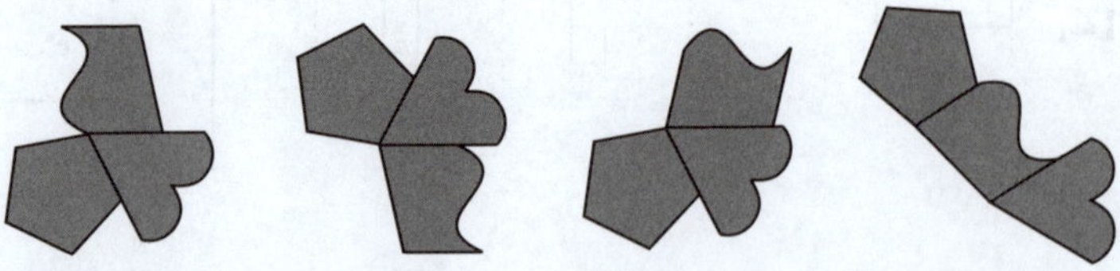

a b c d

 © CGP — not to be photocopied

Work out which 3D figure in the grey box has been rotated to make the new 3D figure.

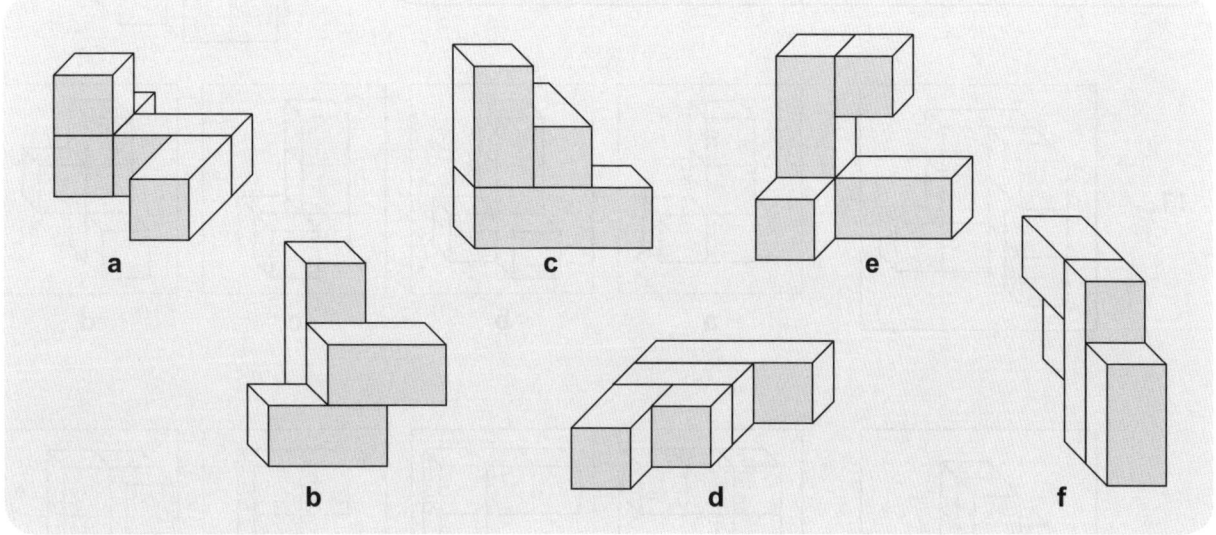

5. 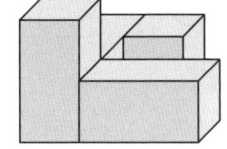 a d
b e
c f

6. 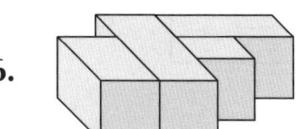 a d
b e
c f

7. 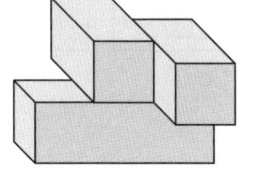 a d
b e
c f

8. 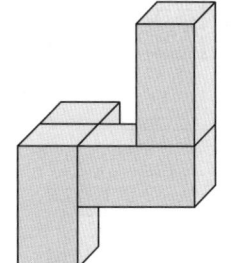 a d
b e
c f

9. 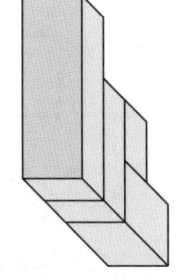 a d
b e
c f

10. 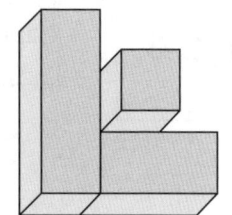 a d
b e
c f

© CGP — not to be photocopied   73   Test 20

Without rotating the figure on the left, work out which option fits onto it to make the 3D shape in the grey box.

11.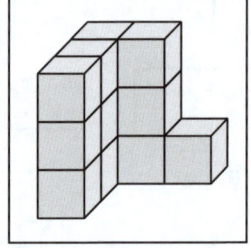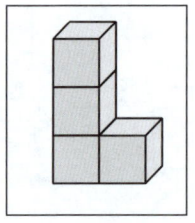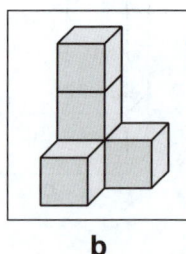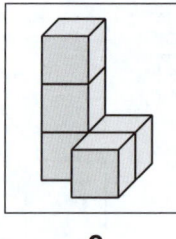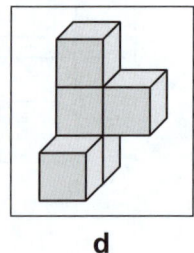
                                  a   b   c   d

12.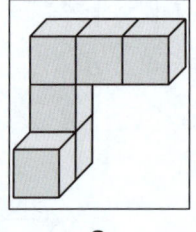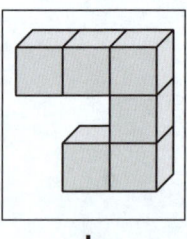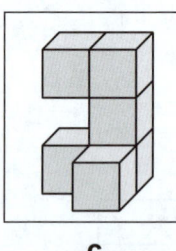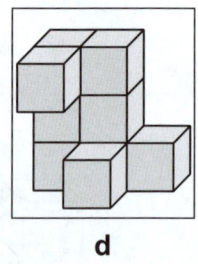
                                  a   b   c   d

13.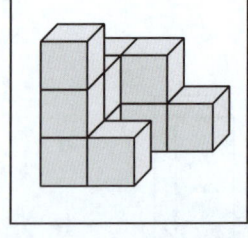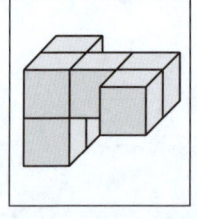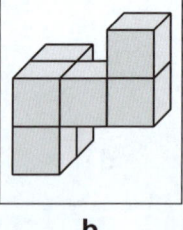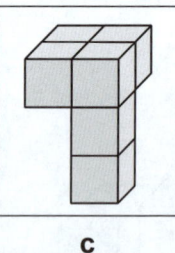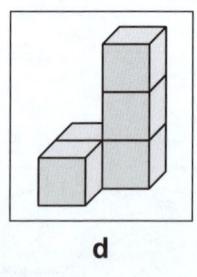
                                  a   b   c   d

14.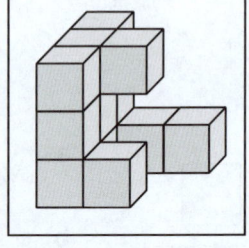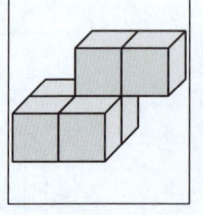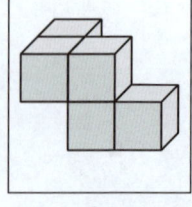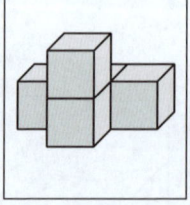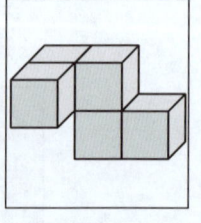
                                  a   b   c   d

/ 14

Test 21

You have **10 minutes** to do this test. Circle the letter for each correct answer.

> Work out which option shows the figure on the left when folded along the dotted line.

1.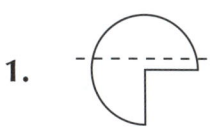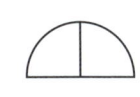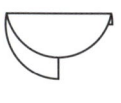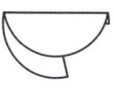
                                               a   b   c   d

2.
                                               a   b   c   d

3.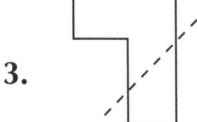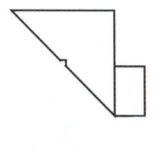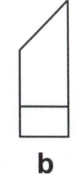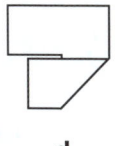
                                               a   b   c   d

4.
                                               a   b   c   d

5.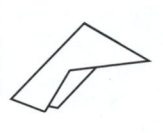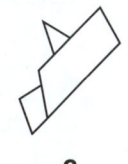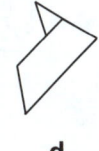
                                               a   b   c   d

Work out which of the four partial nets can be folded to make the cube on the left.

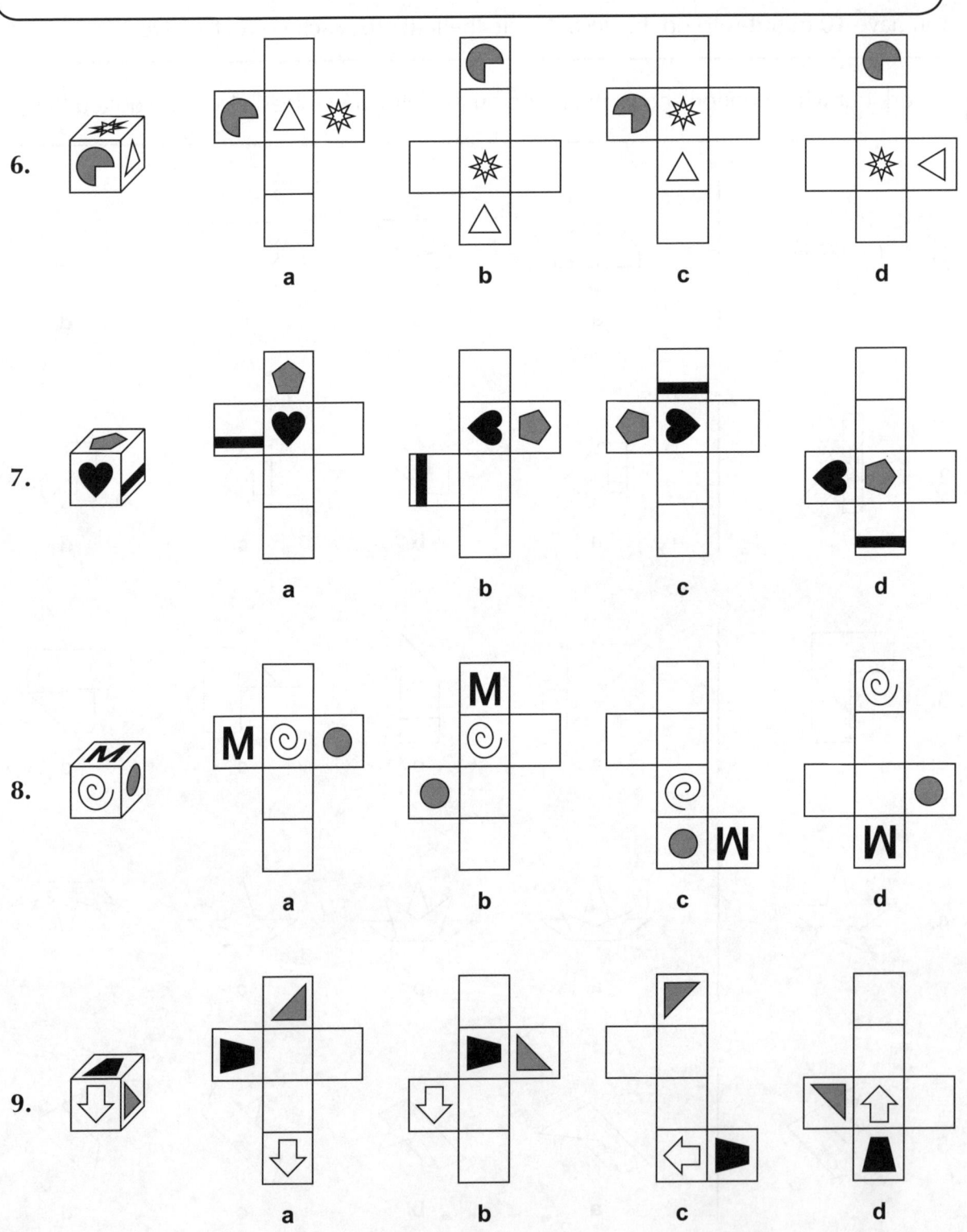

Work out which option contains the hidden shape shown. It should be the same size and orientation.

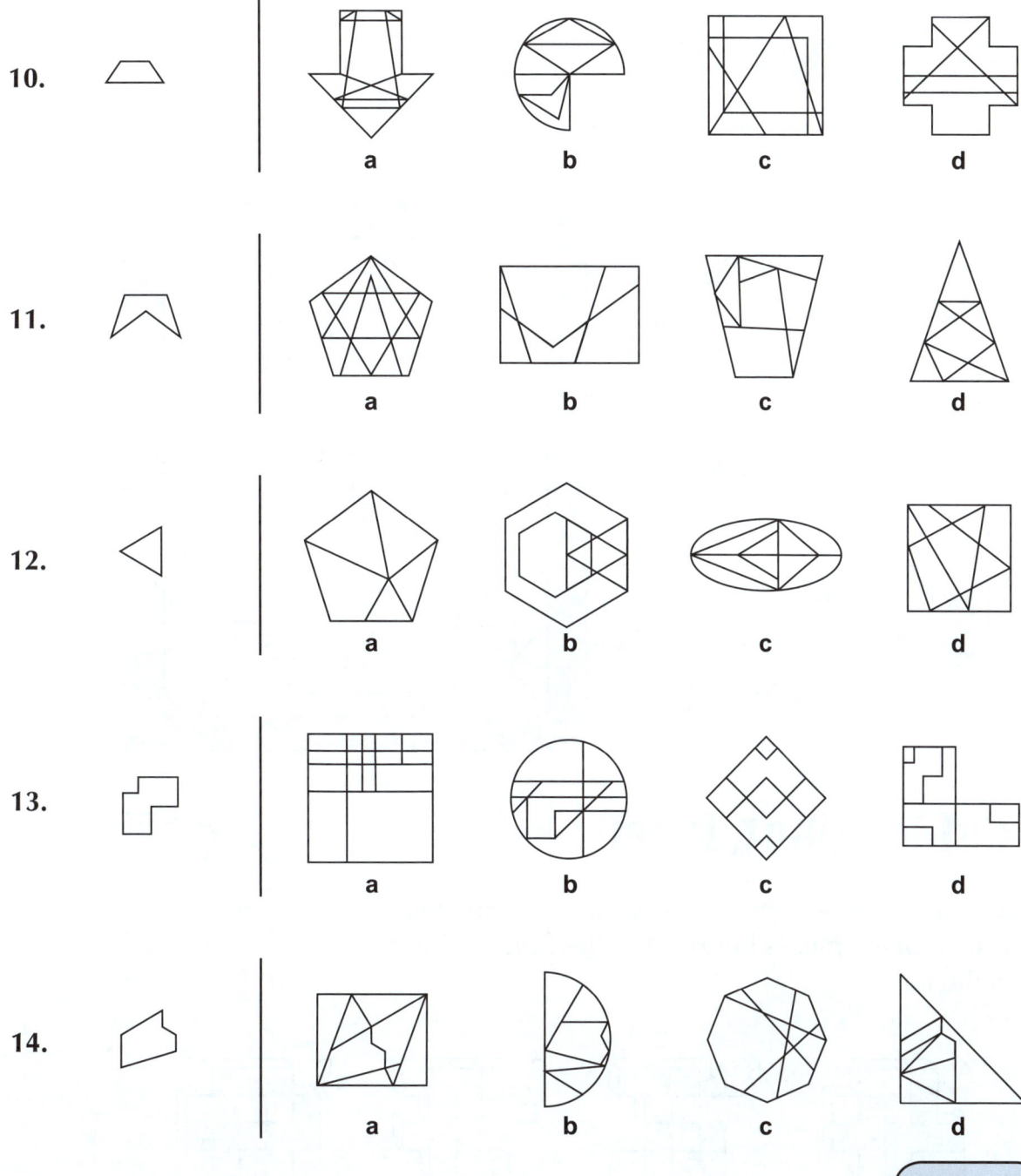

Puzzles 7

These puzzles are a great way of practising your **hidden shape** and **3D rotation** skills.

Shape Shading

Find the shapes below in the picture on the right. Shade them in using one colour. What do you see?

 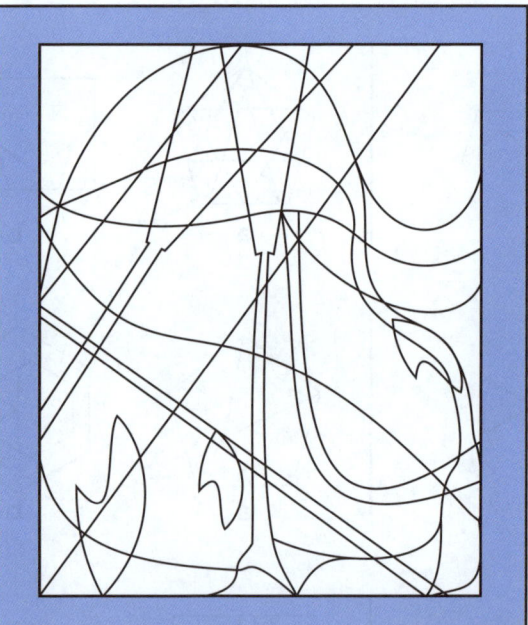

Cubic Conundrum

Part of an open-topped cube is shown on the right. Which of the pieces below form the front and side of the cube?

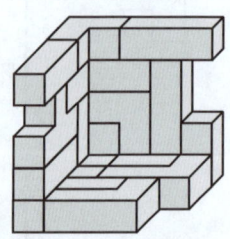

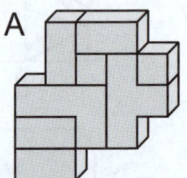 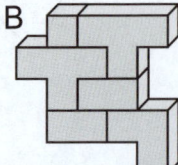 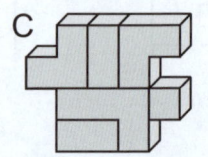 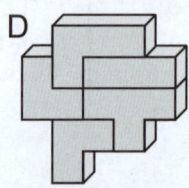

A   B   C   D

Test 22

You have **10 minutes** to do this test. Circle the letter for each correct answer.

Work out which set of blocks can be put together to make the 3D figure on the left.

1.

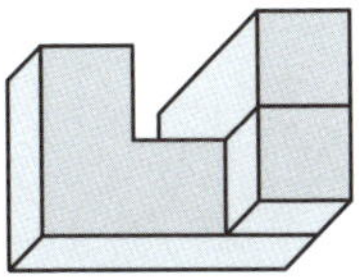

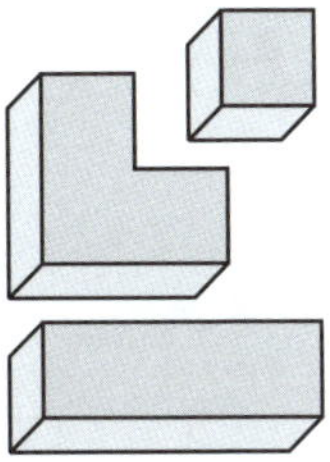

   a 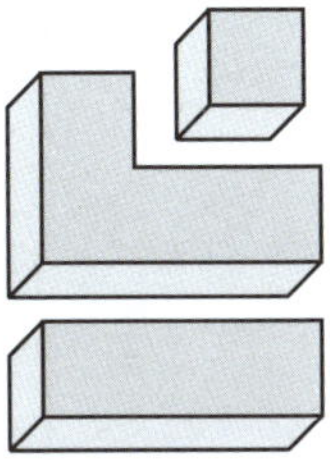   b 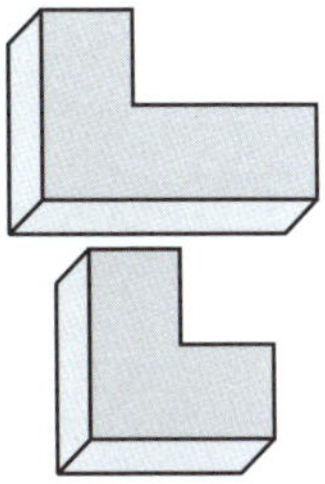   c    d

2.

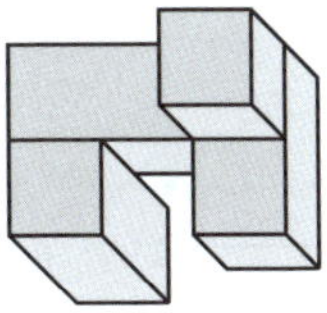

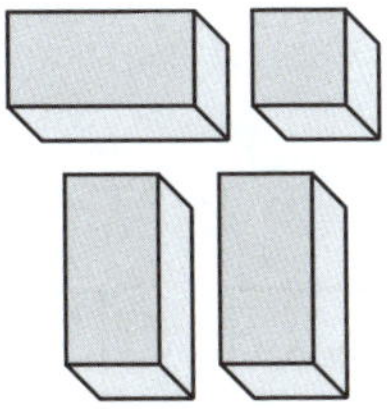

   a 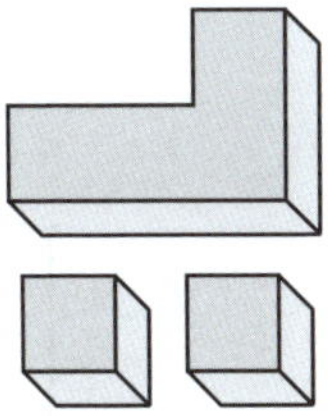   b 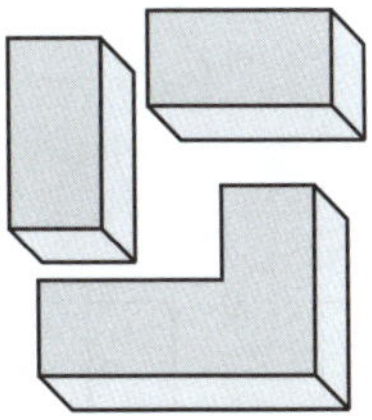   c 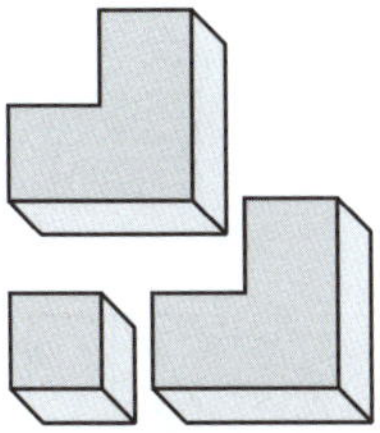   d

3.

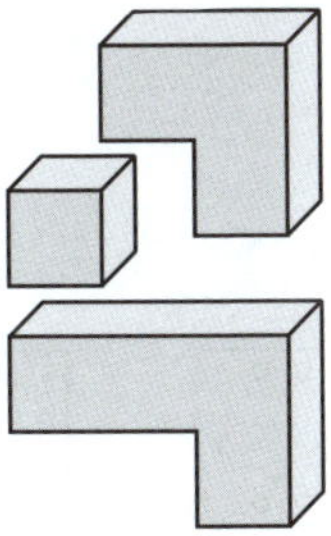

   a 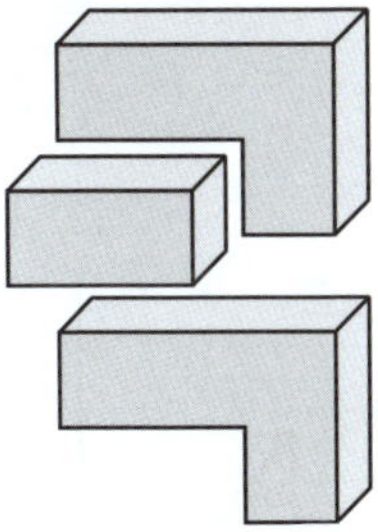   b    c    d

4.

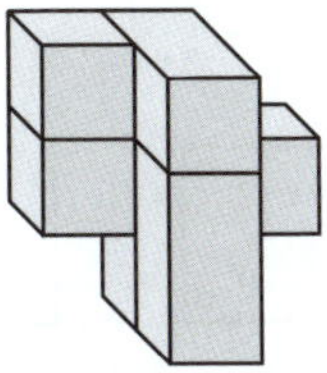

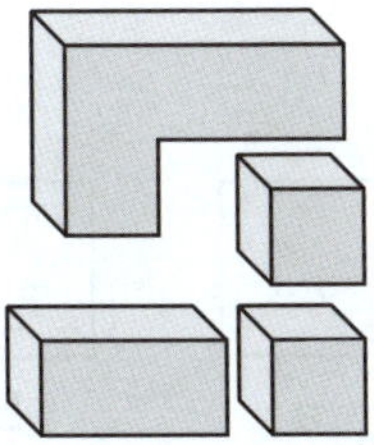

   a 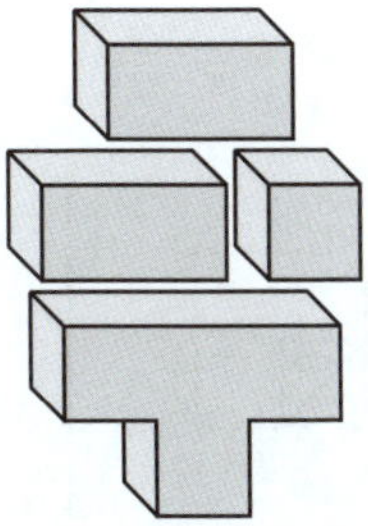   b    c 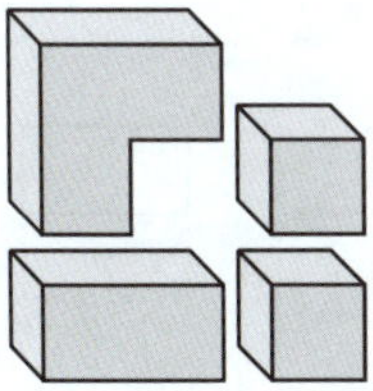   d

© CGP — not to be photocopied   79   Test 22

A square is folded and then a hole is punched, as shown on the left. Work out which option shows the square when unfolded.

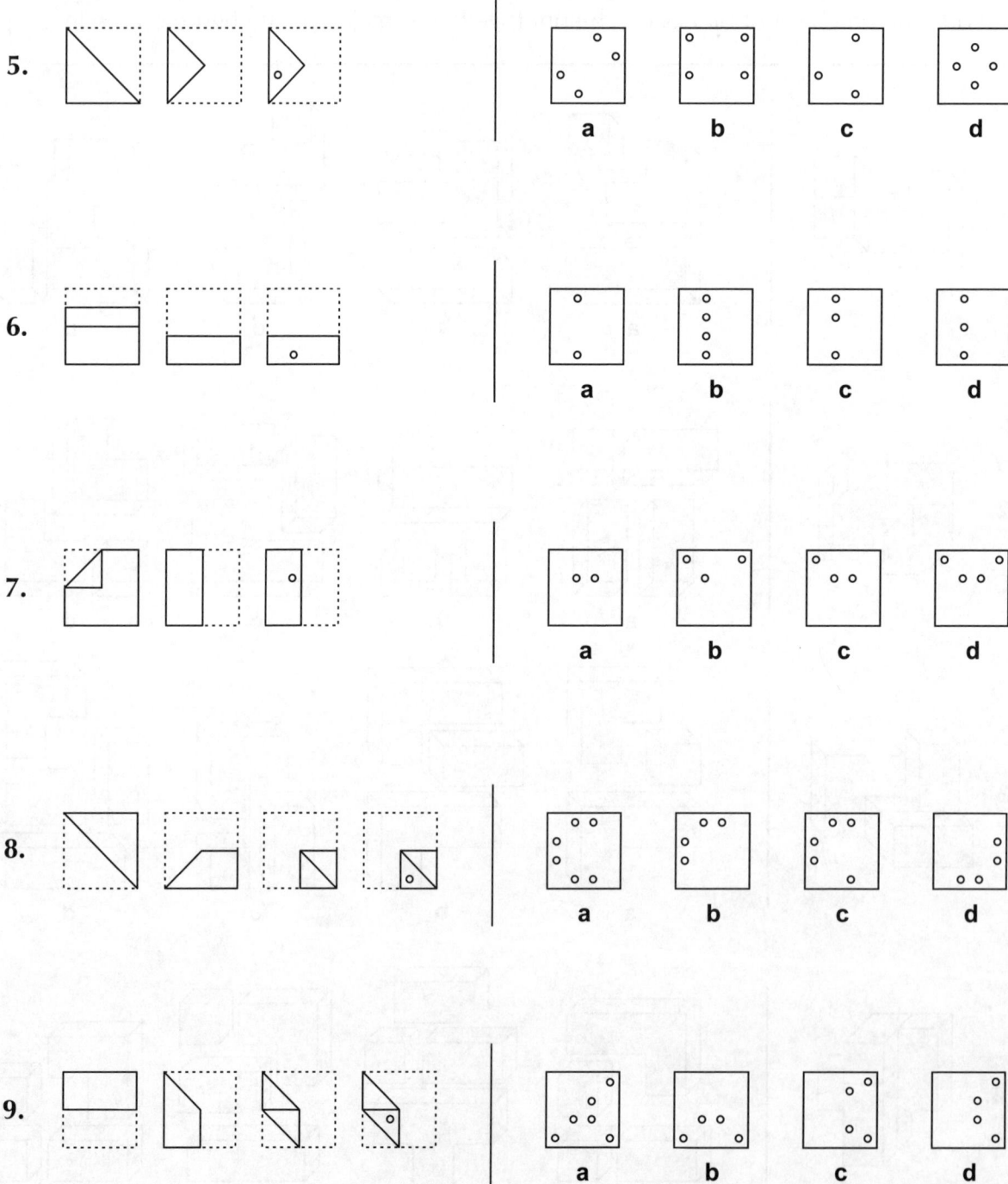

Work out which option contains the hidden shape shown. It should be the same size and orientation.

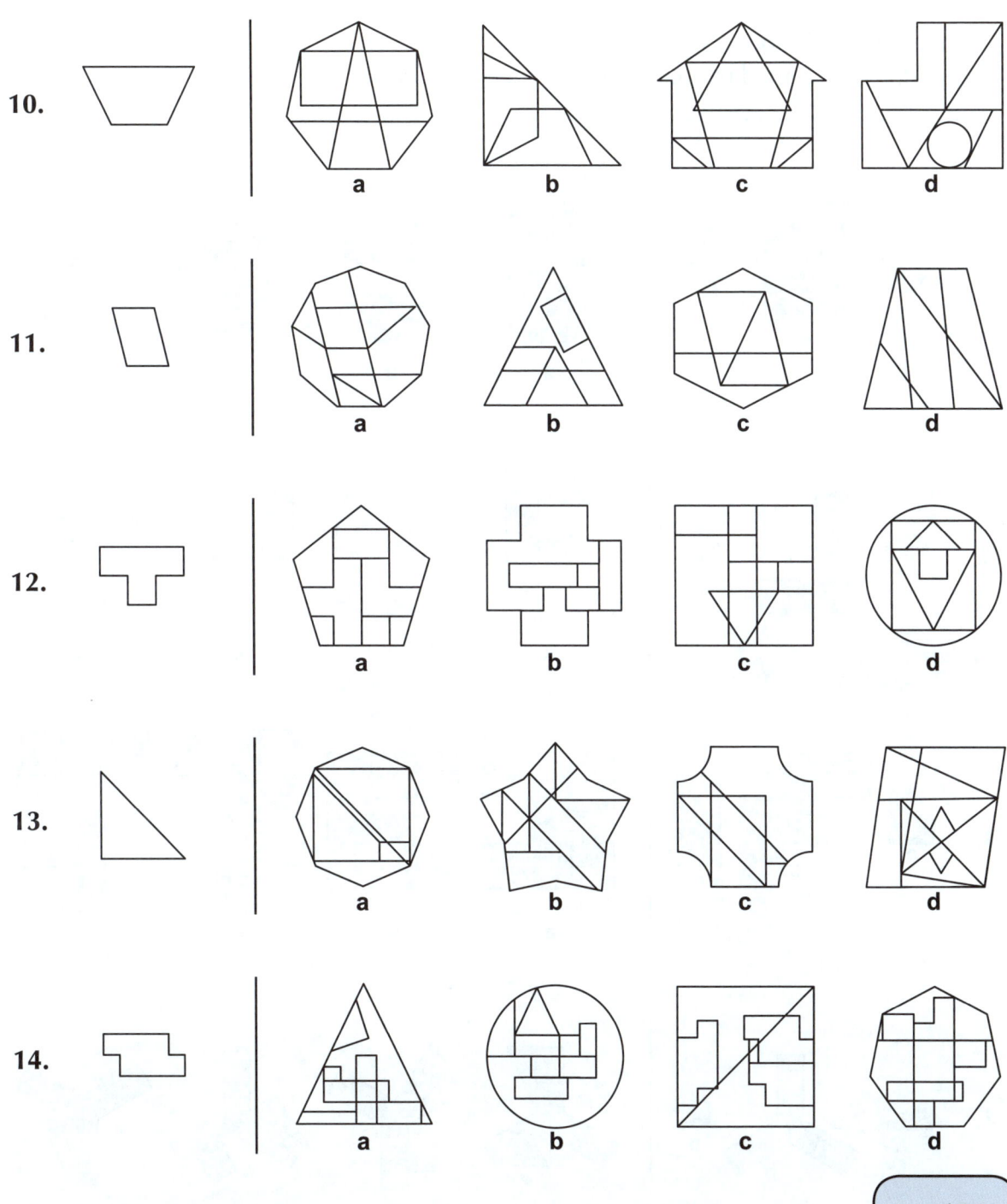

Test 23

You have **10 minutes** to do this test. Circle the letter for each correct answer.

Work out which option shows how the three shapes will look when they are joined by matching the sides with the same letter.

1.

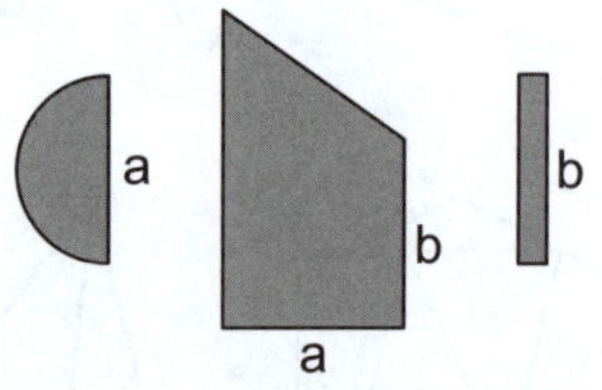

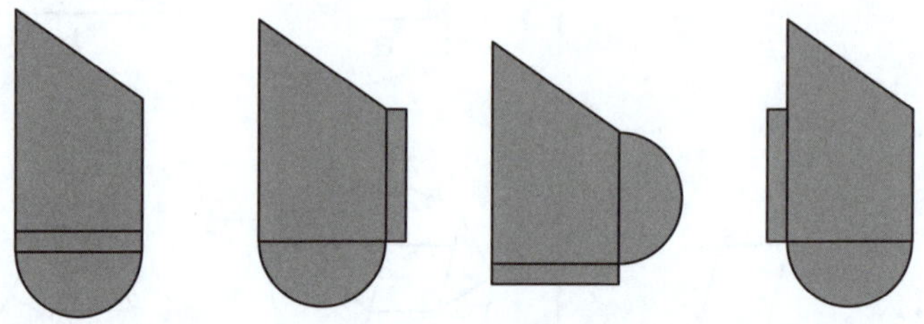

a b c d

2.

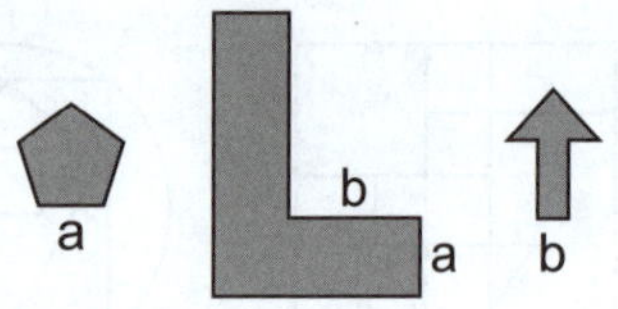

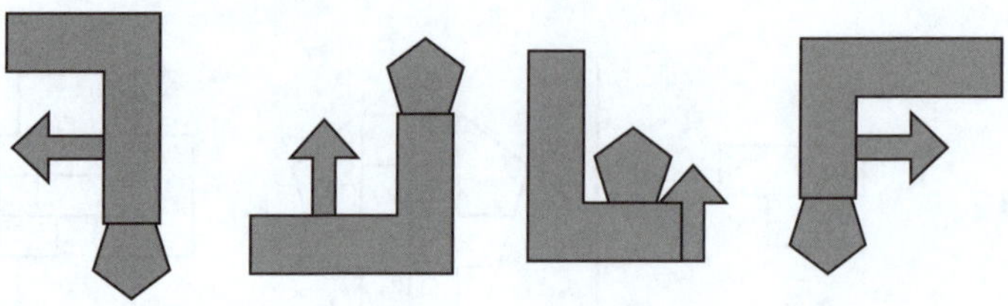

a b c d

3.

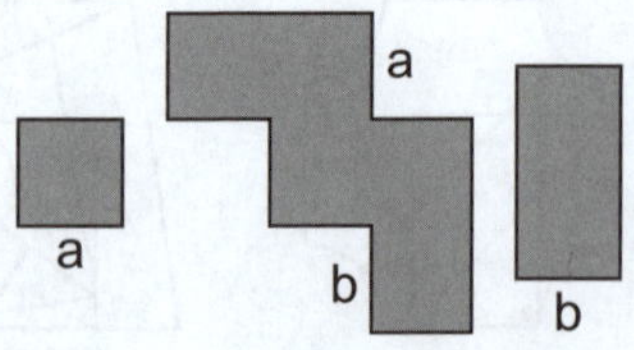

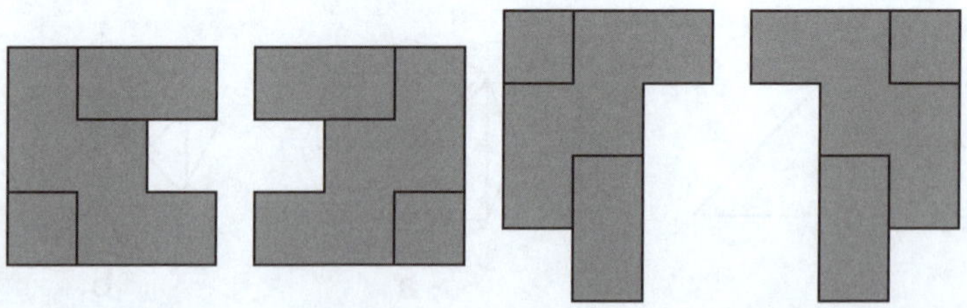

a b c d

4.

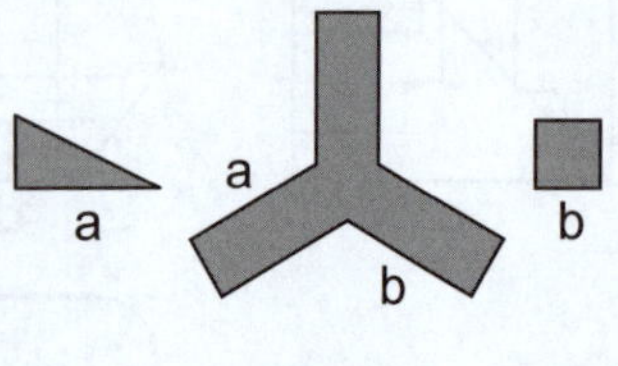

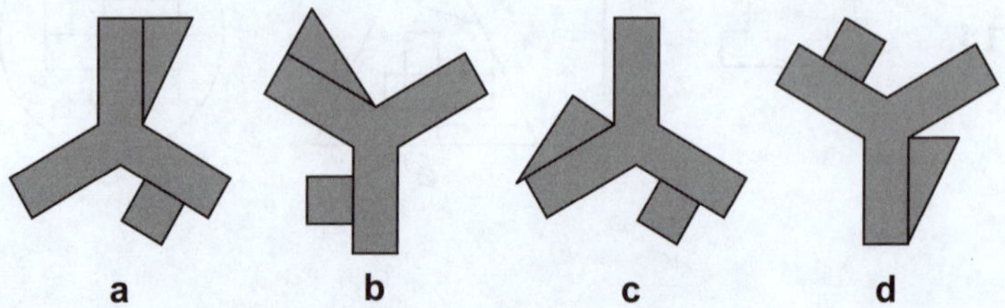

a b c d

© CGP — not to be photocopied

Work out which 3D figure in the grey box has been rotated to make the new 3D figure.

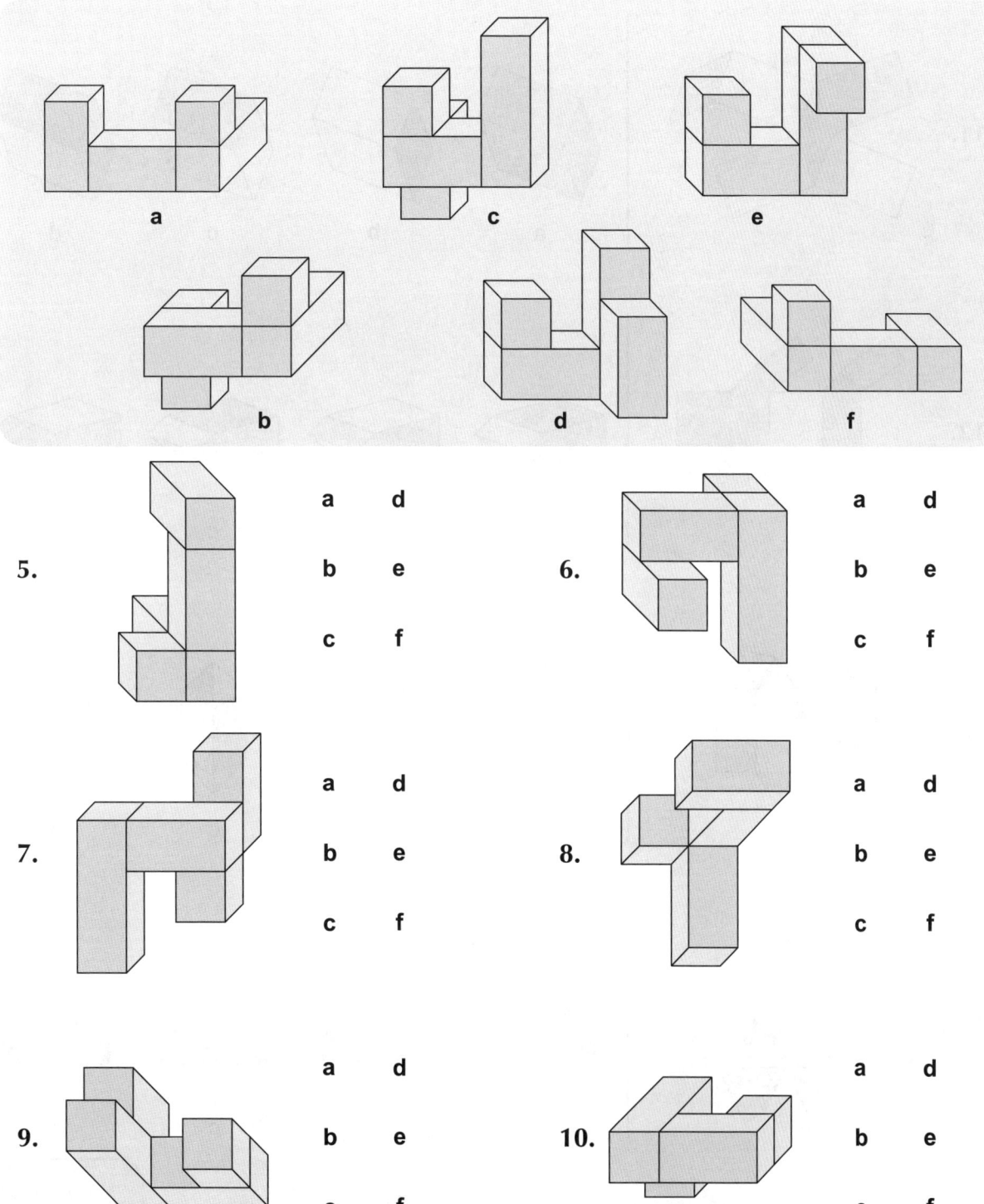

5.

6.

7.

8.

9.

10.

a   d
b   e
c   f

a   d
b   e
c   f

a   d
b   e
c   f

a   d
b   e
c   f

a   d
b   e
c   f

a   d
b   e
c   f

Work out which of the 3D shapes can be made from the net.

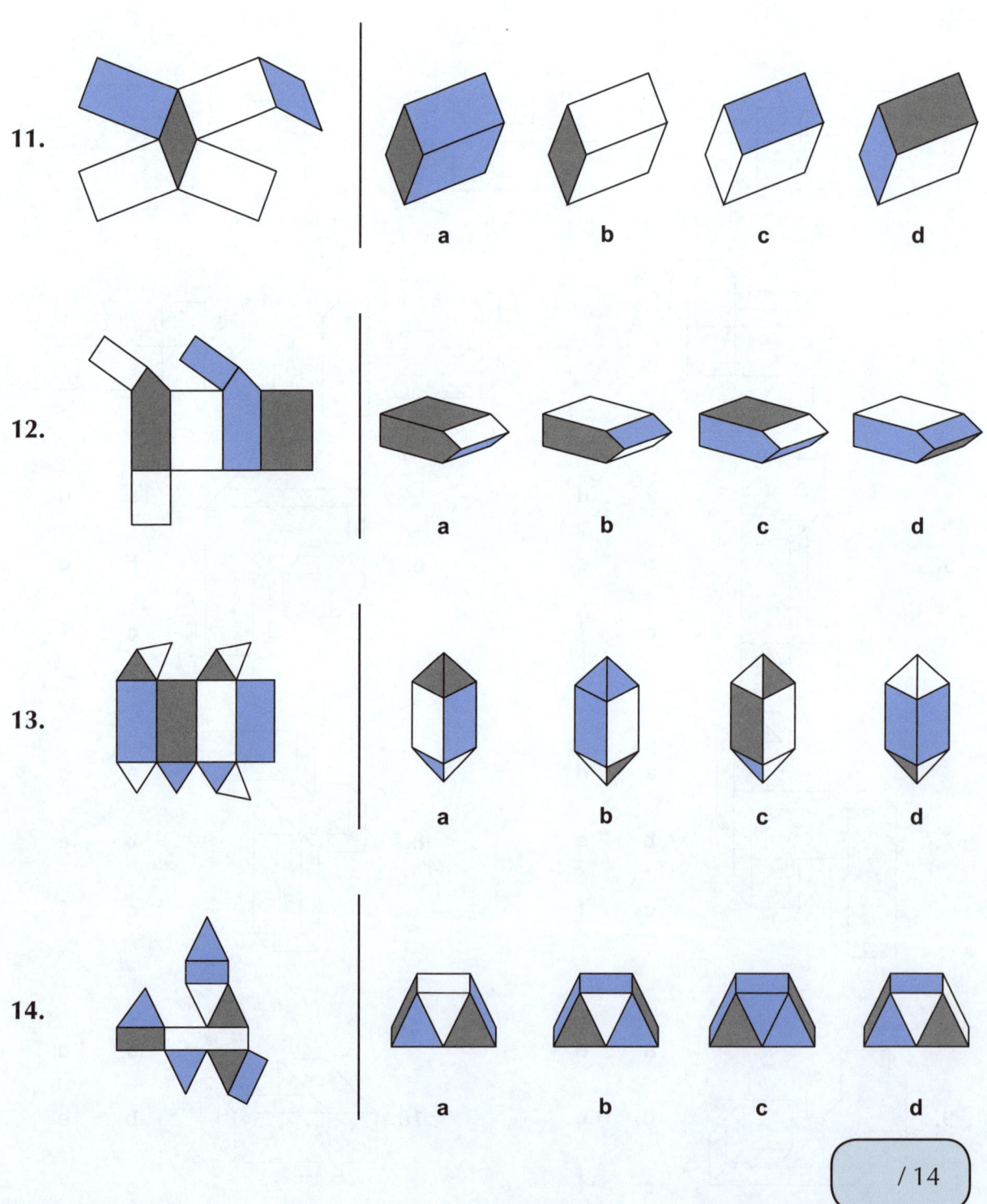

Test 24

You have **10 minutes** to do this test. Circle the letter for each correct answer.

A square is folded and then a hole is punched, as shown on the left. Work out which option shows the square when unfolded.

1.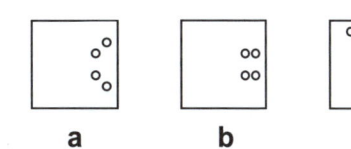

    a   b   c   d

2.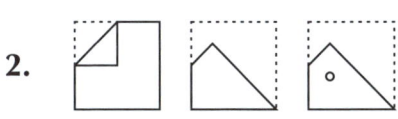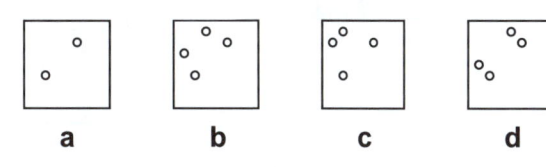

    a   b   c   d

3.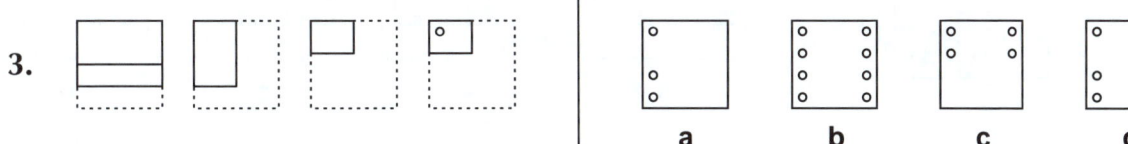

    a   b   c   d

4.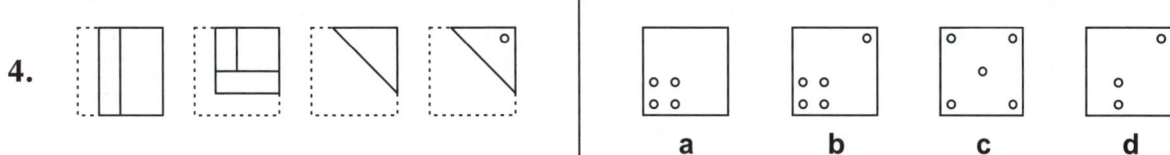

    a   b   c   d

5.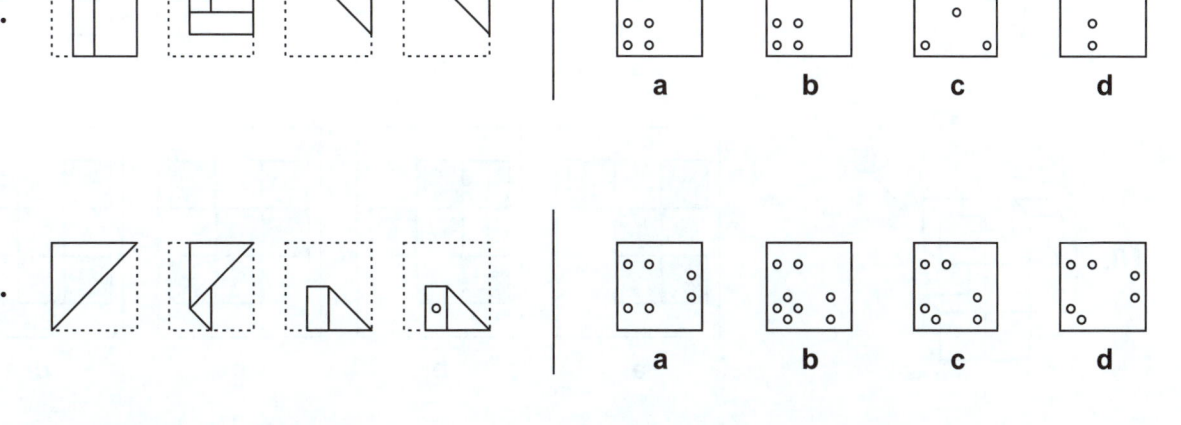

    a   b   c   d

Work out which option is a 2D view from the **back** of the 3D figure shown.

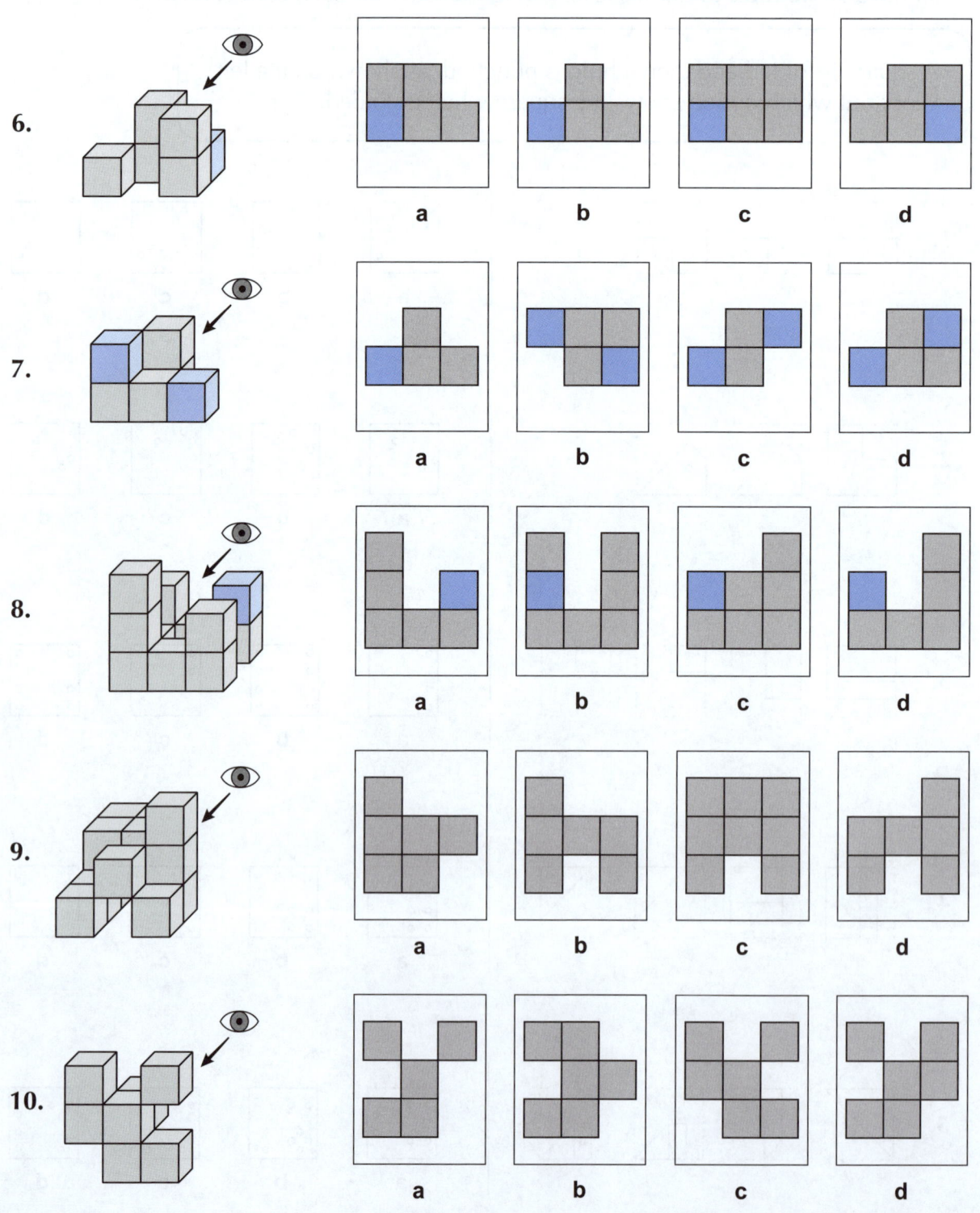

Work out which of the four cubes can be made from the net.

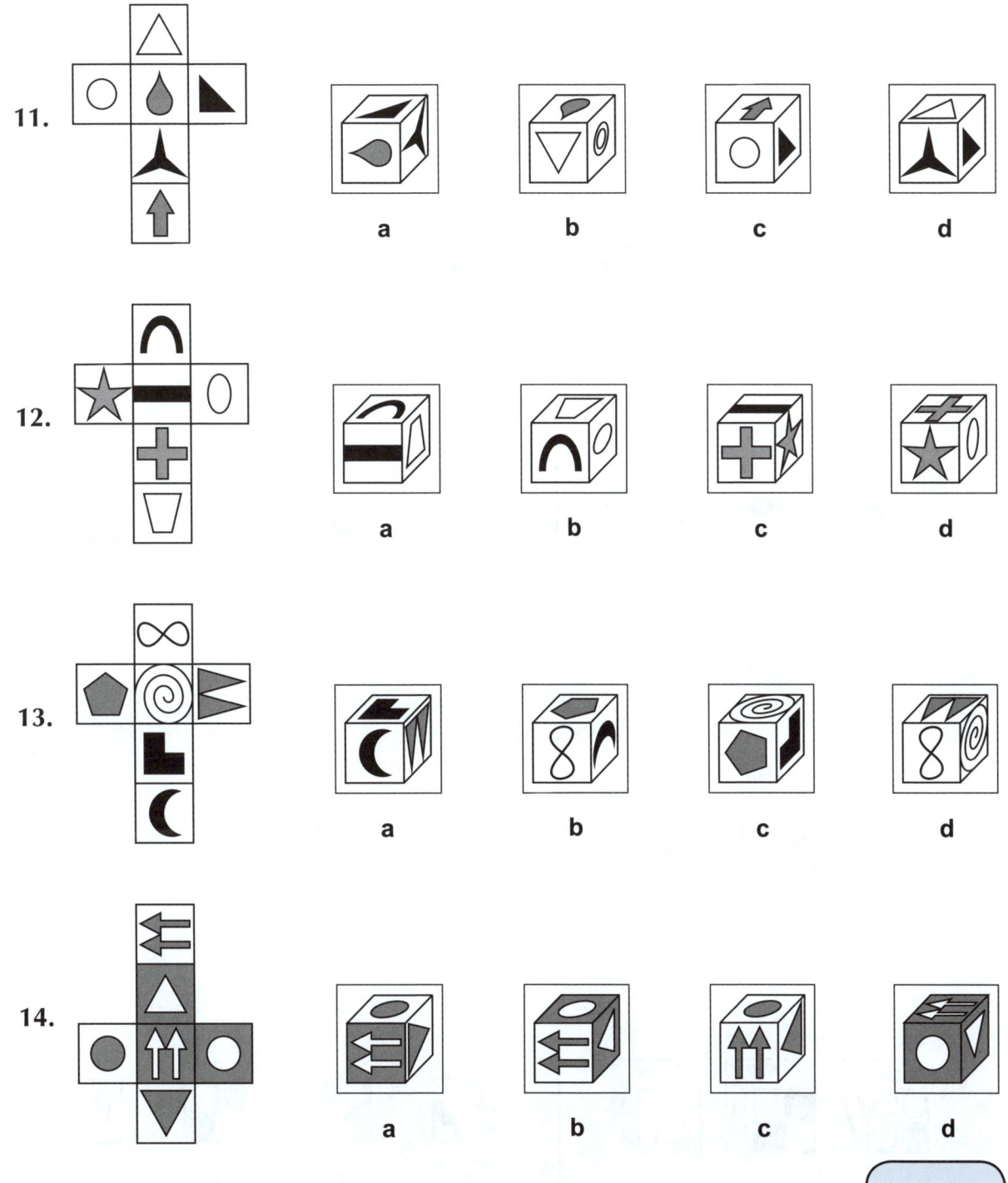

Test 25

You have **10 minutes** to do this test. Circle the letter for each correct answer.

> The figures on the left show different views of the same cube. All the cube faces are different. Work out which of the options should replace the blue cube face.

1.   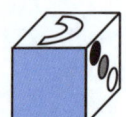   
                                                   a   b   c   d

2. 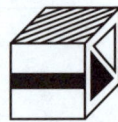     
                                                   a   b   c   d

3.   
                                                   a   b   c   d

4.      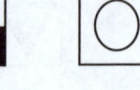
                                                   a   b   c   d

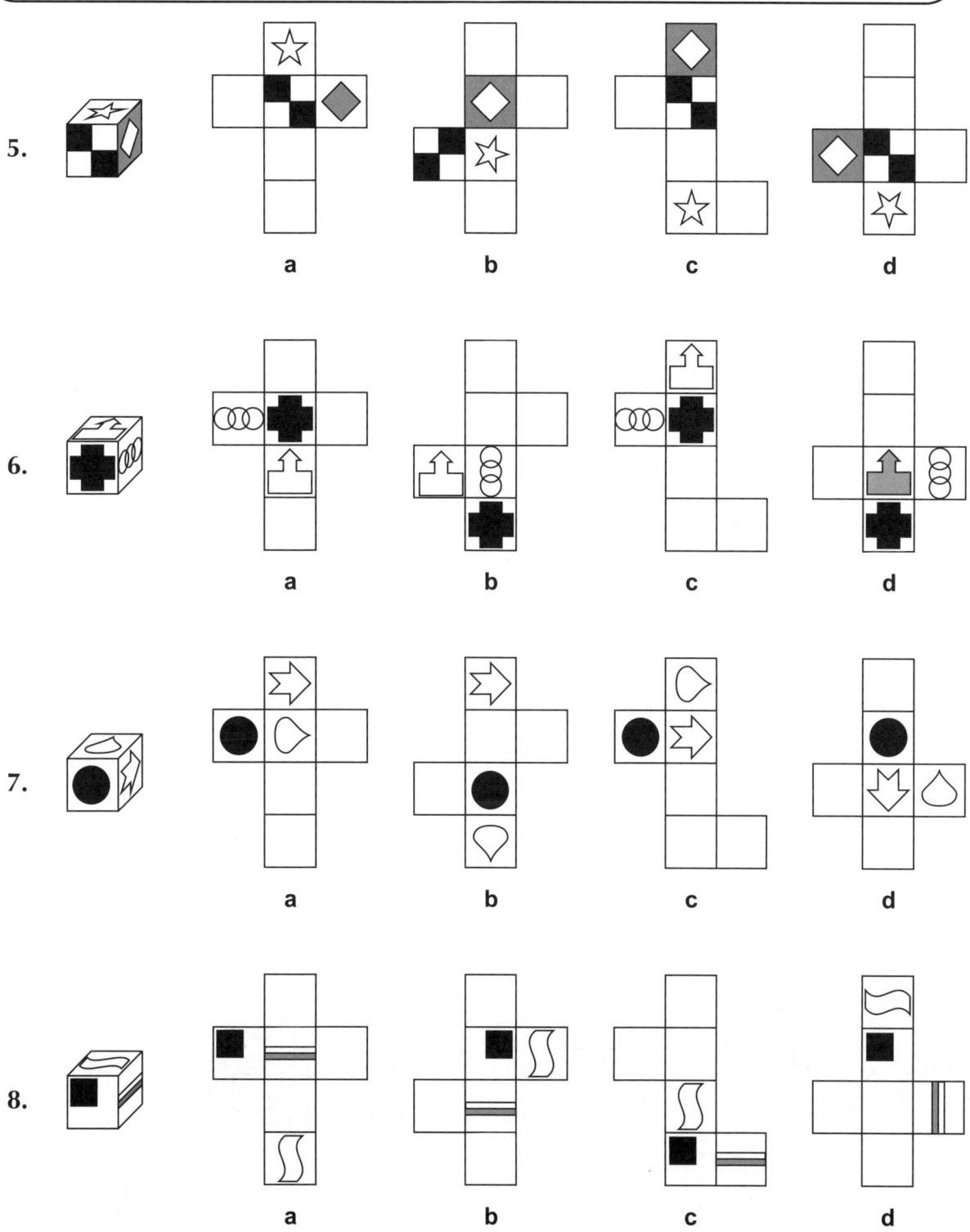

Work out which option is the 3D figure viewed from the **back**.

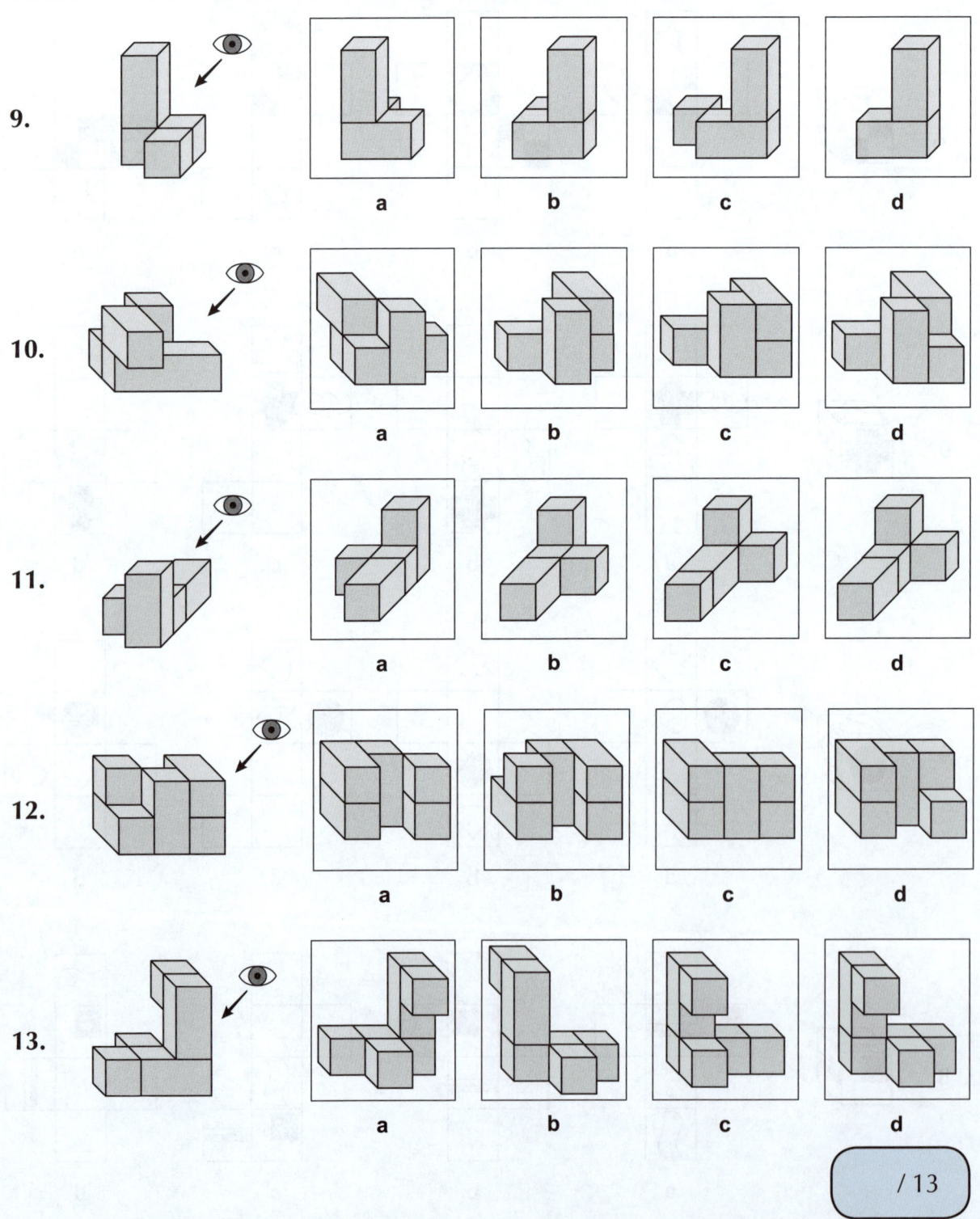

Puzzles 8

It's puzzle time again. Use this page to practise your **cube views** and **net** skills.

Watch Your Step!

Ellie the explorer is trying to reach some treasure. Luckily there's a path made out of identical cubes — but the tops of them have been covered in blue slime. She can only step on cubes that have a four-sided shape on top. The signpost shows two views of the cubes. Draw the path to the treasure.

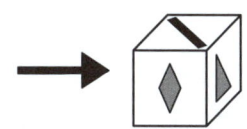 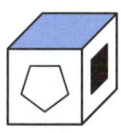 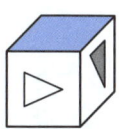 

  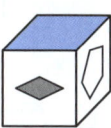 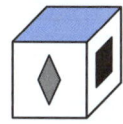

 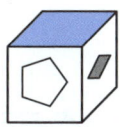  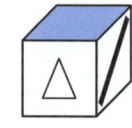

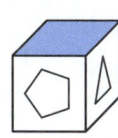   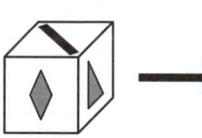

The treasure is protected by a puzzle.

Help Ellie open the chest by completing the net of the cube on the padlock.

Leave the faces that you can't see blank.

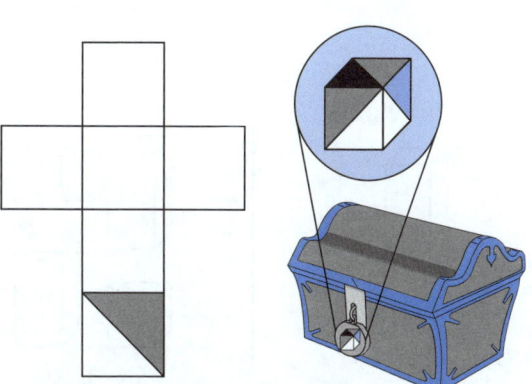

© CGP — not to be photocopied

Test 26

You have **10 minutes** to do this test. Circle the letter for each correct answer.

Work out which set of blocks can be put together to make the 3D figure on the left.

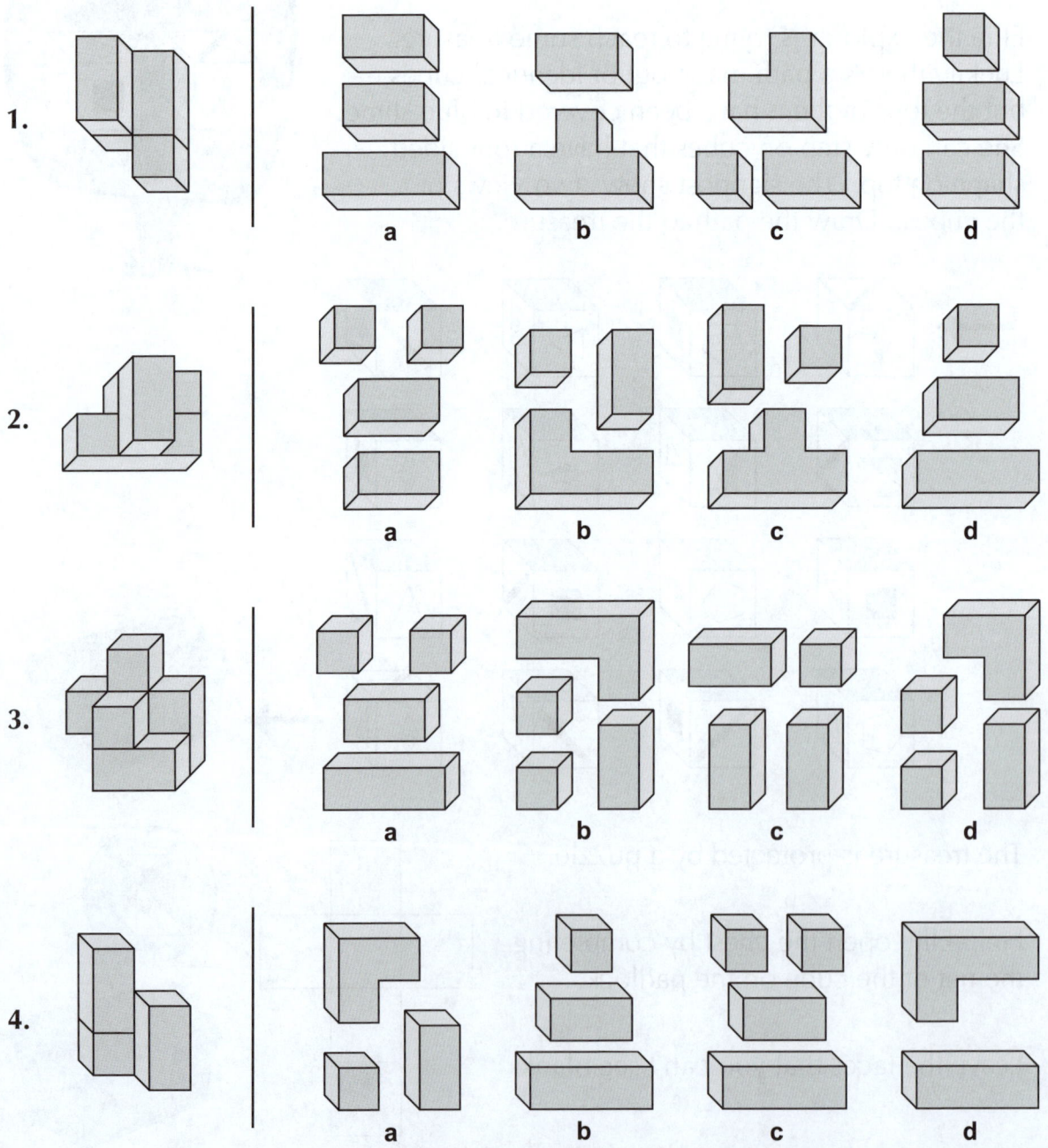

Work out which option is the 3D figure viewed from the **left**.

Work out which option contains the hidden shape shown. It should be the same size and orientation.

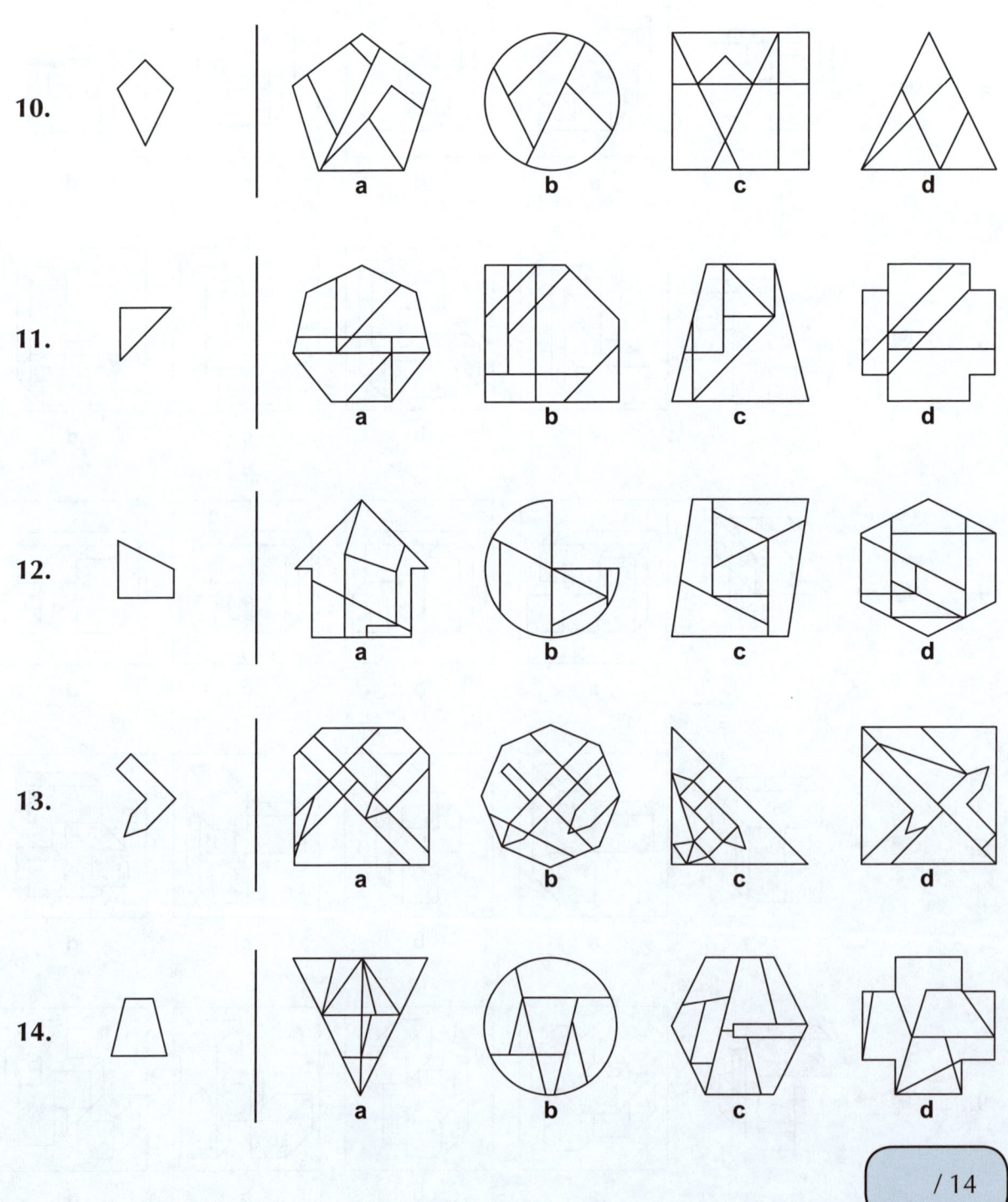

Test 27

You have **10 minutes** to do this test. Circle the letter for each correct answer.

Work out which option shows how the three shapes will look when they are joined by matching the sides with the same letter.

1.

2.

3.

4.

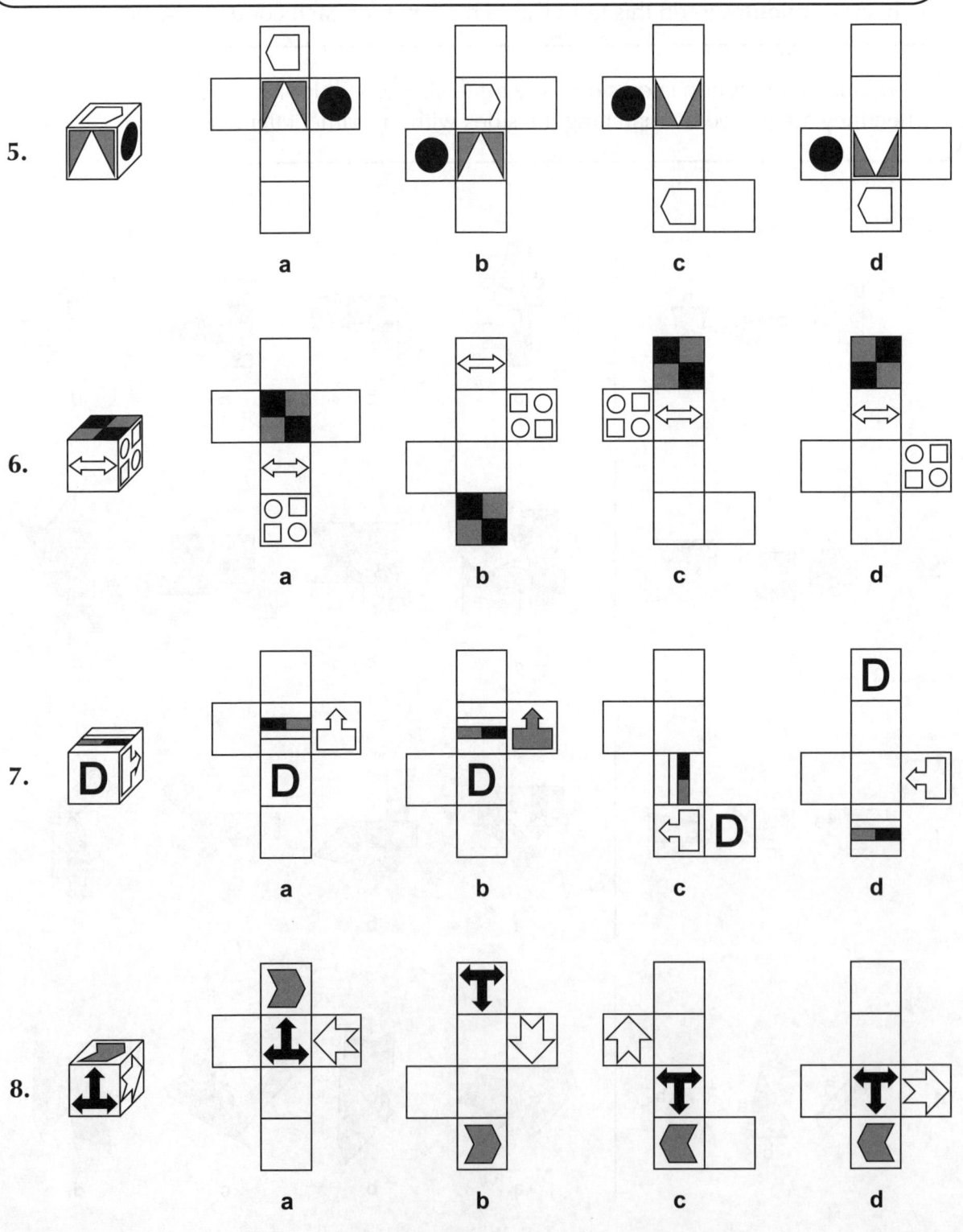

A square is folded and then a hole is punched, as shown on the left. Work out which option shows the square when unfolded.

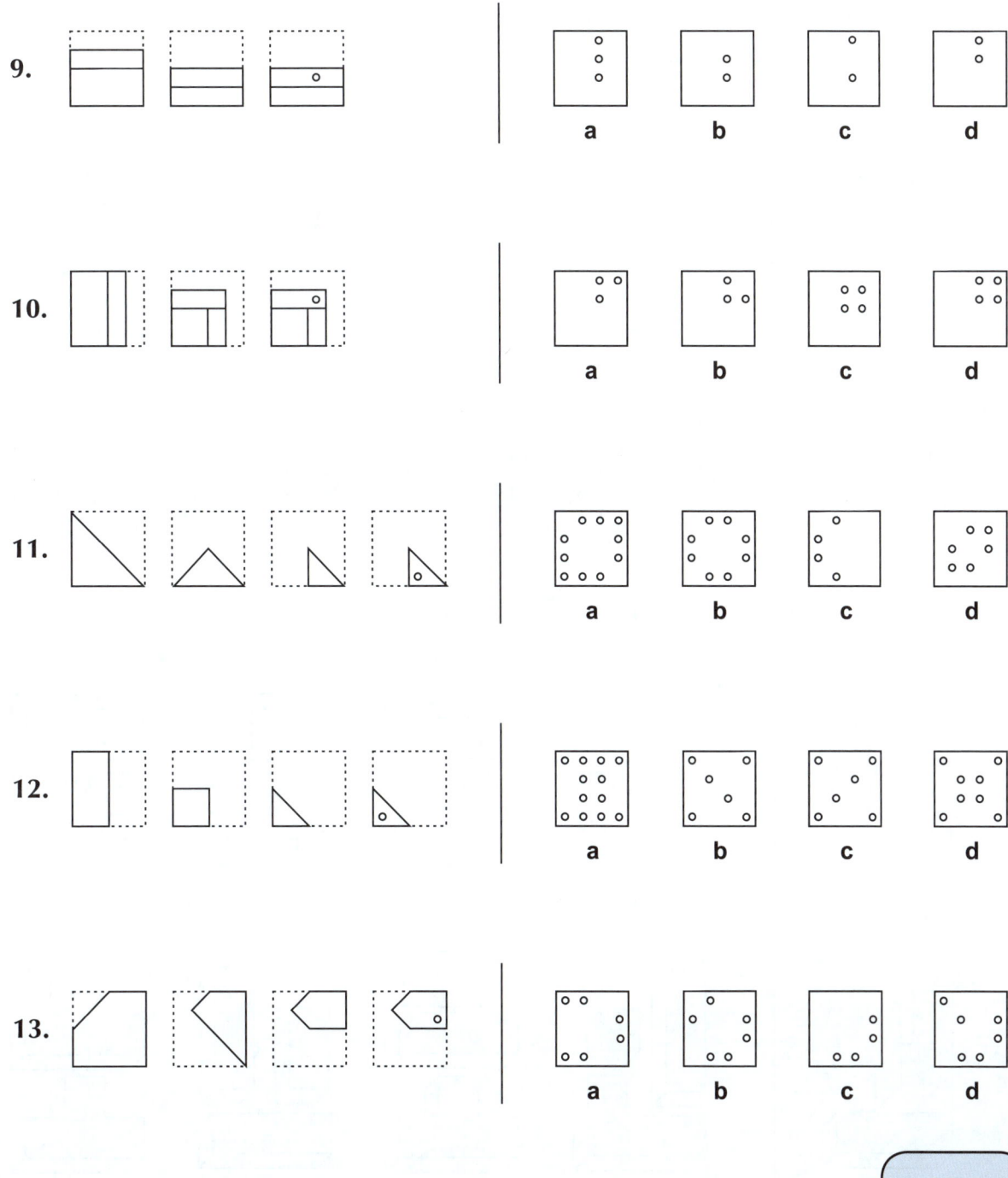

Test 28

You have **10 minutes** to do this test. Circle the letter for each correct answer.

Work out which set of blocks can be put together to make the 3D figure on the left.

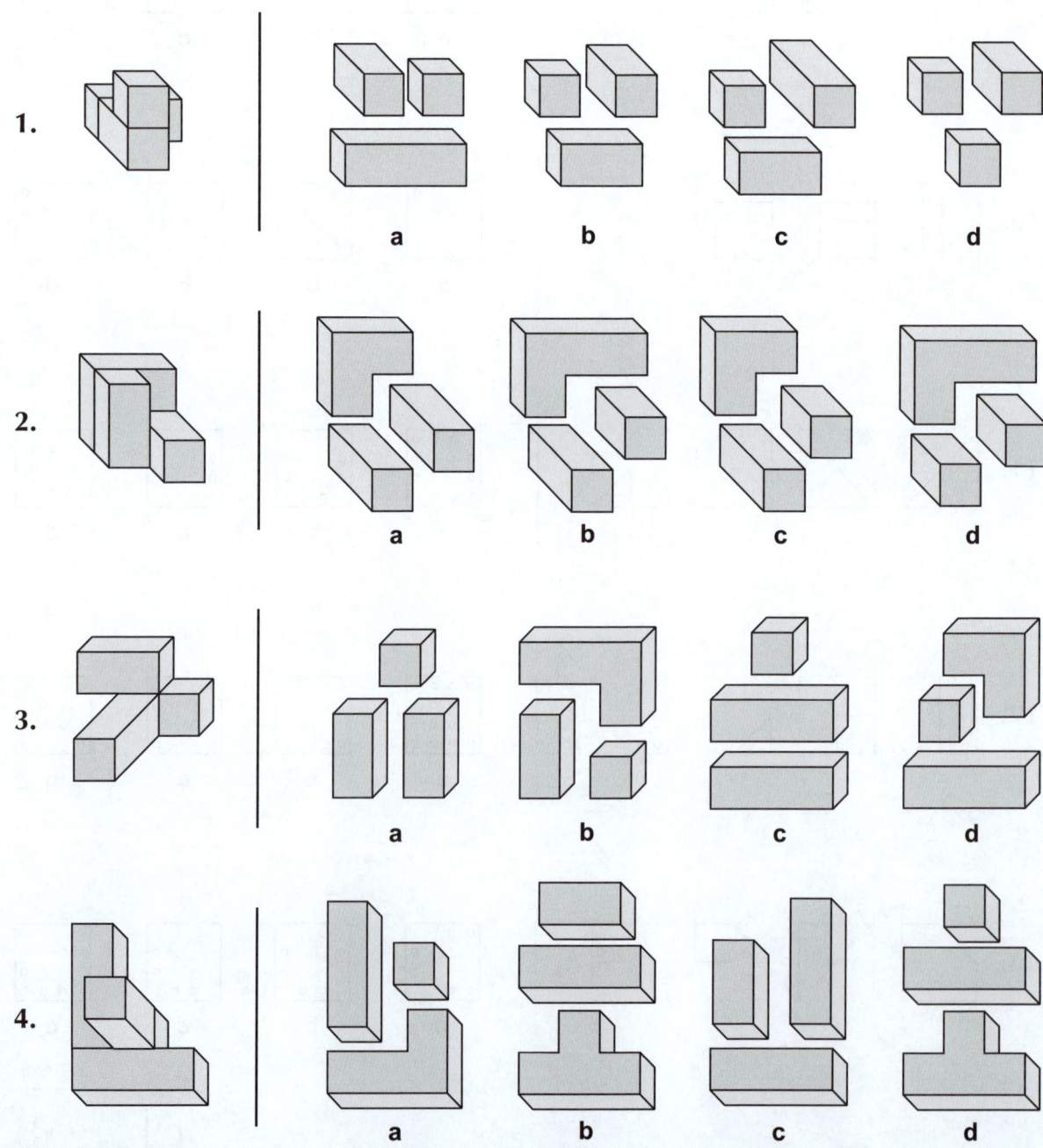

Without rotating the figure on the left, work out which option fits onto it to make the 3D shape in the grey box.

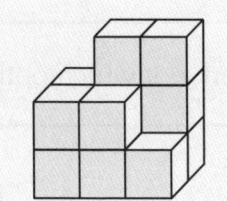

5.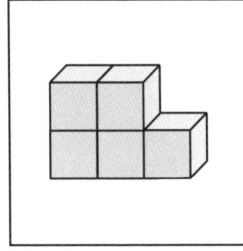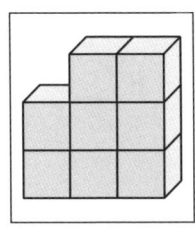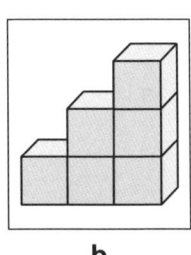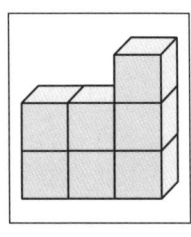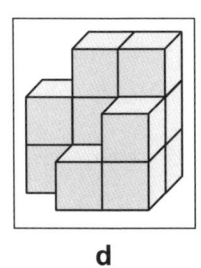
                                 a   b   c   d

6.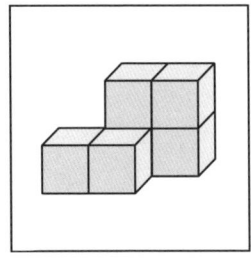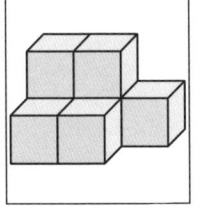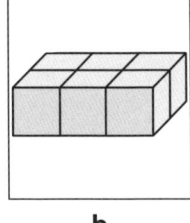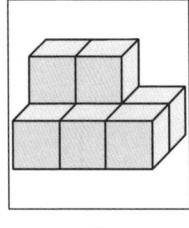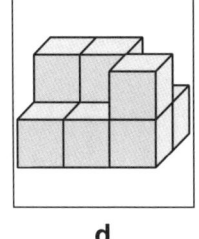
                                 a   b   c   d

7.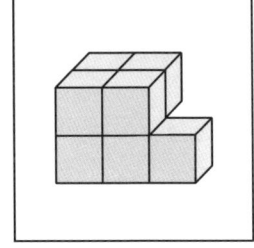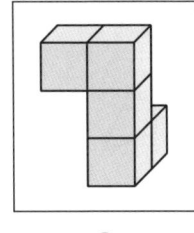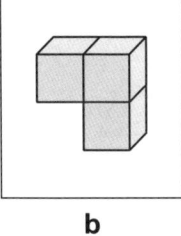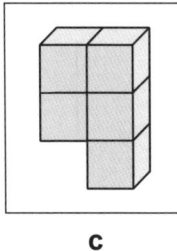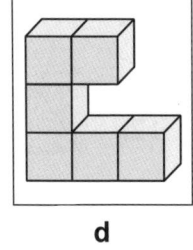
                                 a   b   c   d

8.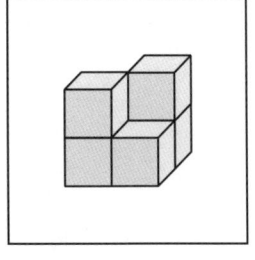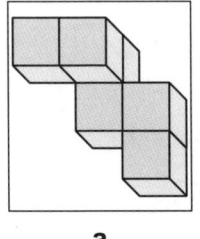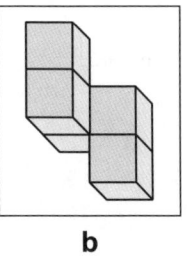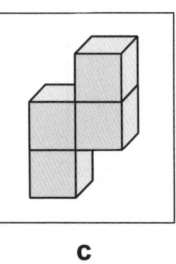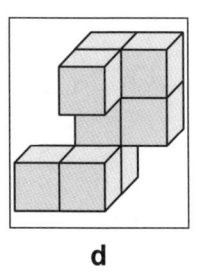
                                 a   b   c   d

© CGP — not to be photocopied   Test 28

Work out which option shows the figure on the left when folded along the dotted line.

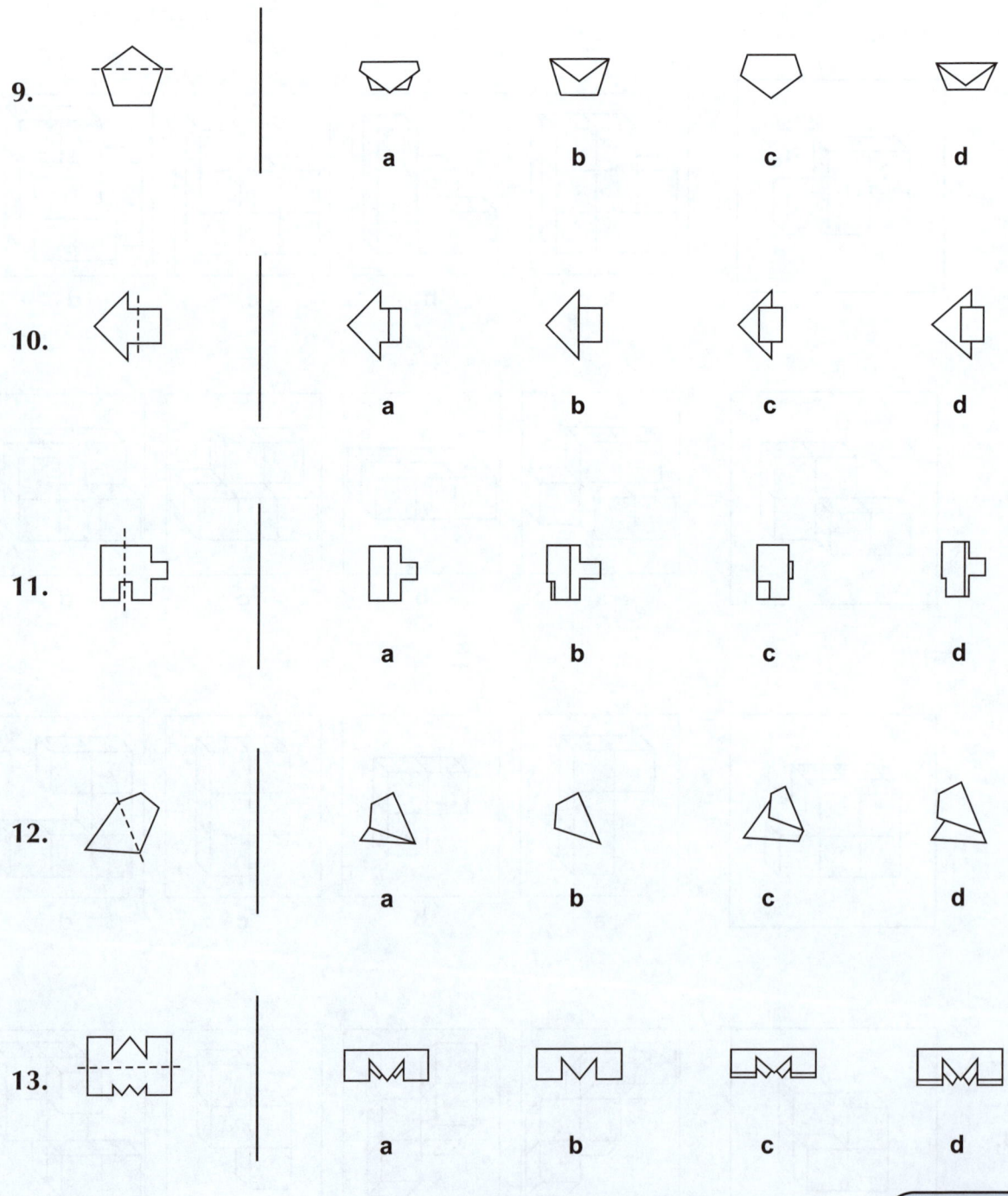

Test 28

Test 29

You have **10 minutes** to do this test. Circle the letter for each correct answer.

The figures on the left show different views of the same cube. All the cube faces are different. Work out which of the options should replace the blue cube face.

1.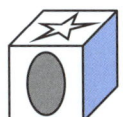
                                                       a   b   c   d

2.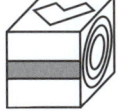
                                                       a   b   c   d

3.
                                                       a   b   c   d

4.
                                                       a   b   c   d

Work out which option is a 2D view from the **left** of the 3D figure shown.

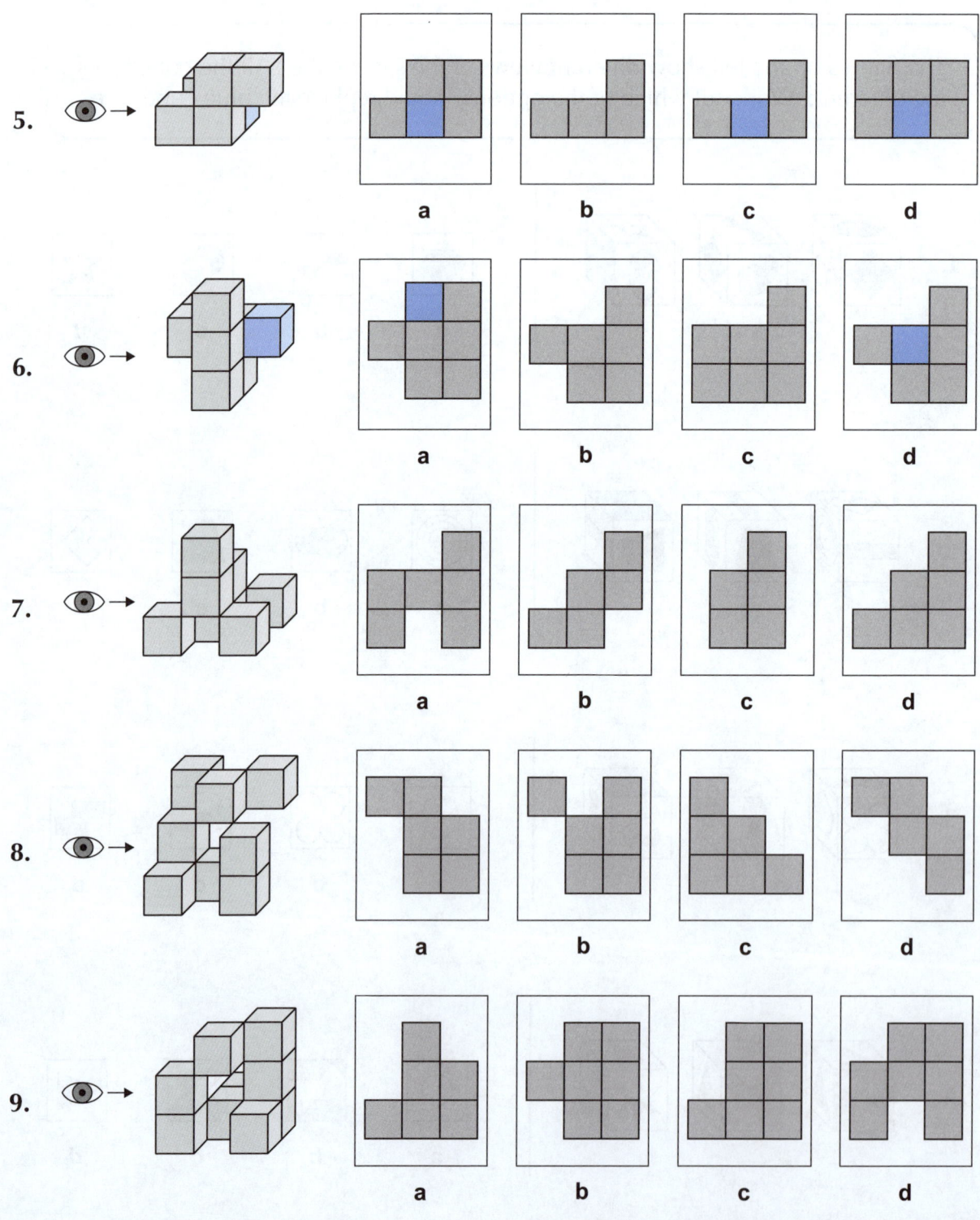

Work out which of the 3D shapes can be made from the net.

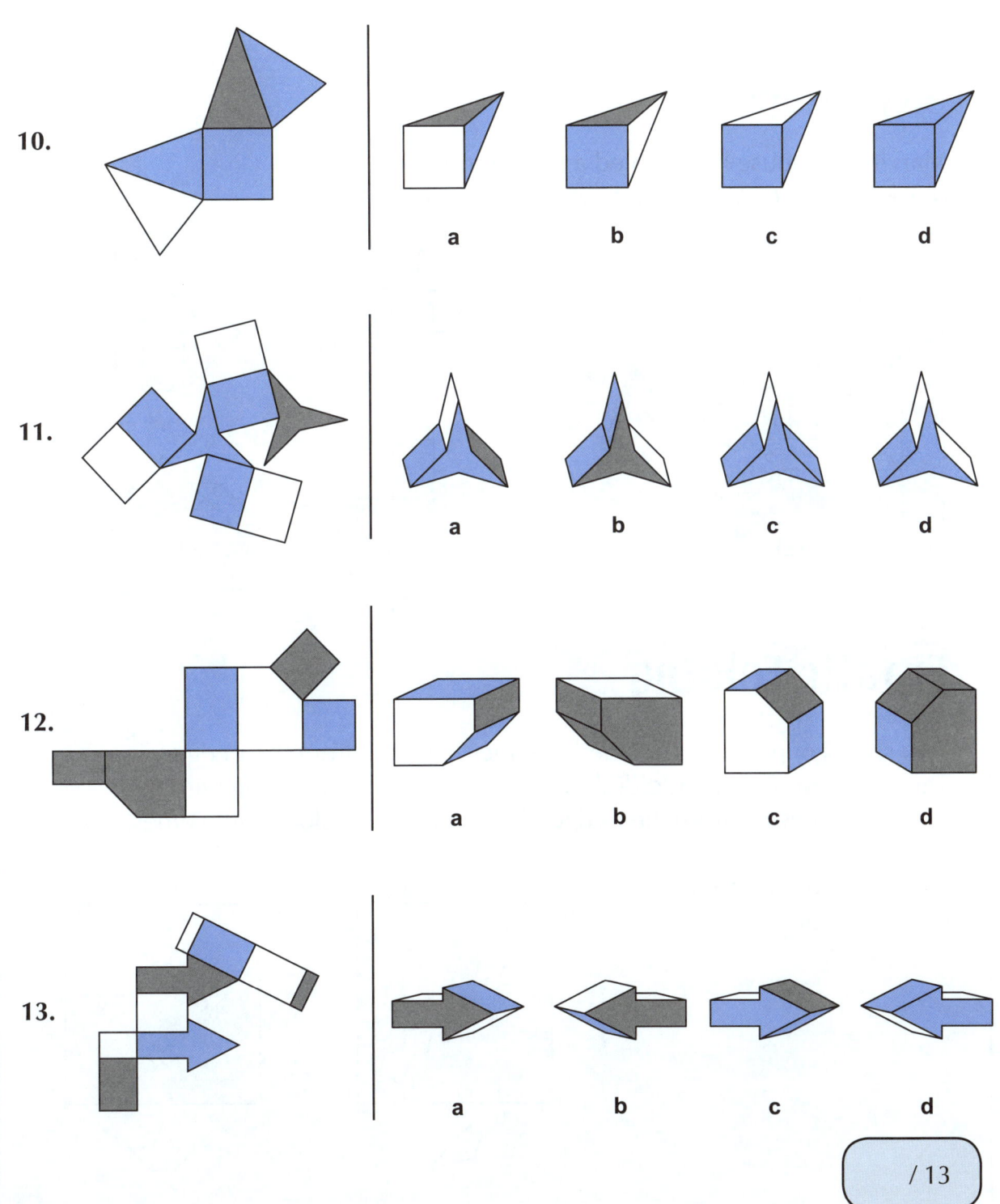

Puzzles 9

Practise your **complete the shape** and **fold and punch** skills with these nifty puzzles.

Say Cheese!

Marvin the mouse has nibbled a section out of a block of cheese. What shape was the piece he ate?

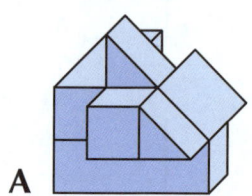
A
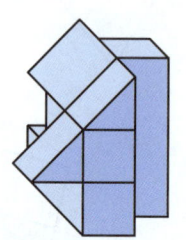
B

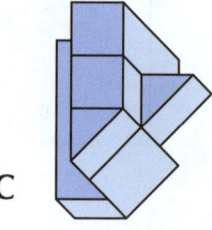
C
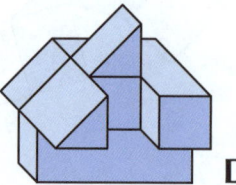
D

Frantic Folding

Two sheets of paper were folded. Shapes were cut from their edges. The sheets were then unfolded. They are shown below, along with the shape that was cut from their edge. Each sheet was folded three times.

Draw dotted lines to show the fold lines.

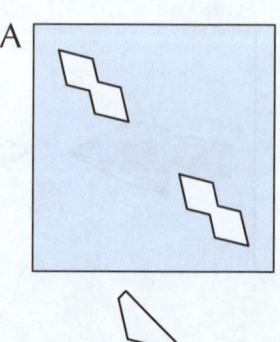
A

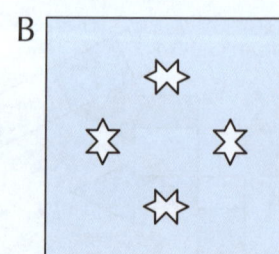
B

Test 30

You have **10 minutes** to do this test. Circle the letter for each correct answer.

Work out which option contains the hidden shape shown. It should be the same size and orientation.

1.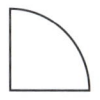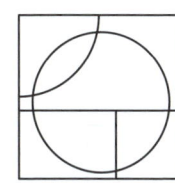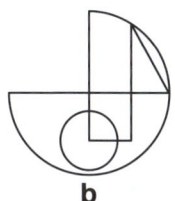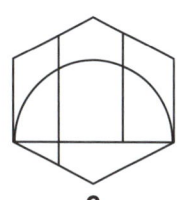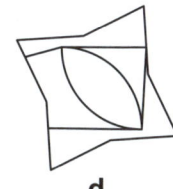
                          a   b   c   d

2.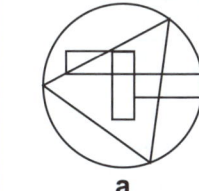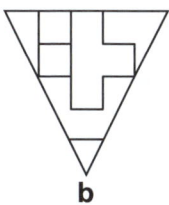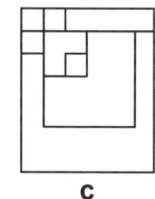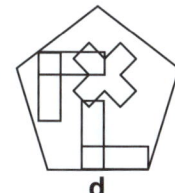
                          a   b   c   d

3.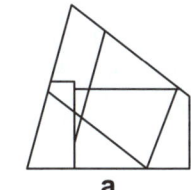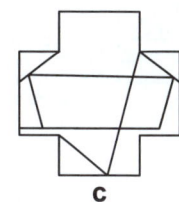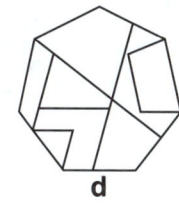
                          a   b   c   d

4.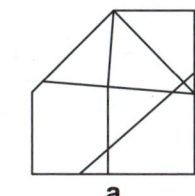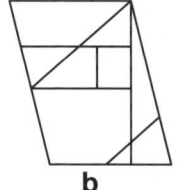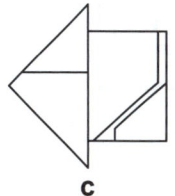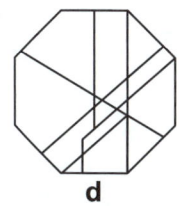
                          a   b   c   d

5.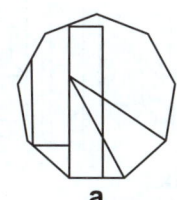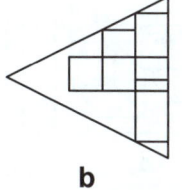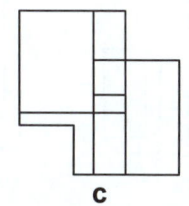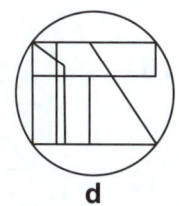
                          a   b   c   d

© CGP — not to be photocopied

Work out which option is the 3D figure viewed from **above**.

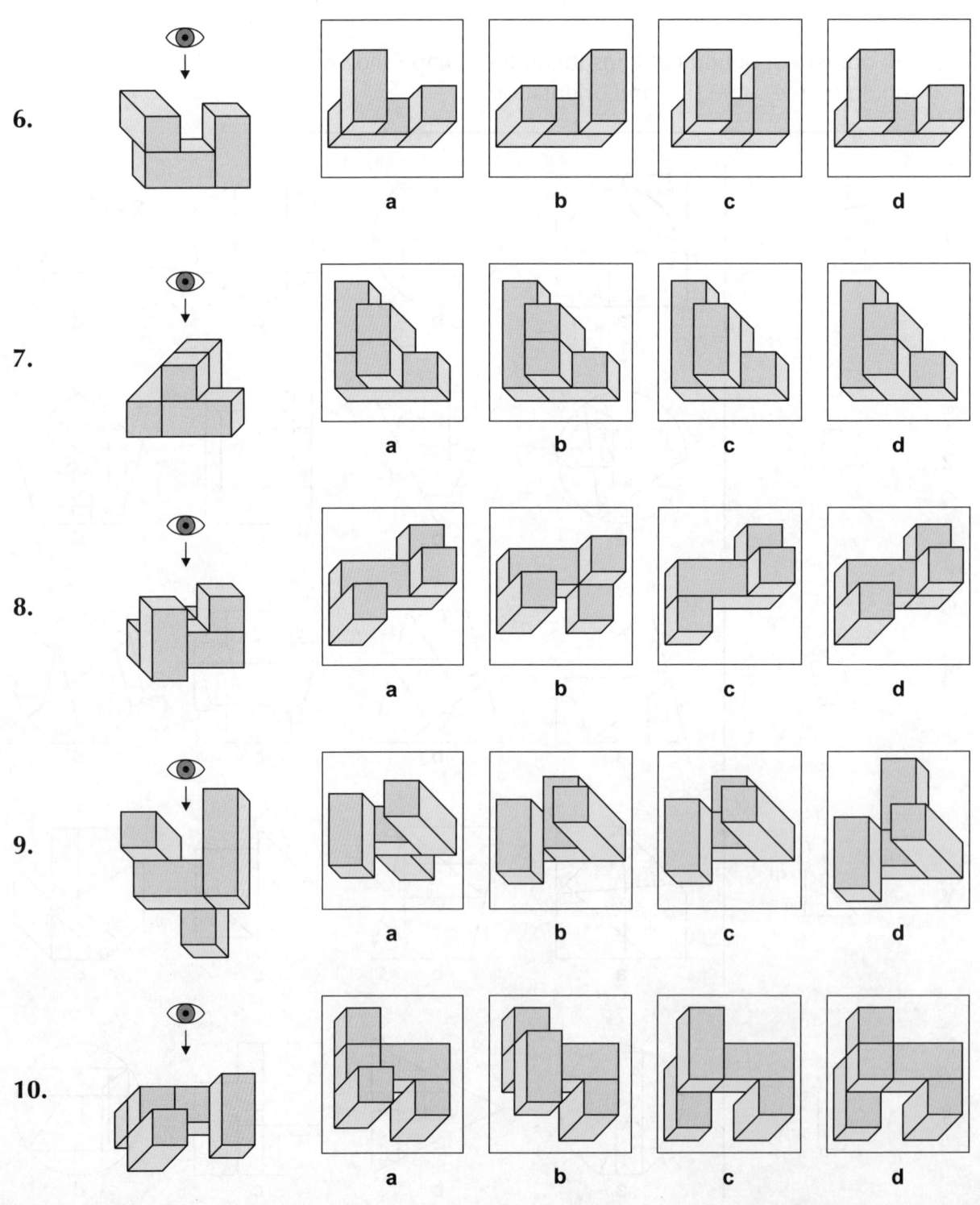

Work out which option shows how the three shapes will look when they are joined by matching the sides with the same letter.

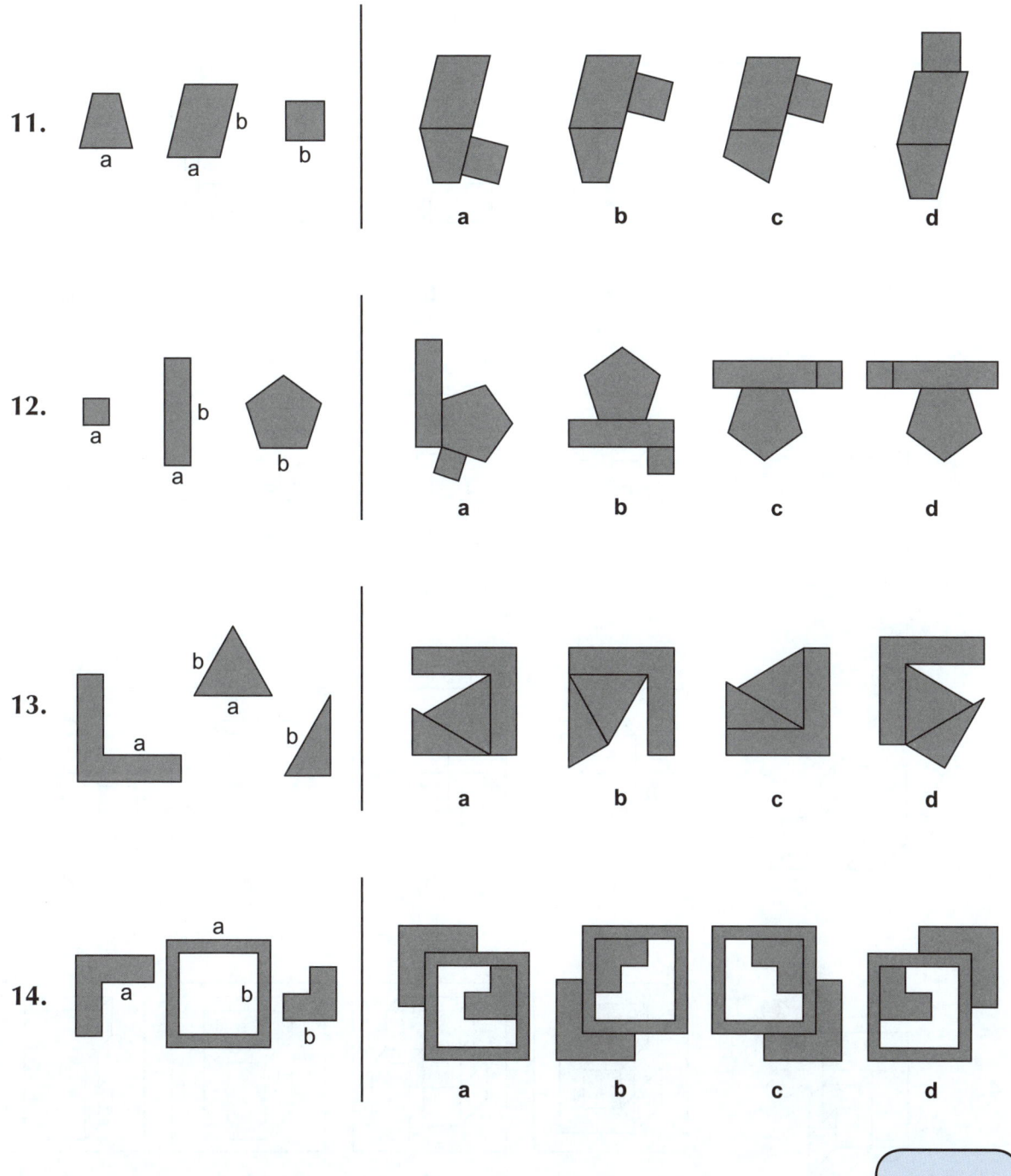

Test 31

You have **10 minutes** to do this test. Circle the letter for each correct answer.

Work out which option is the 3D figure viewed from the **back**.

1.

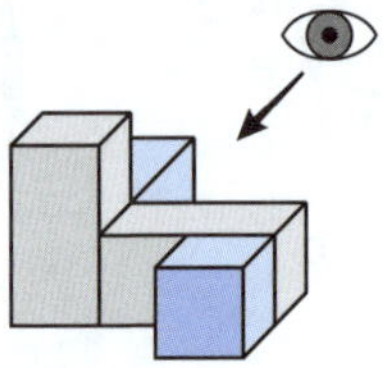

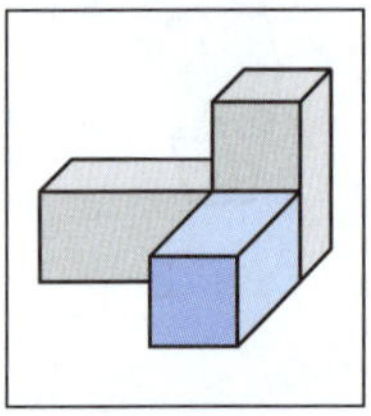
a

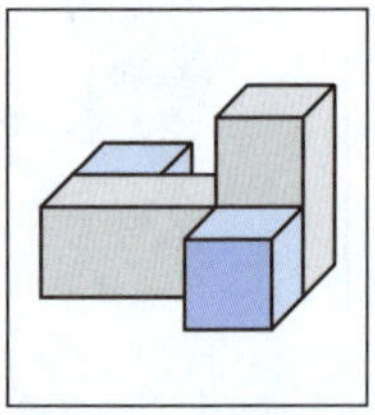
b

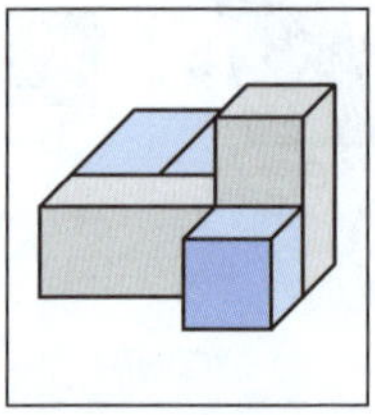
c

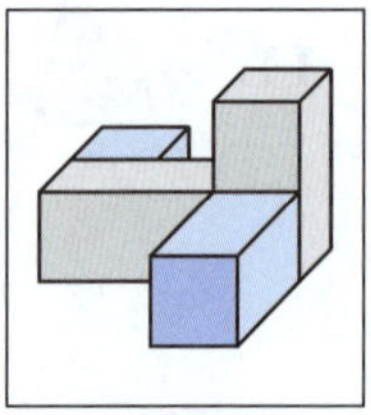
d

2.

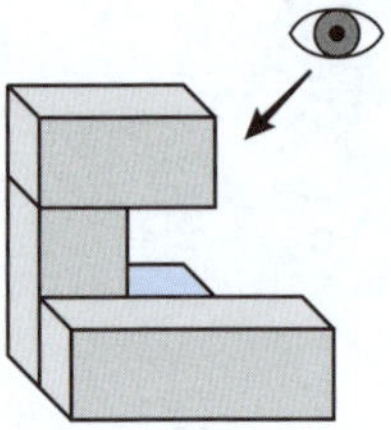

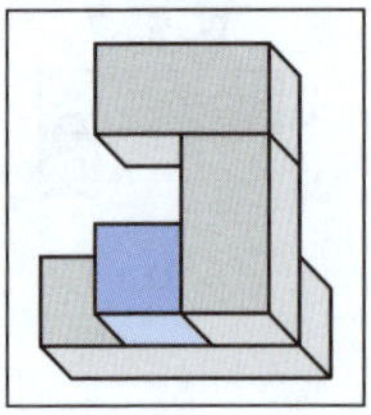
a

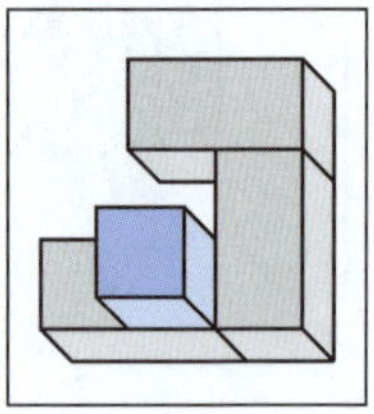
b

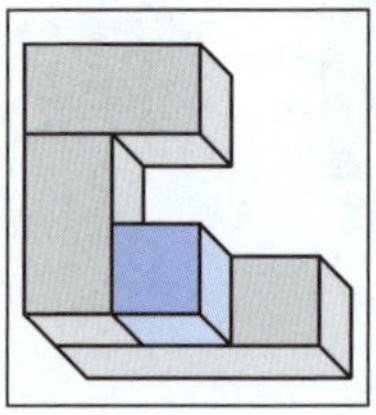
c

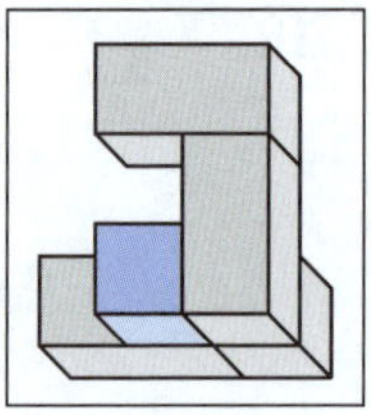
d

3.

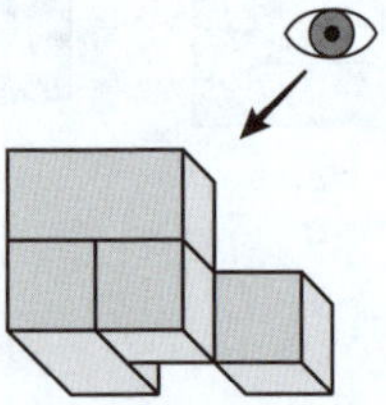

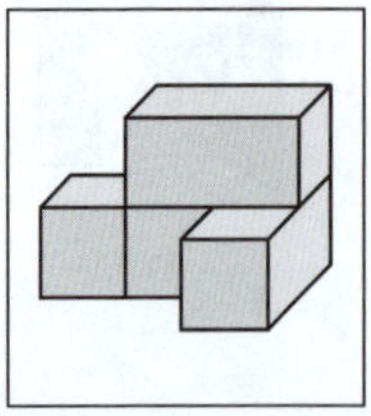
a

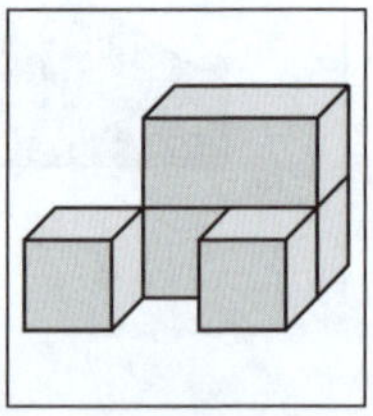
b

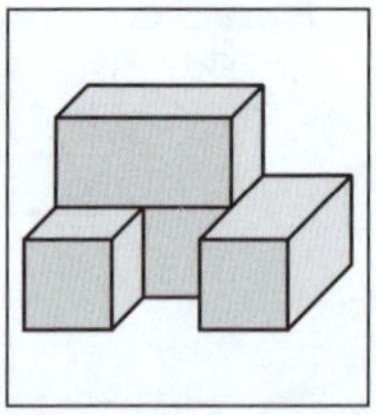
c

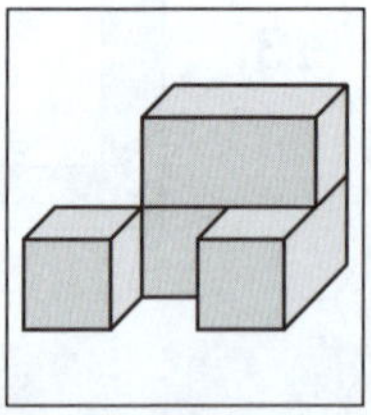
d

4.

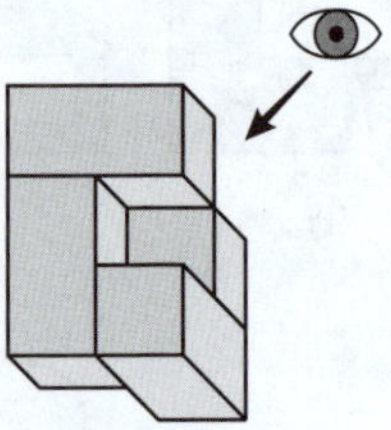

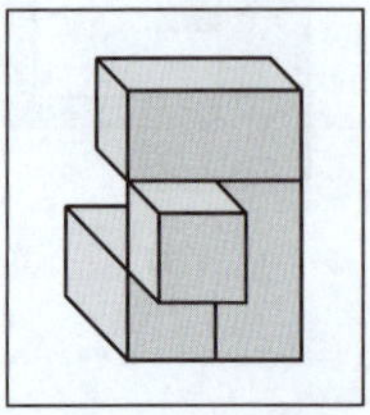
a

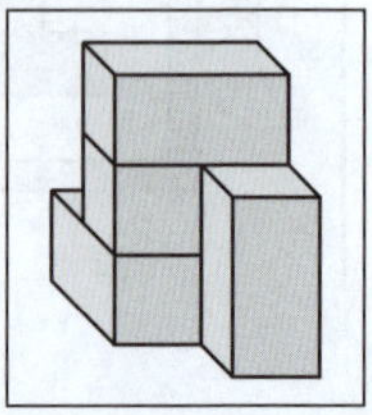
b

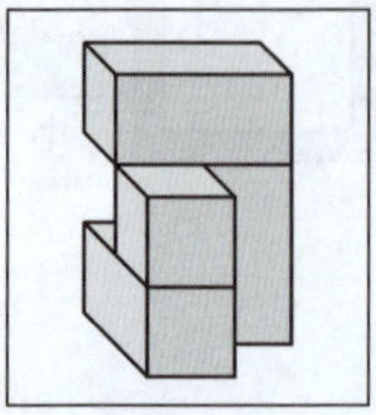
c

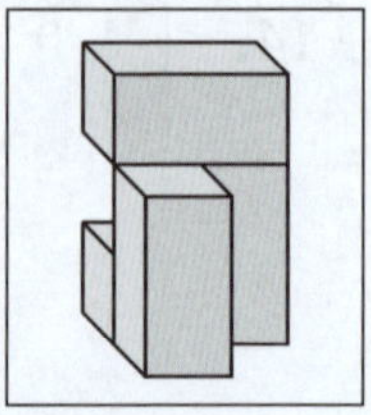
d

© CGP — not to be photocopied

Work out which of the four cubes can be made from the net.

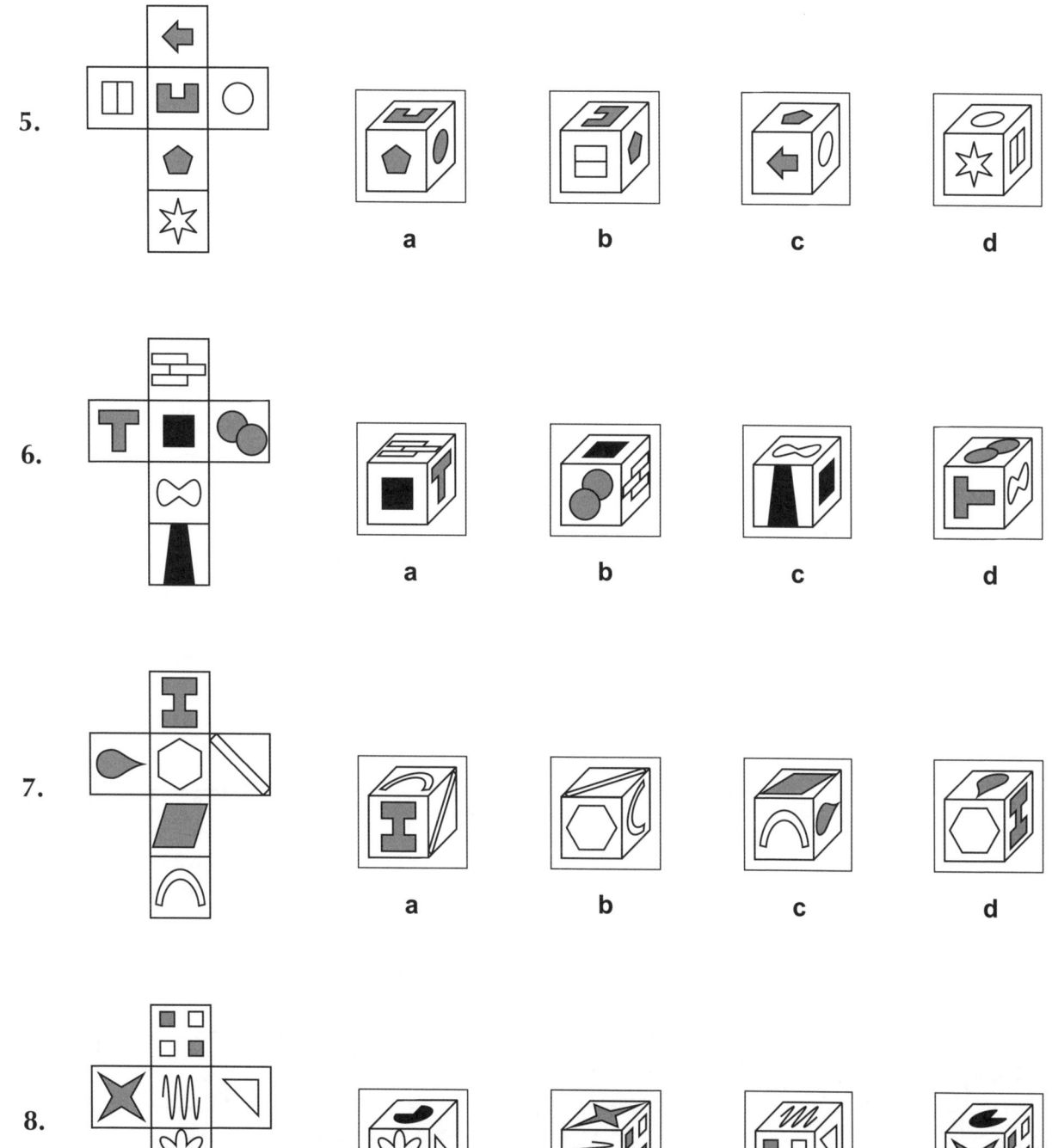

A square is folded and then a hole is punched, as shown on the left. Work out which option shows the square when unfolded.

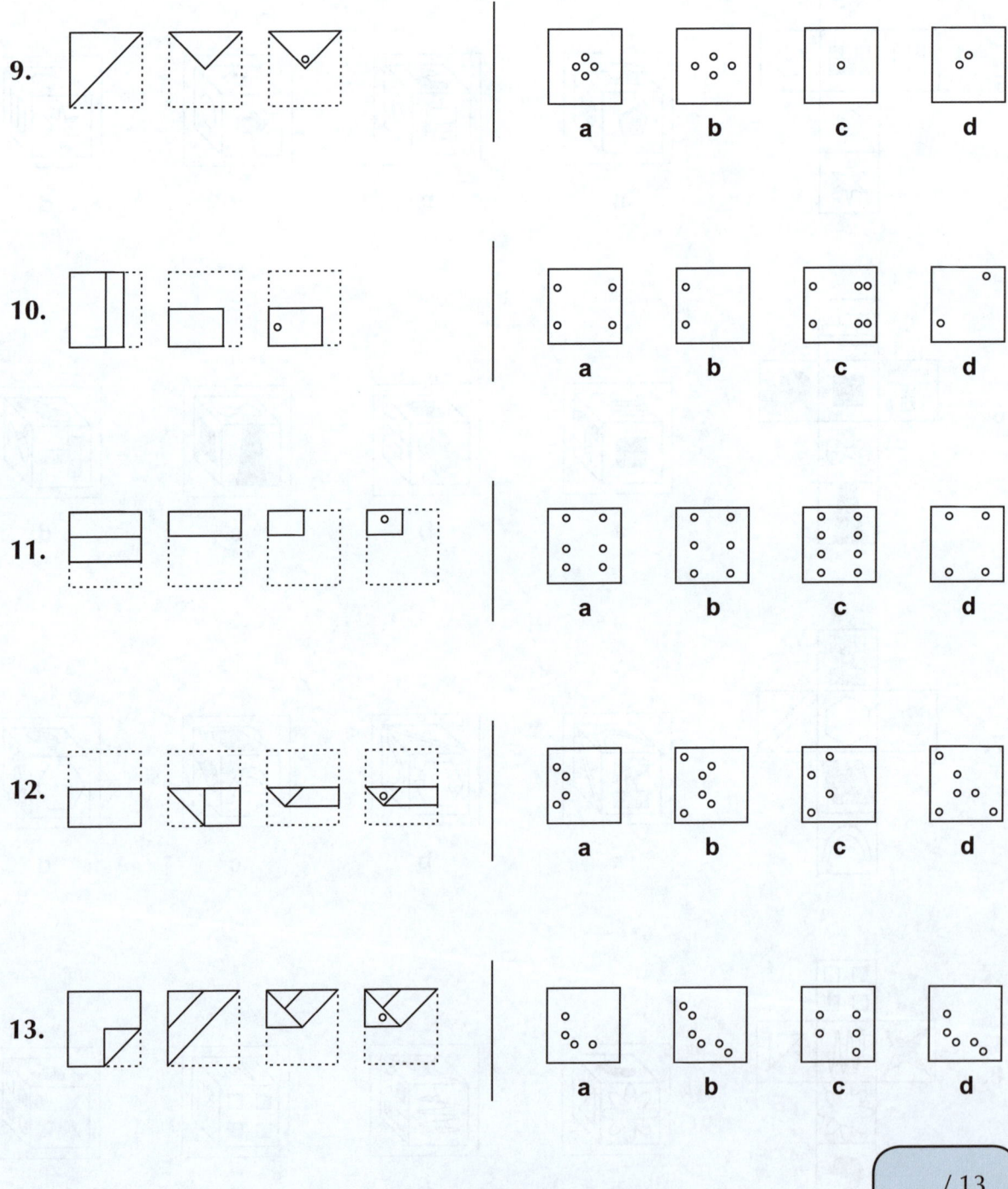

Test 32

You have **10 minutes** to do this test. Circle the letter for each correct answer.

Work out which 3D figure in the grey box has been rotated to make the new 3D figure.

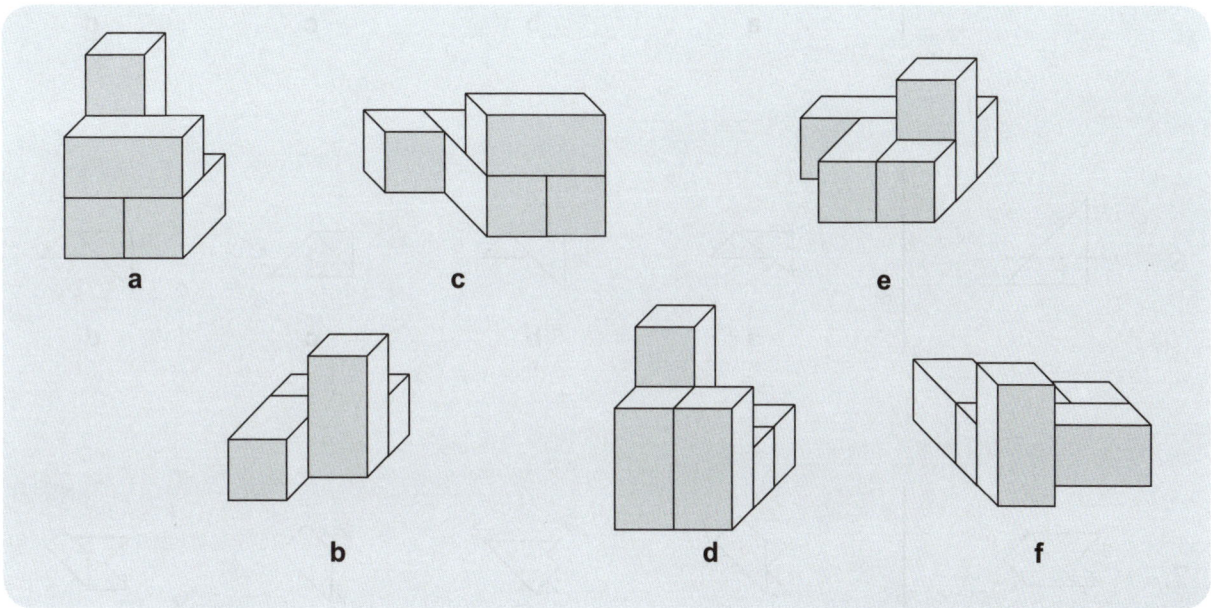

1. 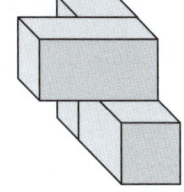   a   d   b   e   c   f

2. 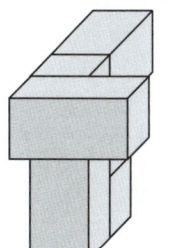   a   d   b   e   c   f

3. 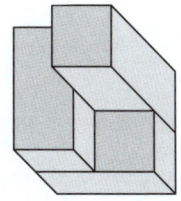   a   d   b   e   c   f

4. 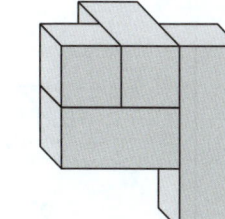   a   d   b   e   c   f

© CGP — not to be photocopied

Work out which option shows the figure on the left when folded along the dotted line.

Work out which set of blocks can be put together to make the 3D figure on the left.

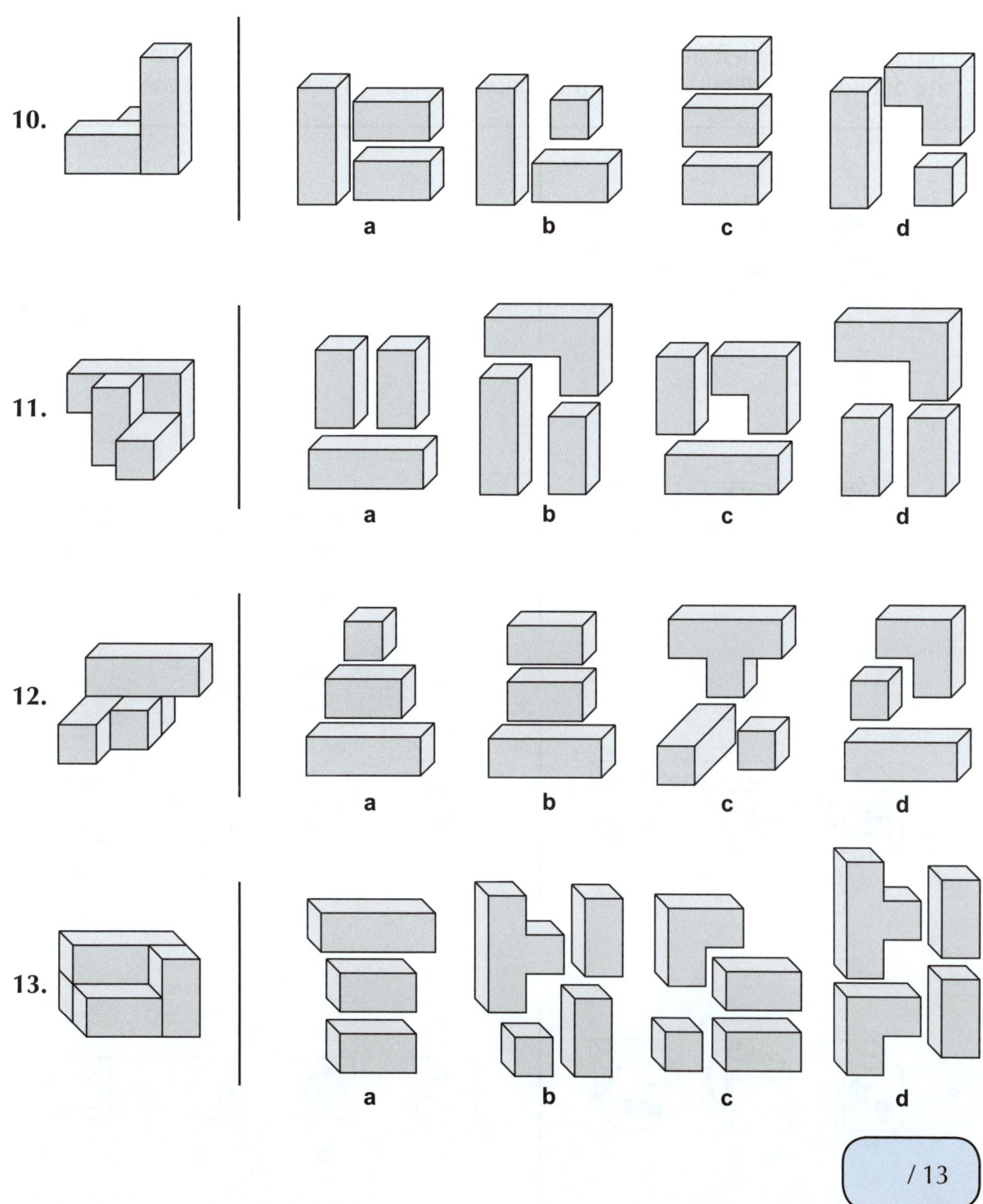

Test 33

You have **10 minutes** to do this test. Circle the letter for each correct answer.

The figures on the left show different views of the same cube. All the cube faces are different. Work out which of the options should replace the blue cube face.

1.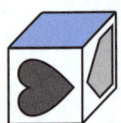

                                                                   a   b   c   d

2.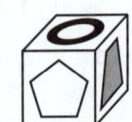

                                                                    a   b   c   d

3.

                                                                    a   b   c   d

4.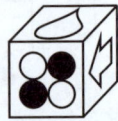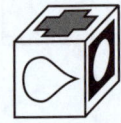

                                                                    a   b   c   d

Work out which option is the 3D figure viewed from the **right**.

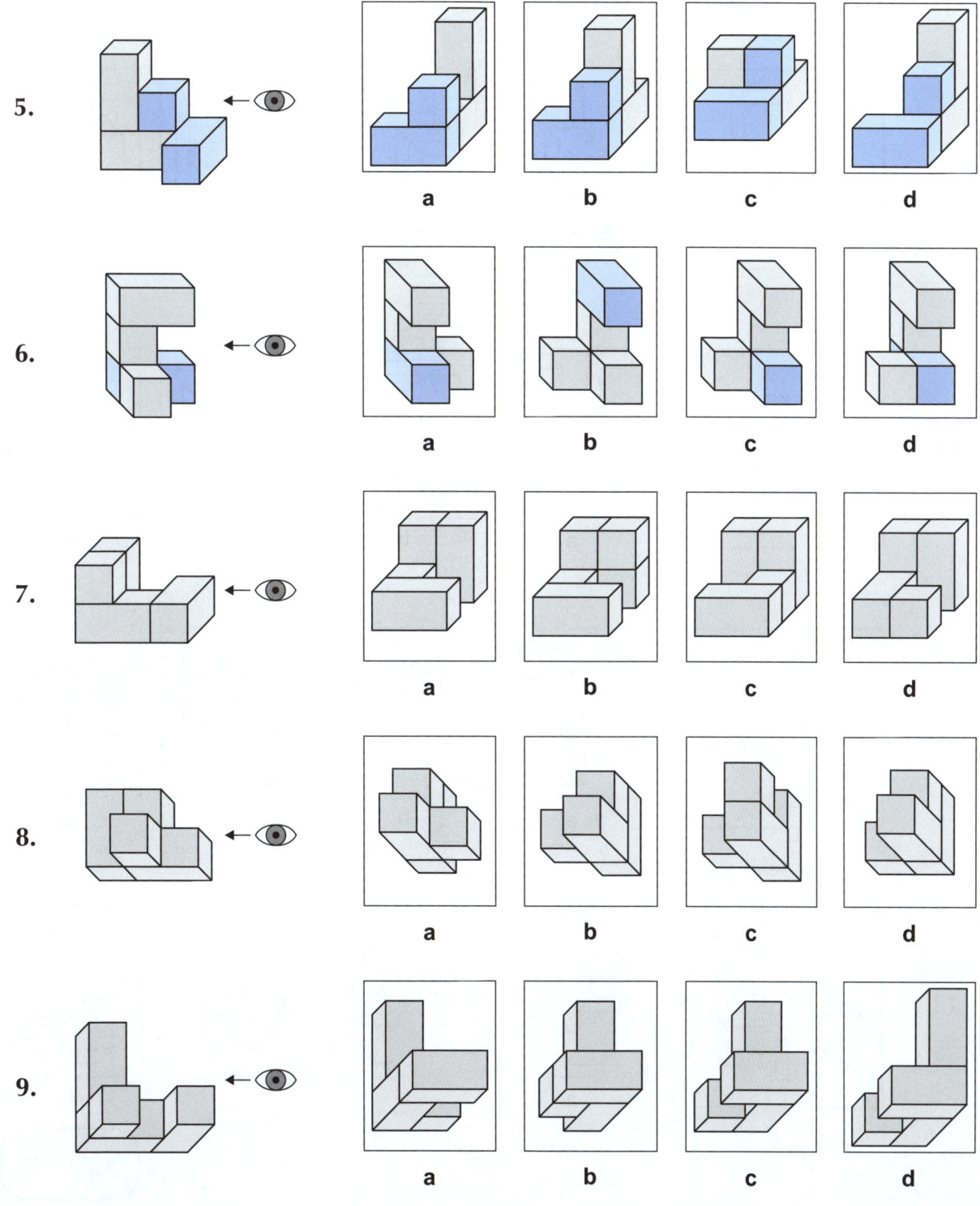

Without rotating the figure on the left, work out which option fits onto it to make the 3D shape in the grey box.

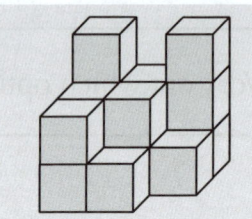

10.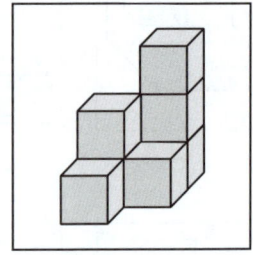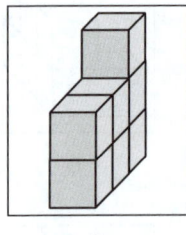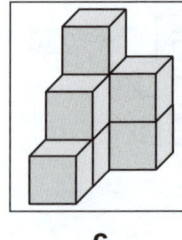
                       a   b   c   d

11.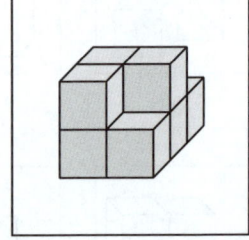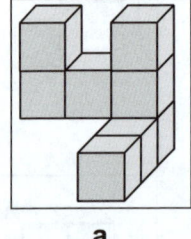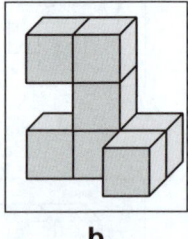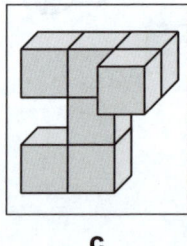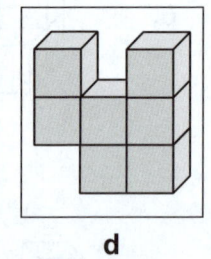
                       a   b   c   d

12.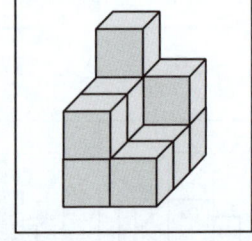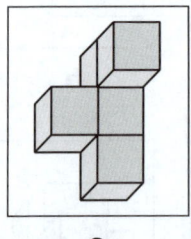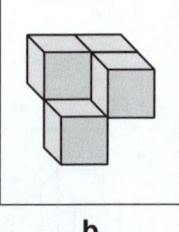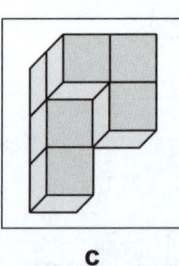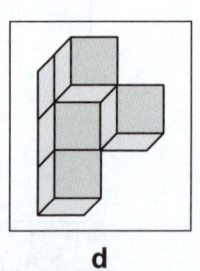
                       a   b   c   d

13.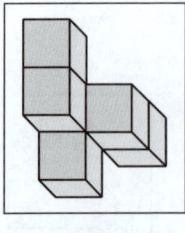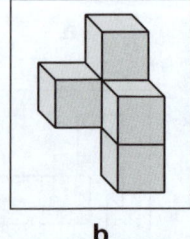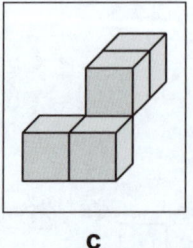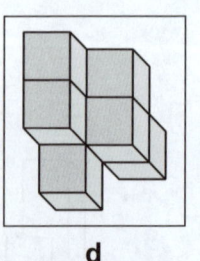
                       a   b   c   d

/ 13

Puzzles 10

Well, that's all the tests done. Just time now for a final page of puzzles.

All for Nought (and Crosses)

Harry and Lily are playing noughts and crosses using identical cubes.
The cubes have a cross on one face and a nought on the opposite face.
Two views of the cubes are shown on the right.
Harry is trying to get a line of three crosses.
Lily is trying to get a line of three noughts.
Who has won the game?

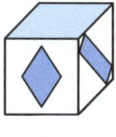 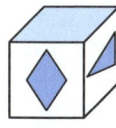 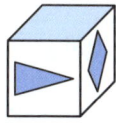

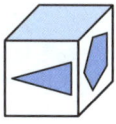 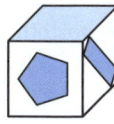 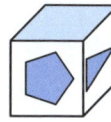

 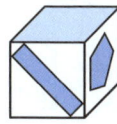 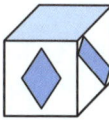

Origami Animals

Alisha wants to make the origami dog shown on the right.
Which option below shows the folds that Alisha needs
to make? Add the shading, the eyes and the nose to the
correct option.

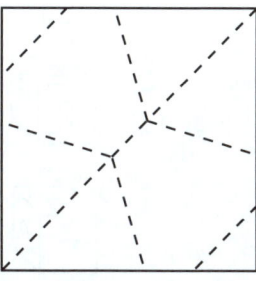 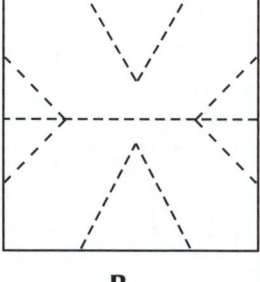 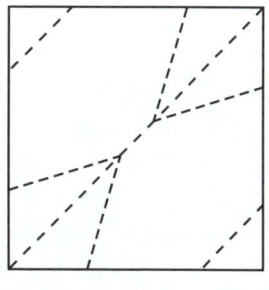 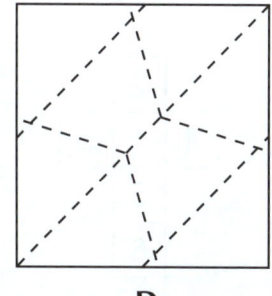

A   B   C   D

Glossary

Folding Nets

Nets should be folded **into the page**.

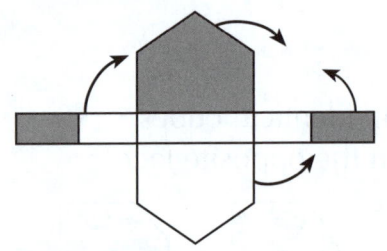

Fold the faces away from you until they all come together.

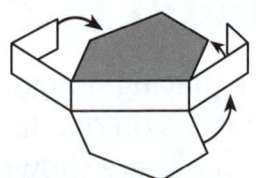

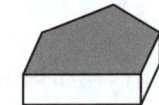

This shape can now be rotated.

3D Rotation

There are **three planes** that a 3D shape can be rotated in.

1. 90 degrees towards you, top-to-bottom / 90 degrees away from you, top-to-bottom

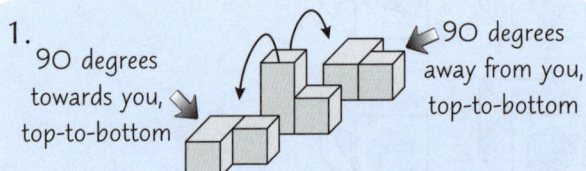

2. 90 degrees left-to-right / 90 degrees right-to-left

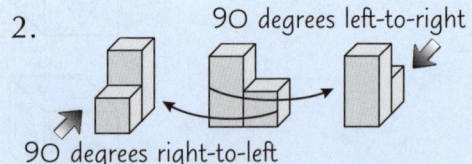

3. 90 degrees anticlockwise in the plane of the page / 90 degrees clockwise in the plane of the page

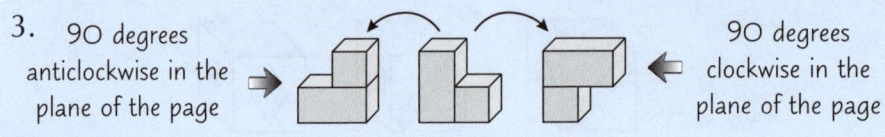

Cubes and Nets

Cubes can be **rotated** in different directions. Start with the cube view shown on the **left**.

Turning 180 degrees...

... left-to-right gives:

... top-to-bottom gives:

... in the plane of the page gives:

Turning 90 degrees...

... left-to-right gives:

... towards you, top-to-bottom gives:

... anticlockwise in the plane of the page gives:

Answers

Test 1 — pages 9-11

1. B
Options A and C are ruled out because the triangle is not connected to the trapezium. Option D is ruled out because the rectangle is not connected to the shortest side of the trapezium.

2. C
Option A is ruled out because neither of the long sides of the smallest rectangle are connected to the square. Options B and D are ruled out because the smallest rectangle is not connected to the square.

3. C
Option A is ruled out because the triangle is not connected to the small arch. Option B is ruled out because the triangle has been reflected. Option D is ruled out because the arches are not connected.

4. C
Option A is ruled out because the two L-shapes are not connected. Options B and D are ruled out because, in both cases, the wrong sides of the L-shapes are connected.

5. F
Shape F has been rotated 90 degrees away from you, top-to-bottom.

6. A
Shape A has been rotated 180 degrees towards you, top-to-bottom.

7. C
Shape C has been rotated 90 degrees left-to-right.

8. E
Shape E has been rotated 90 degrees clockwise in the plane of the page. It has then been rotated 90 degrees left-to-right.

9. D
Shape D has been rotated 90 degrees anticlockwise in the plane of the page. It has then been rotated 90 degrees left-to-right.

10. B
Shape B has been rotated 180 degrees in the plane of the page.

11. B
Option A is ruled out because the single arch shape and the figure made up of two overlapping arches must be on opposite sides. Option C is ruled out because the heart and the star must be on opposite sides. Option D is ruled out because there is no black circle on the cube.

12. D
Option A is ruled out because the black stripe and the triangle must be on opposite sides. Option B is ruled out because the black face and the teardrop are on opposite sides. Option C is ruled out because if the net is folded so that the droplet is at the front and the black stripe is on the top, then the arrow would be on the left.

13. B
Option A is ruled out because the grey rectangle has been rotated. Option C is ruled out because if the net is folded so that the arrow is at the front and the grey rectangle is on the top, then the E-shape would be on the left. Option D is ruled out because the white three-quarter circle and the grey rectangle must be on opposite sides.

14. A
Option B is ruled out because when the net is folded, the pair of black stripes should not run towards the black circle. Option C is ruled out because the grey diamond and the black stripes must be on opposite sides. Option D is ruled out because the division sign has been rotated.

Test 2 — pages 12-14

1. B **2. B**

3. A   **4. D**

5. C

6. C
There should be a block three cubes tall on the left of the figure at the back when viewed from the right. This rules out options A and D. There should be a cube at the front left. This rules out option B.

7. D
There should be two blocks lying on their sides, one on top of the other, in the middle of the figure when viewed from the right. This rules out option C. Neither of these two blocks should protrude forward more than the other. This rules out options A and B.

8. A
There should be a cube on the right of the figure when viewed from the right. This rules out options B and C. This cube should be at the back of the figure. This rules out option D.

9. D
There should be a cube at the front left of the figure at the bottom when viewed from the right. This rules out options B and C. The figure should be two cubes wide. This rules out option A.

10. A
There should be a block two cubes long, lying on its side at the back of the figure when viewed from the right. This rules out option B. The cube at the front left of the figure at the top should be resting on a block two cubes long. This rules out option C. There should be no block at the front left of the figure at the bottom. This rules out option D.

11. B
The third cube view is the second cube view rotated 90 degrees away from you from top-to-bottom, and then rotated 90 degrees right-to-left. So the face with the star is on the right.

12. A
The third cube view is the first cube view rotated 90 degrees right-to-left. So the face with the black circle inside the white part-circle is at the front.

13. C
The third cube view is the second cube view rotated 90 degrees clockwise in the plane of the page. So the face with the grey and white squares is on the right.

14. C
The second cube view is the first cube view rotated 90 degrees away from you, top-to-bottom, and then rotated 90 degrees left-to-right. So the black arch is on the left of the second cube view. The third cube view is the second cube view rotated 90 degrees clockwise in the plane of the page, and then 90 degrees left-to-right. So the face with the black arch is on the top.

Test 3 — pages 15-17

1. D
Options A, B and C are ruled out because the fold lines have moved.

2. B
Options A and C are ruled out because the part of the shape that has been folded is the wrong shape. Option D is ruled out because the fold line has moved.

3. C
Options A and D are ruled out because the part of the shape that has been folded is the wrong shape. Option B is ruled out because the part of the shape originally to the right of the fold line should still be visible.

4. D
Options A, B and C are ruled out because the part of the shape that has been folded is the wrong shape.

5. A
Option B is ruled out because the part of the shape that has been folded is the wrong shape. Option C is ruled out because the part of the shape originally to the left of the fold line is the wrong shape. Option D is ruled out because the fold line has moved.

6. B
There are four blocks visible from the back, which rules out options A and D. The single block at the top is blue, which rules out option C.

7. D
There are six blocks visible from the back, which rules out options B and C. There are three blocks visible on the right, which rules out option A.

8. A
There is only one block visible on the left, which rules out options B, C and D.

9. C
There are six blocks visible from the back, which rules out option A. There are two blocks visible on the right, which rules out options B and D.

10. C
There are five blocks visible from the back, which rules out option A. There is only one blue block visible at the bottom, which rules out option B. This blue block is on the right, which rules out option D.

11. A
Option B is ruled out because the square is not connected to the L-shape. Option C is ruled out because the longest side of the L-shape is not connected to the cross. Option D is ruled out because the square is not connected to the correct side of the L-shape.

12. D
Options A, B and C are ruled out because, in each case, only one side of the small triangle is connected to other shapes.

13. D
Option A is ruled out because the kite shapes should be connected to adjacent sides of the hexagon. Option B is ruled out because the hexagon is only connected to one of the kites. Option C is ruled out because side 'b' of the second kite is not connected to the hexagon.

14. B
Options A and C are ruled out because, in both cases, the parallelogram with side 'a' is connected to side 'b' of the chevron. Option D is ruled out because neither parallelogram is connected to either side 'a' or side 'b' of the chevron.

Puzzles 1 — page 18

Twinkle Twinkle...

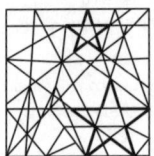

...Chocolate Baa
C

Test 4 — pages 19-21

1. B
Option A is ruled out because the equilateral triangle should be connected to the sloping side of the right-angled triangle. Options C and D are ruled out because in both, the right-angled triangle is only connected to the square, but it should be connected to both of the other shapes.

2. A
Option B is ruled out because the short side of the larger rectangle needs to be connected to the smallest side of the pie shape. Options C and D are ruled out because the two rectangles need to be connected to each other using their longest sides.

3. B
Options A and D are ruled out because both arrows are connected to the wrong sides of the largest shape. Option C is ruled out because the smaller arrow is connected to the wrong side of the largest shape.

4. D
Option A is ruled out because the middle of the longest shape should be connected to the cross. Option B is ruled out because the shortest shape should not be connected to the cross by its end. Option C is ruled out because it is a reflection of the correct answer.

5. C
Option A is ruled out because there is no grey triangle on the net. Option B is ruled out because the spiral and the white star must be on opposite sides. Option D is ruled out because the black cross and the grey trapezium must be on opposite sides.

6. C
Option A is ruled out because the black arrow and the star must be on opposite sides. Option B is ruled out because if the grey squares are at the front and the grey circle is on the right, then the black arrow should be on the top. Option D is ruled out because the black arrow should point toward the grey squares.

7. C
Option A is ruled out because the short sides of the grey rectangles should point towards the grey ring. Option B is ruled out because the black triangle should point away from the grey ring. Option D is ruled out because if the black wave is on the right and the black triangle is on the top then the grey ring must be at the front.

8. C
Option A is ruled out because the grey Z has been rotated. Option B is ruled out because the grey arrow should point towards the bottom of the white Z. Option D is ruled out because the top of the grey Z should be near the side of the white Z.

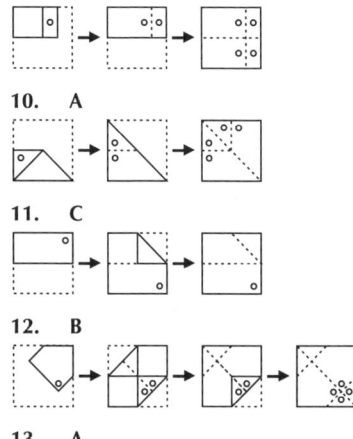

Test 5 — pages 22-24

1. B
One of the bottom two blocks in B goes at the back of the figure. The other block and the cube go at the front.

2. D
Two of the blocks in D are stood next to each other. The third block is arranged on top of the block at the back.

3. A
The bottom block in A goes at the front of the figure. The top two blocks in A are arranged behind the first block. The final block is arranged on top of the two blocks at the back.

4. D
The top block in D is at the back of the figure. The block at the bottom left of D and one of the cubes are arranged in front of it. The other cube is at the front of the figure.

5. B
There are five blocks visible from above, which rules out options C and D. There is only one block visible on the right, which rules out option A.

6. D
There are six blocks visible from above, which rules out options B and C. There is only one block visible on the right, which rules out option A.

7. A
There are six blocks visible from above, which rules out options C and D. There is only one block visible on the left, which rules out option B.

8. B
There are five blocks visible from above, which rules out option C. There are three blocks visible at the front, which rules out options A and D.

9. D
There are six blocks visible from above, which rules out option B. There is one blue block visible from above, which rules out option C. There is only one block visible at the back, which rules out option A.

10. C   **11. B**

12. B   **13. C**

14. D

Test 6 — pages 25-27

1. C
Option A is ruled out because the part of the figure that has been folded is the wrong shape. Option B is ruled out because the part of the figure that has been folded should still be visible. Option D is ruled out because the fold line has moved.

2. B
Option A is ruled out because the part of the figure that has been folded is the wrong shape. Option C is ruled out because the fold line has moved. Option D is ruled out because the part of the figure originally to the right of the fold line has been rotated, not folded.

3. C
Option A is ruled out because the part of the figure originally above the fold line is the wrong shape. Option B is ruled out because the fold line has moved. Option D is ruled out because the part of the figure that has been folded is too big.

4. B
Option A is ruled out because the fold line has moved. Option C is ruled out because the figure has been broken apart along the fold line. Option D is ruled out because the part of the figure that has been folded is the wrong shape.

5. A
Option C is ruled out because the part of the figure originally to the right of the fold line is the wrong shape. Options B and D are ruled out because the part of the figure that has been folded is the wrong shape.

6. B
Option B fits on the right of the figure.

7. C
Option C rotates 90 degrees left-to-right. It then fits on the back of the figure.

8. A
Option A rotates 90 degrees clockwise in the plane of the page. It then fits on top of the figure.

9. D
Option D rotates 90 degrees left-to-right, then 90 degrees clockwise in the plane of the page. It then fits at the back of the figure.

10.   C
Option A is ruled out because the cross is connected to the wrong side of the trapezium. Option B is ruled out because the trapezium and pentagon should not be connected on opposite sides of the cross. Option D is ruled out because the cross should be connected to both shapes.

11.   A
Option B is ruled out because the triangle is connected to the wrong side of the largest shape. Option C is ruled out because the wrong side of the rectangle is connected to the largest shape. Option D is ruled out because both the triangle and the rectangle are connected to the wrong sides of the largest shape.

12.   B
Option A is ruled out because the T-shape is connected to the wrong sides of the smallest shape. Options C and D are ruled out because the smallest shape is connected to the wrong sides of the T-shape.

13.   A
Option B is ruled out because the larger triangle is connected to the wrong side of the parallelogram. Option C is ruled out because the parallelogram is connected to the wrong side of the larger triangle. Option D is ruled out because the smaller triangle is connected to the wrong side of the parallelogram.

Puzzles 2 — page 28

Night Lights
1. C
2. A
3.

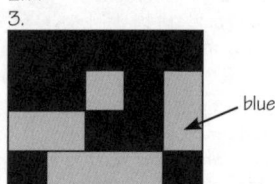
blue

Test 7 — pages 29-31

1.   F
Shape F has been rotated 90 degrees right-to-left. It has then been rotated 180 degrees in the plane of the page.

2.   C
Shape C has been rotated 90 degrees towards you, top-to-bottom.

3.   D
Shape D has been rotated 90 degrees left-to-right. It has then been rotated 90 degrees away from you, top-to-bottom.

4.   A
Shape A has been rotated 90 degrees right-to-left. It has then been rotated 90 degrees away from you, top-to-bottom.

5.   C
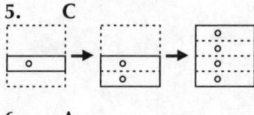

6.   A
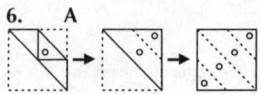

7.   B

8.   A

9.   D

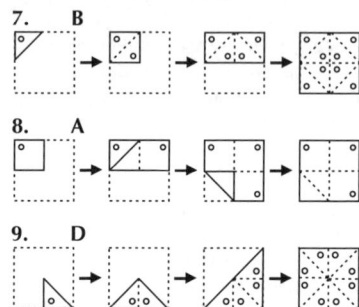

10.   D
Option A is ruled out because the longest rectangular face should not be blue. Option B is ruled out because there is no blue triangular face on the net. Option C is ruled out because there is only one blue face on the net.

11.   C
Option A is ruled out because there is no blue hexagonal face on the net. Option B is ruled out because there is no white rectangular face on the net. Option D is ruled out because there should not be two blue faces next to each other.

12.   B
Option A is ruled out because if the front face is grey, the vertical rectangular face at the top right should also be grey. Option C is ruled out because the top face should not be grey. Option D is ruled out because if the front face is blue, the vertical face at the top right should be white.

13.   C
Option A is ruled out because if the front face is grey, the face on the left-hand side should be blue. Options B and D are ruled out because the face at the front should be grey.

Test 8 — pages 32-34

1.   D   **2.   B**

3.   B   **4.   A**

5.   D

6.   A
Option B is ruled out because the square and the circle are on opposite sides. Option C is ruled out because there is no pentagon on the cube. Option D is ruled out because the square and the triangle are on opposite sides.

7.   D
Option A is ruled out because the cross and the triangle are on opposite sides. Option B is ruled out because if it is folded so that the horseshoe shape is on top of the cube and the cross is at the front, the triangle would be on the left. Option C is ruled out because the horseshoe shape and the cross are on opposite sides.

8. C
Option A is ruled out because the arrow and the black teardrop are on opposite sides. Option B is ruled out because the arrow should point towards the white side of the hexagon. Option D is ruled out because the narrow end of the black teardrop should point towards the arrow.

9. C
Option A is ruled out because one of the points on the star should point towards the oval. Option B is ruled out because the narrow end of the rectangle should point towards the oval. Option D is ruled out because if it is folded so that the rectangle is on the front of the cube and the oval is on the top, the star would be on the left.

10. B
There are five blocks visible from the left, which rules out options A and C. There is only one block visible on the right, which rules out option D.

11. A
There are six blocks visible from the left, which rules out options C and D. There are three blocks visible at the bottom, which rules out option B.

12. B
There are six blocks visible from the left, which rules out option C. There is only one block visible on the left, which rules out option D. There are no blue blocks visible, which rules out option A.

13. C
There are six blocks visible from the left, which rules out options A and B. There is only one block visible at the top, which rules out option D.

Test 9 — pages 35-37

1. C
Option A is ruled out because the figure has been broken apart along the fold line. Option B is ruled out because the fold line has moved. Option D is ruled out because the part of the figure that has been folded is the wrong shape.

2. D
Option A is ruled out because the part of the figure originally to the left of the fold line should still be visible. Option B is ruled out because the part of the figure that has been folded is the wrong shape. Option C is ruled out because the fold line has moved.

3. D
Option A is ruled out because the part of the figure that has been folded is the wrong shape. Options B and C are ruled out because the fold line has moved.

4. B
Option A is ruled out because the part of the figure that has been folded is the wrong shape. Options C and D are ruled out because the part of the figure originally to the right of the fold line is the wrong shape.

5. A
Option B is ruled out because the fold line has moved. Option C is ruled out because the part of the figure originally to the left of the fold line has been rotated, not folded. Option D is ruled out because the part of the figure originally to the right of the fold line is the wrong shape.

6. B
Options A and C are ruled out because the semicircle should be connected to both of the other shapes. Option D is ruled out because the crescent is connected to the wrong part of the semicircle.

7. C
Option A is ruled out because the squares should be connected to adjacent sides of the rectangle. Option B is ruled out because both squares are connected to the wrong sides of the rectangle. Option D is ruled out because it is a reflection of the correct answer.

8. A
Option B is ruled out because the right-angled triangle is connected to the wrong side of the cross. Option C is ruled out because the equilateral triangle is connected to the wrong side of the cross. Option D is ruled out because both triangles are connected to the wrong sides of the cross.

9. B
Option A is ruled out because both the square and the rectangle are connected to the wrong sides of the largest shape. Option C is ruled out because the rectangle is connected to the wrong side of the largest shape. Option D is ruled out because the square is connected to the wrong side of the largest shape.

10. C
Option A is ruled out because the moon and the triangle must be on opposite sides. Option B is ruled out because there aren't two black triangles on the net. Option D is ruled out because the cross and the square must be on opposite sides.

11. A
Option B is ruled out because if the trapezium is on the front and the star is on the top, then the pentagon should be on the left. Option C is ruled out because there is no grey star on the net. Option D is ruled out because the semicircle and the trapezium must be on opposite sides.

12. C
Option A is ruled out because the A and the D must be on opposite sides. Option B is ruled out because if the F is on the front and the D is on the top, then the E should be on the left. Option D is ruled out because the F has been rotated.

13. D
Option A is ruled out because the arch has been rotated. Option B is ruled out because if the arrow is on the front and the lightning bolt is on the right, then the three-pointed star should be on the bottom. Option C is ruled out because the arrow has been rotated.

Puzzles 3 — page 38

Disorganised Dinos
B

String It Together

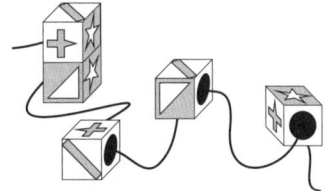

Test 10 — pages 39-41

1. C
The third cube view is the first cube view rotated 90 degrees anticlockwise in the plane of the page. So the triangle is on the front.

2. D
The third cube view is the second cube view rotated 90 degrees towards you, top-to-bottom, then 180 degrees in the plane of the page. So the split rectangle is on the top.

3. D
The first cube view is the second cube view rotated 180 degrees left-to-right. So the pentagon is on the left of the first cube view. The third cube view is the first cube view rotated 90 degrees left-to-right. So the pentagon is on the front.

4. B
The third cube view is the first cube view rotated 90 degrees right-to-left, then rotated 180 degrees in the plane of the page. So the circle is on the right.

5. D **6. C**
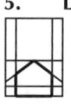

7. C **8. B**

9. A

10. B
Option B fits at the front of the figure.

11. D
Option D rotates 90 degrees clockwise in the place of the page. It then fits at the left of the figure.

12. A
Option A rotates 90 degrees right-to-left. It then rotates 90 degrees clockwise in the plane of the page. It then fits at the left of the figure.

13. D
Option D rotates 90 degrees towards you, top-to-bottom. It then fits at the back of the figure.

Test 11 — pages 42-44

1. D
Option A is ruled out because the pentagon is not connected to the triangle. Option B is ruled out because the arrow and pentagon are connected to the wrong sides of the triangle. Option C is ruled out because the arrow is not connected to the triangle.

2. D
Option A is ruled out because the wrong side of the rectangle is connected to the thin triangle. Option B is ruled out because the rectangle is connected to the wrong side of the thin triangle. Option C is ruled out because the wide triangle is connected to the wrong side of the thin triangle.

3. A
Option B is ruled out because the wrong side of the parallelogram is connected to the trapezium. Option C is ruled out because the arrow is connected to the wrong side of the trapezium. Option D is ruled out because neither the arrow nor the parallelogram are connected to the correct sides of the trapezium.

4. C
Option A is ruled out because the L-shape is not connected to the correct side of the T-shape. Option B is ruled out because the L-shape is connected to the wrong side of the T-shape. Option D is ruled out because the L-shape is not connected to the rectangle.

5. D
There should be a blue cube at the top left, which rules out option A. There should be a block three cubes wide at the top at the back, which rules out options B and C.

6. B
There should be three blocks stacked on top of each other at the bottom, which rules out options A, B and C.

7. C
There should be a blue cube at the bottom left, which rules out option D. There should be a blue block two cubes long on the left, which rules out option A. The block at the back should be on the right, which rules out option B.

8. D
There should be a block two cubes long in the centre, going top-to-bottom, which rules out options A and B. There should be a cube to the left of this block, in line with its bottom, which rules out option C.

9. A
There should be a blue cube on the left at the centre, which rules out options B and C. There should be a blue block at the back, going top-to-bottom, which rules out option D.

10. C
Options A and D are ruled out because the part of the figure that has been folded is the wrong shape. Option B is ruled out because the fold line has moved.

11. C
Option A is ruled out because the fold line has moved. Options B and D are ruled out because the part of the figure that has been folded is the wrong shape.

12. B
Options A and D are ruled out because the part of the figure that has been folded is the wrong shape. Option C is ruled out because the part of the figure that has been folded should still be visible.

13. A
Options B and C are ruled out because the part of the figure that has been folded is the wrong shape. Option D is ruled out because the fold line has moved.

14. D
Options A and B are ruled out because the fold line has moved. Option C is ruled out because the part of the shape originally to the right of the fold line should still be visible.

Test 12 — pages 45-47

1. B
Shape B has been rotated 90 degrees away from you, top-to-bottom.

2. D
Shape D has been rotated 90 degrees anticlockwise in the plane of the page. It has then been rotated 90 degrees left-to-right.

3. A
Shape A has been rotated 90 degrees left-to-right. It has then been rotated 180 degrees top-to-bottom.

4. E
Shape E has been rotated 90 degrees away from you, top-to-bottom. It has then been rotated 90 degrees right-to-left.

5. C
Option A is ruled out because there are no small blue rectangular faces on the net. Option B is ruled out because there are no large grey rectangular faces on the net. Option D is ruled out because the top face should be blue.

6. C
Option A is ruled out because there are no grey rectangular faces on the net. Option B is ruled out because if the grey triangle is at the front, the right rectangular face should be white and the left rectangular face should be blue. Option D is ruled out because there aren't two white rectangular faces on the net.

7. A
Option B is ruled out because if the grey five-sided face is on top, the face to the left of the blue rectangular face should be grey. Option C is ruled out because if the grey five-sided face is on top, the face to the right of the blue rectangular face should be white. Option D is ruled out because there aren't two grey rectangular faces on the net.

8. C
Option A is ruled out because the horizontal triangular face should be blue. Option B is ruled out because the front rectangular face should be blue. Option D is ruled out because the trapezium-shaped face next to the blue rectangular face should be white.

9. C   **10. B**
   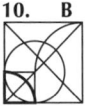

11. D   **12. B**

13. B

Puzzles 4 — page 48

Folding Flowers
B
12 holes

Test 13 — pages 49-51

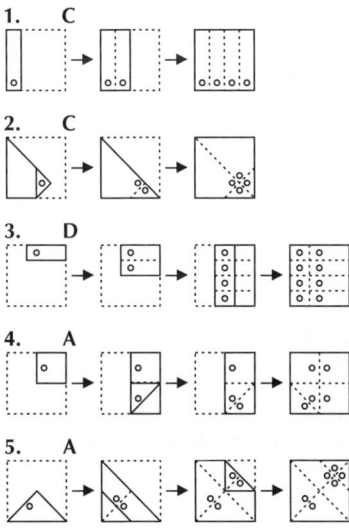

6. C
There are five blocks visible from the right, which rules out options A and D. There are two grey blocks visible on the right, which rules out option B.

7. B
There are five blocks visible from the right, which rules out options A and C. There is a blue block visible on the bottom row, which rules out option D.

8. D
There are six blocks visible from the right, which rules out option A. There is only one block visible on the left, which rules out option B. There are three blocks visible on the bottom row, which rules out option C.

9. C
There are eight blocks visible from the right, which rules out option B. There are two blue blocks visible, which rules out option A. There are only two blocks visible on the right, which rules out option D.

10. A
There are six blocks visible from the right, which rules out option D. There is only one blue block visible, which rules out option B. There are only two blocks visible in the middle row, which rules out option C.

11. C
Option A is ruled out because the wrong side of the triangle is connected to the parallelogram. Option B is ruled out because only the square is connected to the parallelogram. Option D is ruled out because the triangle is connected to the wrong side of the parallelogram.

12. A
Option B is ruled out because the wrong side of the L-shape is connected to the trapezium. Option C is ruled out because both the L-shape and the semicircle are connected to the wrong sides of the trapezium. Option D is ruled out because the semicircle is connected to the wrong side of the trapezium.

13. A
Option B is incorrect because the wrong side of the arc is connected to the pentagon. Option C is ruled out because the wrong side of the triangle is connected to the pentagon. Option D is ruled out because the triangle is connected to the wrong side of the pentagon.

14. B
Options A and C are ruled out because the cross is connected to the wrong side of the middle shape. Option D is ruled out because the triangle is connected to the wrong side of the middle shape.

Test 14 — pages 52-54

1. B
Option A is ruled out because the part of the figure originally above the fold line is the wrong shape. Option C is ruled out because the fold line has moved. Option D is ruled out because the part of the figure originally below the fold line should still be visible.

2. D
Option A is ruled out because the figure has been broken apart along the fold line. Options B and C are ruled out because the part of the figure that has been folded is the wrong shape.

3. A
Options B and D are ruled out because the fold line has moved. Option C is ruled out because the part of the figure that has been folded is the wrong shape.

4. B
Option A is ruled out because the fold line has moved. Options C and D are ruled out because the part of the figure that has been folded is the wrong shape.

5. B
Option A is ruled out because the figure has been broken apart along the fold line. Option C is ruled out because the part of the figure originally to the left of the fold line is the wrong shape. Option D is ruled out because the fold line has moved.

6. A
The top block in A goes at the back of the figure. The bottom block in A goes at the front of the figure.

7. A
The top block in A goes at the back of the figure. The corner block in A goes on top and to the right of it. The bottom left block in A goes at the front of the figure.

8. C
The top left block in C goes at the back of the figure. The block on the right in C goes in front of it. The bottom left block in C goes on the right of the figure.

9. C
The bottom block in C goes at the bottom left of the figure. The top block in C goes above it. The middle block in C goes at the front of the figure.

10. A
The third cube view is the second cube view rotated 90 degrees right-to-left, then 90 degrees clockwise in the plane of the page. So the sun shape is on the top.

11. B
The third cube view is the first cube view rotated 90 degrees clockwise in the plane of the page. So the grey cross is at the front.

12. A
The second cube view is the first cube view rotated 180 degrees towards you, top-to-bottom. So the joined triangles are on the bottom. The third cube view is the second cube view rotated 90 degrees away from you, top-to-bottom, then 90 degrees left-to-right. So the joined triangles are on the right.

13. A
The second cube view is the first cube view rotated 90 degrees right-to-left, then 90 degrees towards you, top-to-bottom. So the black triangle is on the left. The third cube view is the second cube view rotated 90 degrees clockwise in the plane of the page, then 90 degrees right-to-left. So the black triangle is on the top.

Test 15 — pages 55-57

1. B 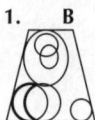   2. B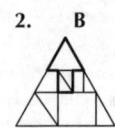

3. C 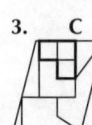   4. D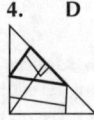

5. D

6. A
There are five blocks visible from above, which rules out options B and C. There is only one block visible on the left, which rules out option D.

7. C
There are six blocks visible from above, which rules out options A and D. There is one blue block visible in the middle row, which rules out option B.

8. C
There are seven blocks visible from above, which rules out option D. There is one blue block visible, which rules out option A. There is only one block visible on the top row, which rules out option B.

9. D
There are six blocks visible from above, which rules out option C. There is one blue block visible in the middle row, which rules out option A. There are two blocks visible in the top row, which rules out option B.

10. A
There are seven blocks visible from above, which rules out option B. There are no blue blocks visible, which rules out option C. There are three blocks visible on the left, which rules out option D.

11. D
Option B is ruled out because there are no blue pentagonal faces on the net. Options A and C are ruled out because there are no blue rectangular faces next to each other on the net.

12. A
Option B is ruled out because the rectangular face on the right should be white. Option C is ruled out because the rectangular face on the right should be blue. Option D is ruled out because the front, five-sided face should be blue.

13. B
Option A is ruled out because the rectangular face on the left should be white. Option C is ruled out because the small rectangular face on the right should be white. Option D is ruled out because the rectangular face on the top should be grey.

14. D
Option A is ruled out because the vertical white rectangular face should be grey. Option B is ruled out because the vertical grey rectangular face should be white. Option C is ruled out because the horizontal grey rectangular face should be white.

Puzzles 5 — page 58

Daylight Robbery

Test 16 — pages 59-61

1. B
Option A is ruled out because the part of the figure originally to the left of the fold line is the wrong shape. Options C and D are ruled out because the fold line has moved.

Answers

2.   C
Options A and B are ruled out because the part of the figure originally to the right of the fold line is the wrong shape. Option D is ruled out because the fold line has moved.

3.   B
Options A and C are ruled out because the fold line has moved. Option D is ruled out because the part of the figure originally to the left of the fold line is the wrong shape.

4.   D
Options A and B are ruled out because the fold line has moved. Option C is ruled out because the part of the shape originally below the fold line should still be visible.

5.   A
Option B is ruled out because the fold line has moved. Option C is ruled out because the part of the figure originally to the right of the fold line is the wrong shape. Option D is ruled out because the figure has been broken apart along the fold line.

6.   B
The third cube view is the second cube view rotated 90 degrees left-to-right, and then 90 degrees towards you, top-to-bottom. So the circles are on the front.

7.   D
The third cube view is the first cube view rotated 90 degrees left-to-right. So the arrow is on the top.

8.   B
The third cube view is the first cube view rotated 180 degrees in the plane of the page, then 90 degrees away from you, top-to-bottom. So the bone is on the top.

9.   C
The second cube view is the first cube view rotated 90 degrees towards you, top-to-bottom, so the cross is at the bottom. The third cube view is the second cube view rotated 180 degrees top-to-bottom. So the cross is at the top.

10.   A
Shape A has been rotated 90 degrees clockwise in the plane of the page.

11.   F
Shape F has been rotated 90 degrees anticlockwise in the plane of the page. It has then been rotated 90 degrees left-to-right.

12.   E
Shape E has been rotated 90 degrees towards you, top-to-bottom. It has then been rotated 90 degrees clockwise in the plane of the page.

13.   D
Shape D has been rotated 90 degrees left-to-right. It has then been rotated 180 degrees top-to-bottom.

Test 17 — pages 62-64

1.   B    **2.   B**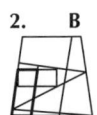

3.   D   **4.   C**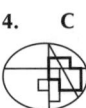

5.   D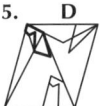

6.   B
Option A is ruled out because the circle and teardrop must be on opposite sides. Option C is ruled out because the arrowhead and black and white triangles must be on opposite sides. Option D is ruled out because the net doesn't have a lightning bolt.

7.   B
Option A is ruled out because the net doesn't have a grey trapezium. Option C is ruled out because the black circles and the white trapezium must be on opposite sides. Option D is ruled out because the star and crossed arrows must be on opposite sides.

8.   D
Option A is ruled out because the circle and the lightning bolt must be on opposite sides. Option B is ruled out because if the arrow is at the front and the lightning bolt is on the top, then the star should be on the left. Option C is ruled out because the arrow is pointing in the wrong direction.

9.   D
Option A is ruled out because the spiral and single-headed arrow must be on opposite sides. Option B is ruled out because if it is folded so that the stars are at the front and the black shape is on top, then the arrow would be on the left. Option C is ruled out because the face with the three squares has been rotated.

10.   D
The top block in D goes at the top left of the figure, on top of the bottom block in D. The middle block in D is arranged at the front of the figure.

11.   C
The bottom block in C goes at the left of the figure. The other two blocks in C are arranged behind and to the right of it.

12.   B
The top block in B goes at the back of the figure. The other two blocks in B are arranged below and in front of it.

13.   A
The bottom block in A goes at the back of the figure. The other two blocks in A are arranged in front of it.

Test 18 — pages 65-67

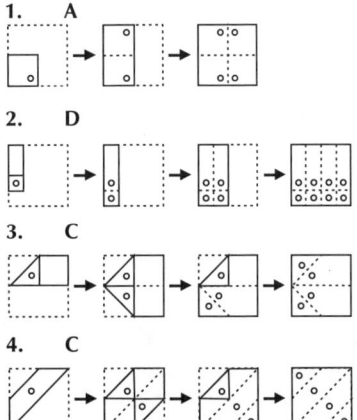

5. A

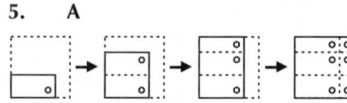

6. B
Option A is ruled out because the circles and the diamond are on opposite sides. Option C is ruled out because if it is folded so that the circles are on the top and the diamond is at the front, then the star would be on the left. Option D is ruled out because the diamond and the star are on opposite sides.

7. C
Option A is ruled out because the triangle and black quadrilateral are on opposite sides. Options B and D are ruled out because if it is folded so that the squares are on the front and the quadrilateral is on the top, then the triangle would be on the left.

8. D
Option A is ruled out because the black squares have been rotated. Option B is ruled out because the black squares and the white shape are on opposite sides. Option C is ruled out because if the white shape is at the front and the grey shape is on the top, then the black squares should be on the left.

9. B
Option A is ruled out because the teardrop has been rotated. Option C is ruled out because if the arrow is on the top and the teardrop is at the front, then the S would be on the left. Option D is ruled out because the arrow has been rotated.

10. B
Option A is ruled out because the trapezium and the pentagon are connected to the wrong sides of the triangle. Option C is ruled out because the trapezium is connected to the wrong side of the triangle. Option D is ruled out because the pentagon is connected to the trapezium instead of the triangle.

11. D
Option A is ruled out because the first shape is connected to the second shape by the wrong side. Option B is ruled out because the rectangle is connected to the wrong side of the second shape. Option C is ruled out because the rectangle and the first shape are connected to the wrong sides of the second shape.

12. A
Option B is ruled out because the triangle is connected to the first shape instead of the square. Option C is ruled out because the square is connected to the wrong side of the first shape. Option D is ruled out because the wrong side of the triangle is connected to the square.

13. C
Option A is ruled out because the rectangle is connected to the wrong side of the L-shape. Option B is ruled out because the L-shape and the T-shape are connected by the wrong sides. Option D is ruled out because the rectangle is connected to the T-shape instead of the L-shape.

Puzzles 6 — page 68

Hear Me Roar
B

Crown Calamity
D

Test 19 — pages 69-71

1. B
The top block in B has been rotated 90 degrees towards you, top-to-bottom, to become the block at the bottom of the figure. The other block in B is on top of it.

2. D
The top block in D is the block at the front of the figure. The other two blocks in D are arranged underneath and behind it.

3. B
The middle block in B is at the back of the figure, on the left. The other two blocks in B are arranged in front and to the right of it.

4. B
The top block in B is rotated 90 degrees clockwise in the plane of the page. The bottom left block in B is arranged on top of it. The bottom right block in B goes at the front of the figure.

5. C
There should be a horizontal blue block at the very front of the figure at the top. This rules out options A, B and D.

6. D
There should be a vertical block three cubes high at the right of the figure, which rules out options A and B. There should be a horizontal block two cubes wide at the back of the figure, which rules out option C.

7. A
There should be a block two cubes wide at the front of the figure at the top, which rules out option B. The block at the back of the figure on the right should not have any other block on top of it, which rules out options C and D.

8. B
There should be a vertical block two cubes high at the front centre of the figure, which rules out option C. This block is only connected to the rest of the figure along one edge, which rules out options A and D.

9. D
There should be a vertical block two cubes high at the front centre of the figure, which rules out option A. There should be no block immediately behind this block, which rules out option C. There should be a block lying on its side at the front right of the figure, which rules out option B.

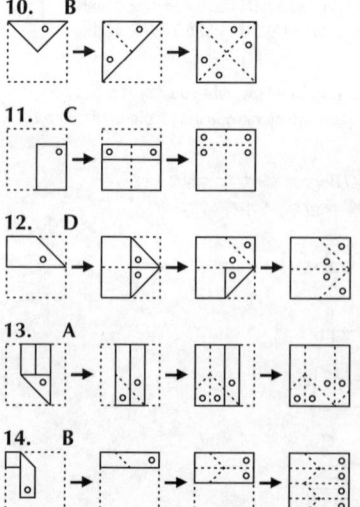

Test 20 — pages 72-74

1. B
Option A is ruled out because the semicircle is connected to the wrong side of the rectangle. Options C and D are ruled out because the arch is not connected to the rectangle.

2. A
Option B is ruled out because the large rectangle is not connected to the small rectangle. Option C is ruled out because the square is connected to the wrong side of the small rectangle. Option D is ruled out because the wrong side of the large rectangle is connected to the small rectangle.

3. C
Option A is ruled out because the square is not connected to the star. Option B is ruled out because the square and the triangle should not be connected to adjacent sides of the star. Option D is ruled out because the square and the triangle are connected to the wrong sides of the star.

4. A
Option B is ruled out because the pentagon and the wavy shape are connected to the wrong sides of the heart. Option C is ruled out because the wrong side of the wavy shape is connected to the heart. Option D is ruled out because the pentagon is not connected to the heart.

5. E
Shape E has been rotated 90 degrees away from you top-to-bottom.

6. F
Shape F has been rotated 90 degrees anticlockwise in the plane of the page. It has then been rotated 90 degrees right-to-left.

7. B
Shape B has been rotated 90 degrees away from you from top-to-bottom. It has then been rotated 90 degrees left-to-right.

8. A
Shape A has been rotated 90 degrees away from you, top-to-bottom.

9. D
Shape D has been rotated 180 degrees top-to-bottom. It has then been rotated 90 degrees anticlockwise in the plane of the page.

10. C
Shape C has been rotated 90 degrees anticlockwise in the plane of the page. It has then been rotated 180 degrees left-to-right.

11. B
Option B fits at the front of the figure on the right.

12. A
Option A is rotated 90 degrees left-to-right. It then fits at the front of the figure.

13. B
Option B rotates 90 degrees clockwise in the plane of the page. It then fits at the right of the figure.

14. D
Option D is rotated 90 degrees anticlockwise in the plane of the page. It is then rotated 90 degrees from left-to-right. It then fits at the right of the figure.

Test 21 — pages 75-77

1. B
Option A is ruled out because the fold line has moved. Option C is ruled out because the part of the figure that has not been folded is the wrong shape. Option D is ruled out because the part of the figure originally below the fold line should still be visible.

2. C
Option A is ruled out because the part of the figure that has been folded is the wrong shape. Option B is ruled out because the part of the figure originally above the fold line should still be visible. Option D is ruled out because the fold line has moved.

3. D
Options A and B are ruled out because the fold line has moved. Option C is ruled out because the part of the figure originally below the fold line should still be visible.

4. A
Options B and D are ruled out because the part of the figure that has been folded is the wrong shape. Option C is ruled out because the fold line has moved.

5. B
Options A and D are ruled out because the part of the figure that has been folded is the wrong shape. Option C is ruled out because the figure has been broken apart along the fold line.

6. C
Options A, B and D are ruled out because the sun and the part-circle are on opposite sides.

7. D
Option A is ruled out because if the cube is folded so that the heart is on the front and the pentagon is on the top, the black stripe would be on the left. Option B is ruled out because the pentagon and the black stripe are on opposite sides. Option C is ruled out because the end of the black stripe should point towards the heart.

8. C
Option A is ruled out because the M and the circle are on opposite sides. Option B is ruled out because if the cube is folded so that the spiral is on the front and the M is on the top, the circle would be on the left. Option D is ruled out because if the cube is folded the top of the M would point towards the spiral.

9. C
Option A is ruled out because if the cube is folded the arrow will point towards the triangle. Option B is ruled out because the arrow and the triangle are on opposite sides. Option D is ruled out because the trapezium has been rotated.

10. C   **11. D**

12. C   **13. A**

14. D

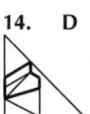

Puzzles 7 — page 78

Shape Shading

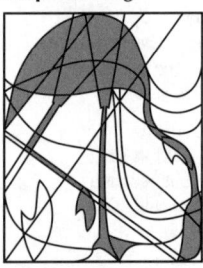

Cubic Conundrum
B at the front. D at the side.

Test 22 — pages 79-81

1. B
The top block in B goes at the front of the figure. The middle block in B goes behind it. The bottom block in B is arranged on top of the other two blocks.

2. A
The top right block in A goes at the front of the figure. The other three blocks are arranged behind it.

3. D
One of the middle blocks in D goes at the front of the figure. The other middle block and the bottom block in D go behind it. The top block in D goes at the back of the figure.

4. B
The bottom block in B goes at the back of the figure. The top block in B goes in front of it. The other two blocks are arranged on top.

5. A
6. C
7. C
8. B
9. D

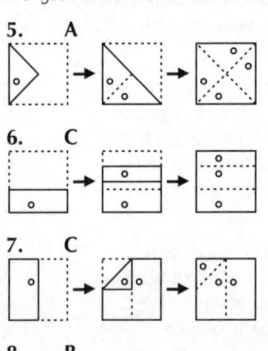

10. D   **11. A**

Test 23 — pages 82-84

12. D   **13. D**

   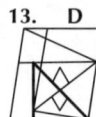

14. B

1. B
Option A is ruled out because the semicircle is not connected to the largest shape. Option C is ruled out because the rectangle and the semicircle are connected to the wrong sides of the largest shape. Option D is ruled out because the rectangle is connected to the wrong side of the largest shape.

2. D
Options A and C are ruled out because the pentagon and the arrow shape are connected to the wrong sides of the L shape. Option B is ruled out because the arrow shape is connected to the wrong side of the L shape.

3. A
Options B and C are ruled out because the rectangle is connected to the wrong side of the largest shape. Option D is ruled out because the wrong side of the rectangle is connected to the largest shape.

4. B
Options A and D are ruled out because the triangle is connected to the wrong side of the largest shape. Option C is ruled out because the wrong side of the triangle is connected to the largest shape.

5. F
Shape F is rotated 90 degrees anticlockwise in the plane of the page.

6. B
Shape B is rotated 90 degrees away from you, top-to-bottom.

7. C
Shape C is rotated 180 degrees in the plane of the page.

8. A
Shape A is rotated 90 degrees anticlockwise in the plane of the page. It is then rotated 90 degrees away from you, top-to-bottom.

9. D
Shape D is rotated 180 degrees left-to-right. It is then rotated 90 degrees towards you, top-to-bottom.

10. E
Shape E is rotated 180 degrees left-to-right. It is then rotated 90 degrees away from you, top-to-bottom.

11. B
Option A is ruled out because there is only one blue rectangular face on the net. Option C is ruled out because there are no white diamond-shaped faces on the net. Option D is ruled out because there are no grey rectangular faces on the net.

12. A
Option B is ruled out because the grey five-sided face should be blue. Option C is ruled out because the blue five-sided face should be grey. Option D is ruled out because the grey rectangular face should be white.

13. D
Option A is ruled out because the top right triangular face should be white. Option B is ruled out because the top left triangular face should be white. Option C is ruled out because the bottom right triangular face should be blue.

14. C
Option A is ruled out because the top rectangular face should be blue. Option B is ruled out because the middle triangular face should be blue. Option D is ruled out because the right rectangular face should be blue.

Test 24 — pages 85-87

1. A
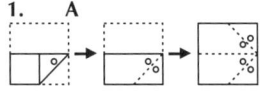

2. A
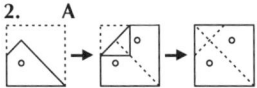

3. D
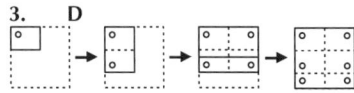

4. B
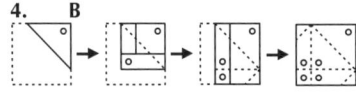

5. C
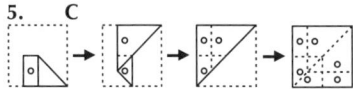

6. A
There are five blocks visible from the back, which rules out options B and C. There is one blue block visible on the left, which rules out option D.

7. D
There are five blocks visible from the back, which rules out options A and C. There is only one grey block visible on the top row, which rules out option B.

8. D
There are six blocks visible from the back, which rules out options B and C. There are two blocks visible on the left, which rules out option A.

9. B
There are six blocks visible from the back, which rules out option C. There are three blocks visible on the left, which rules out option D. There are two blocks visible on the right, which rules out option A.

10. D
There are six blocks visible from the back, which rules out option A. There are two blocks visible on the right, which rules out option B. There is a block visible on the bottom left, which rules out option C.

11. A
Option B is ruled out because there is no white ring shape on the net. Option C is ruled out because the white circle and the black triangle must be on opposite sides. Option D is ruled out because the black three-pointed star and the white triangle must be on opposite sides.

12. B
Option A is ruled out because the black rectangle and the white trapezium must be on opposite sides. Option C is ruled out because if the grey cross is on the front and the black rectangle is on the top, then the white oval should be on the right. Option D is ruled out because the grey star and the white oval must be on opposite sides.

13. B
Option A is ruled out because the grey triangles should point towards the black moon shape. Option C is ruled out because the black L-shape has been rotated. Option D is ruled out because the bases of the grey triangles should be near the spiral.

14. C
Option A is ruled out because if the white arrows are on the front and the grey triangle is on the right, then the white circle should be on the top. Option B is ruled out because the face with the grey arrows has been rotated. Option D is ruled out because the white arrows should point towards the base of the white triangle.

Test 25 — pages 88-90

1. C
The third cube view is the second cube view rotated 90 degrees away from you, top-to-bottom, then rotated 90 degrees right-to-left, so the arrow is on the front.

2. D
The third cube view is the first cube view rotated 90 degrees right-to-left, then rotated 180 degrees in the plane of the page, so the line is on the right.

3. C
The third cube view is the first cube view rotated 90 degrees right-to-left, then rotated 180 degrees in the plane of the page, so the teardrop is on the right.

4. B
The second cube view is the first cube view rotated 180 degrees right-to-left, so the circles are at the back. The third cube view is the second cube view rotated 90 degrees right-to-left, so the circles are on the right.

5. D
Option A is ruled out because the diamond is the wrong colour. Option B is ruled out because if it was folded so that the star is on top and the squares are at the front, then the diamond would be on the left. Option C is ruled out because the star is opposite the squares.

6. B
Option A is ruled out because the rectangle with the arrow has been rotated. Option C is ruled out because if it was folded so that the rectangle with the arrow is on top and the cross is at the front, then the circles would be on the left. Option D is ruled out because the rectangle with the arrow is the wrong colour.

7. C
Option A is ruled out because if it was folded so that the teardrop is on top and the circle is at the front, then the arrow would be on the left. Option B is ruled out because the circle and arrow are on opposite sides. Option D is ruled out because the teardrop has been rotated.

8. D
Option A is ruled out because the banner and the lines are on opposite sides. Option B is ruled out because the lines have been rotated. Option C is ruled out because the banner has been rotated.

9. B
There should be a vertical block two cubes tall at the front of the figure on the right, which rules out option A. There should be a block two cubes long lying on its side at the bottom of the figure at the front. There should be a cube directly behind this. This rules out options C and D.

10. D
There should be a cube on the right of the figure at the front, which rules out options A and B. There should not be a block on top of the cube, which rules out option C.

11. B
There should be a block two cubes tall at the back of the figure on the left. This rules out option A. There should be a block two cubes long at the front of the figure on the left. This rules out option C. There should not be a cube at the back of the figure, which rules out option D.

12. A
There should be a block two cubes long at the top of the figure on the left. This rules out option B. There should be a cube on the front right of the figure at the top. This rules out option D. There should be a block two cubes tall at the back of the figure, in the middle. This rules out option C.

13. D
There should be a vertical block two cubes tall on the left of the figure, which rules out option A.
The vertical block should have a cube directly in front of it, at the top. This rules out option B. There should be a cube in the centre of the figure at the bottom. This rules out option C.

Puzzles 8 — page 91

Watch Your Step!

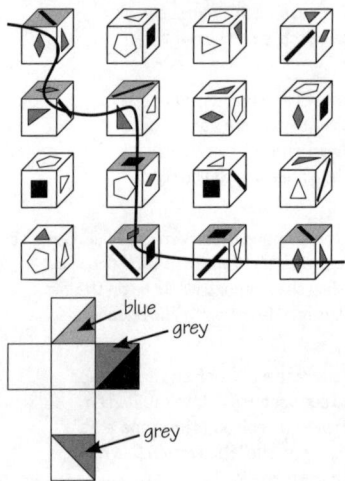

Test 26 — pages 92-94

1. C
The top block in C goes at the back of the figure. The bottom left block in C is arranged beneath it. The bottom right block in C goes at the front of the figure.

2. C
The bottom block in C goes at the back of the figure. The top right block in C goes on top of it. The top left block in C goes at the front of the figure.

3. B
The top block in B goes at the back of the figure. One of the single cubes in B is arranged on top of it. The other two blocks in B are arranged at the front of the figure.

4. A
The top block in A is arranged at the right of the figure, pointing backwards into the page. The bottom left and bottom right blocks in A are arranged to the left of it.

5. B
There should be a blue block two cubes long on the left of the figure, which rules out options C and D. There should be a grey block two cubes long at the front of the figure, which rules out option A.

6. D
There should be a blue block two cubes long at the back left of the figure, which rules out options A and C. There should be a single cube at the back of the figure on the right, which rules out option B.

7. C
There shouldn't be a cube at the back bottom left of the figure, which rules out options B and D. The blue cube should be beneath the top horizontal grey block, which rules out option A.

8. C
The top block in the figure should be coming out of the page, which rules out option D. There should be a horizontal block two cubes long on the left of the figure, which rules out options A and B.

9. D
The block on the left-hand side of the figure should be coming out of the page, which rules out options A and C. The block on the left-hand side of the figure should not be beneath any other block, which rules out option B.

10. C   **11. B**

12. D 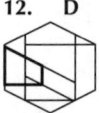 **13. C**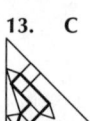

14. A

Test 27 — pages 95-97

1. D
Option A is ruled out because the trapezium is connected to the wrong side of the rectangle. Option B is ruled out because the rectangle is connected to the wrong side of the T-shape. Option C is ruled out because the trapezium is connected to the T-shape instead of the rectangle.

2. B
Option A is ruled out because the third shape is connected to the cross instead of the pentagon. Option C is ruled out because the pentagon is connected to the wrong side of the cross. Option D is ruled out because the third shape is connected to the wrong side of the pentagon.

3. **C**
Option A is ruled out because the third shape is connected to the wrong side of the second shape. Option B is ruled out because the third shape is connected to the rectangle with the arrow instead of the second shape. Option D is ruled out because the second shape is connected to the wrong side of the rectangle with the arrow.

4. **B**
Option A is ruled out because the parallelogram is connected to the wrong side of the triangle. Option C is ruled out because the wrong side of the parallelogram is connected to the triangle. Option D is ruled out because the third shape is connected to the parallelogram instead of the triangle.

5. **D**
Option A is ruled out because the pentagon has been rotated. Option B is ruled out because if the pentagon is on the top and the triangles are at the front, then the circle should be on the left. Option C is ruled out because the pentagon and triangles are on opposite sides.

6. **B**
Option A is ruled out because the black and grey squares and the circles and squares are on opposite sides. Option C is ruled out because if the black and grey squares are on the top, and the double arrow is at the front, then the circles and squares should be on the left. Option D is ruled out because the circles and squares have been rotated.

7. **D**
Option A is ruled out because the rectangles have been rotated. Option B is ruled out because the rectangle with the arrow is the wrong colour. Option C is ruled out because if the rectangles are on the top and the D is at the front, then the rectangle with the arrow should be on the left.

8. **C**
Option A is ruled out because the white arrow has been rotated. Option B is ruled out because the black three-headed arrow has been rotated. Option D is ruled out because if the grey arrow is on the top and the black arrow is at the front, then the white arrow should be on the left.

9. **A**
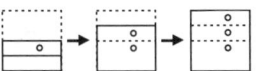

10. **D**
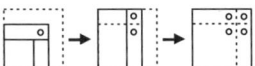

11. **B**
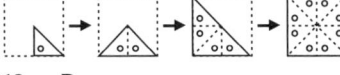

12. **D**
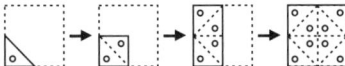

13. **C**
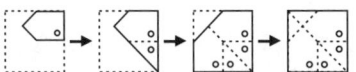

Test 28 — pages 98-100

1. **B**
The bottom block in B goes at the back of the figure. The other blocks in B are arranged in front of it.

2. **C**
The top block in C goes at the back of the figure. The other two blocks are arranged below and in front of it.

3. **D**
The bottom block in D goes at the front of the figure. The other two blocks are arranged behind it.

4. **B**
The middle block in B goes at the back left of the figure. The bottom block in B goes at the back of the figure at the bottom. The top block in B is arranged on top of it.

5. **A**
Shape A fits on the back of the figure.

6. **C**
Shape C fits underneath the figure.

7. **D**
Shape D rotates 180 degrees right-to-left. It then fits on the back right of the figure.

8. **A**
Shape A rotates 90 degrees anticlockwise in the plane of the page. It then fits on the back left of the figure.

9. **B**
Options A and C are ruled out because the fold line has moved. Option D is ruled out because the part of the figure originally below the fold line is the wrong shape.

10. **C**
Option A is ruled out because the fold line has moved. Option B is ruled out because the figure has broken apart along the fold line. Option D is ruled out because the part of the figure originally to the left of the fold line is the wrong shape.

11. **D**
Options A and C are ruled out because the fold line has moved. Option B is ruled out because the part of the figure originally to the right of the fold line is the wrong shape.

12. **A**
Option B is ruled out because the part of the figure to the left of the fold line should still be visible. Option C is ruled out because the fold line has moved. Option D is ruled out because the figure has broken apart at the fold line.

13. **A**
Option B is ruled out because the part of the figure originally below the fold line should still be visible. Option C is ruled out because the part of the figure originally above the fold line is the wrong shape. Option D is ruled out because the figure has been broken apart along the fold line.

Test 29 — pages 101-103

1. **A**
The third cube view is the first cube view rotated 90 degrees towards you, top-to-bottom, then 90 degrees anticlockwise in the plane of the page. So the black diamond is on the right.

2.   D
The second cube view is the first cube view rotated 90 degrees away from you, top-to-bottom, then 90 degrees left-to-right. So the white V-shape is on the left. The third cube view is the second cube view rotated 90 degrees clockwise in the plane of the page. So the white V-shape is on the top.

3.   B
The second cube view is the first cube view rotated 90 degrees right-to-left, then 90 degrees towards you, top-to-bottom. So the four-leafed clover shape is on the left. The third cube view is the second cube view rotated 90 degrees right-to-left, then 90 degrees towards you, top-to-bottom. So the four-leafed clover shape is on the top.

4.   A
The first cube view is the second cube view rotated 90 degrees right-to-left, then 90 degrees away from you, top-to-bottom. So the white circle is at the back. The third cube view is the first cube view rotated 90 degrees right-to-left, then 90 degrees away from you, top-to-bottom. So the white circle is on the right.

5.   C
There are four blocks visible from the left, which rules out options A and D. There is one blue block visible on the bottom row, which rules out option B.

6.   B
There are six blocks visible from the left, which rules out options A and C. The are no blue blocks visible, which rules out option D.

7.   D
There are six blocks visible from the left, which rules out options B and C. There are three blocks visible in the bottom row, which rules out option A.

8.   A
There are six blocks visible from the left, which rules out option D. There are three blocks visible in the middle column, which rules out options B and C.

9.   C
There are seven blocks visible from the left, which rules out option A. There are three blocks visible in the bottom row, which rules out options B and D.

10.   C
Option A is ruled out because there are no white square faces on the net. Option B is ruled out because there are no grey triangular faces next to white triangular faces on the net. Option D is ruled out because there are no blue triangular faces next to each other on the net.

11.   D
Option A is ruled out because there are no grey rectangular faces on the net. Option B is ruled out because there are no blue rectangular faces next to each other on the net. Option C is ruled out because the blue rectangular face on the right should be white.

12.   D
Option A is ruled out because the rectangular face on the bottom right should be grey. Option B is ruled out because the white rectangular face should be blue. Option C is ruled out because the top blue rectangular face should be grey.

13.   B
Option A is ruled out because the white rectangular face on the left should be grey. Option C is ruled out because the grey rectangular face should be white. Option D is ruled out because the white rectangular face on the right should be grey.

Puzzles 9 — page 104

Say Cheese!
D

Frantic Folding

A B

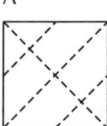 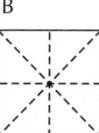

Test 30 — pages 105-107

1. B   2. C

 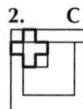

3. C   4. D

 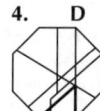

5. C

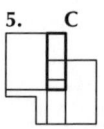

6.   A
There should be a block two cubes long on the left-hand side at the bottom, which rules out options B and D. There should be a block two cubes long coming out of the page on the right-hand side, which rules out option C.

7.   B
There should be a block two cubes long on the right-hand side at the bottom, which rules out options A and D. There should be a cube at the front, which rules out option C.

8.   A
There should be a single cube at the top, which rules out option B. There should be a block two cubes long coming out of the page on the bottom left-hand side, which rules out option C. There should be a block at least two cubes long at the bottom on the right-hand side, which rules out option D.

9.   C
There should be a block two cubes long going into the page at the back, which rules out options B and D. This block should not be directly below any other block, which rules out option A.

10.   D
There should be a block two cubes long lying on its side on the left-hand side at the back, which rules out options A and B. There should be two cubes on the left-hand side at the front, which rules out option C.

11.   B
Option A is ruled out because the square should be connected to the parallelogram. Option C is ruled out because the wrong side of the trapezium is connected to the parallelogram. Option D is ruled out because the square is connected to the wrong side of the parallelogram.

12. D
Option A is ruled out because the square should be connected to the rectangle. Option B is ruled out because the square is connected to the wrong side of the rectangle. Option C is ruled out because the pentagon is connected to the wrong side of the rectangle.

13. C
Option A is ruled out because the wrong side of the L-shape is connected to the equilateral triangle. Option B is ruled out because the right-angled triangle and the equilateral triangle are connected by the wrong sides. Option D is ruled out because the right-angled triangle is connected to the wrong side of the equilateral triangle.

14. B
Option A is ruled out because the wrong side of the smaller L-shape is connected to the square. Option C is ruled out because the larger L-shape is connected to the wrong side of the square. Option D is ruled out because the smaller L-shape is connected to the wrong side of the square.

Test 31 — pages 108-110

1. D
There should be a blue block two cubes long at the front, which rules out options B and C. There should be a blue cube at the back, which rules out option A.

2. A
There should be a grey block three cubes long at the back, which rules out options B and D. There should be a grey block two cubes tall on the right-hand side, which rules out option C.

3. D
There should be a cube at the front on the left, which rules out option A. There should be a block two cubes long at the bottom right, which rules out option B. There should be a block two cubes long on the right-hand side at the top, which rules out option C.

4. C
There should be a cube at the front, which rules out options B and D. There should be a block two cubes long directly beneath the cube, which rules out option A.

5. B
Option A is ruled out because there is no grey circle on the net. Option C is ruled out because the arrow and the pentagon must be on opposite sides. Option D is ruled out because the rectangles and the circle must be on opposite sides.

6. B
Option A is ruled out because if the square is on the front and the three rectangles are on the top, then the T-shape would be on the left. Option C is ruled out because the trapezium and the square must be on opposite sides. Option D is ruled out because the T-shape and the grey circles must be on opposite sides.

7. A
Option B is ruled out because the hexagon and the arch must be on opposite sides. Option C is ruled out because if the arch is on the front and the parallelogram is on the top, then the teardrop would be on the left. Option D is ruled out because the I-shape has been rotated.

8. D
Option A is ruled out because if the flower shape is on the front and the pie shape is on the top, then the triangle would be on the left. Option B is ruled out because the four squares have been rotated. Option C is ruled out because if the four squares are on the front and the wave is on the top, then the triangle would be on the left.

9. A

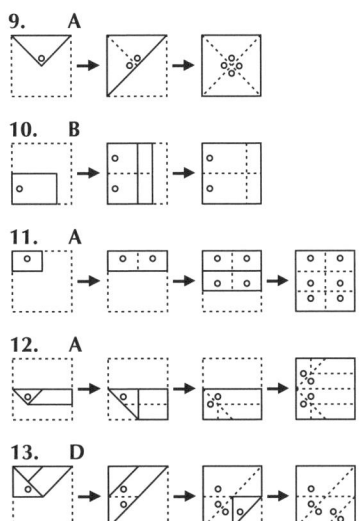

10. B

11. A

12. A

13. D

Test 32 — pages 111-113

1. B
Shape B has been rotated 90 degrees anticlockwise in the plane of the page.

2. F
Shape F has been rotated 90 degrees clockwise in the plane of the page.

3. A
Shape A has been rotated 90 degrees towards you, top-to-bottom. It has then been rotated 90 degrees clockwise in the plane of the page.

4. E
Shape E has been rotated 90 degrees away from you, top-to-bottom. It has then been rotated 90 degrees anticlockwise in the plane of the page.

5. B
Options A and C are ruled out because the fold line has moved. Option D is ruled out because the part of the figure originally below the fold line is the wrong shape.

6. B
Option A is ruled out because the part of the figure originally above the fold line is the wrong shape. Option C is ruled out because the fold line has moved. Option D is ruled out because the figure has broken apart along the fold line.

7. A
Option B is ruled out because the figure has broken apart along the fold line. Option C is ruled out because the part of the figure originally to the left of the fold line is the wrong shape. Option D is ruled out because the fold line has moved.

8. C
Option A is ruled out because the part of the figure originally to the left of the fold line should still be visible. Option B is ruled out because the figure has broken apart along the fold line. Option D is ruled out because the fold line has moved.

9. D
Option A is ruled out because the part of the figure originally to the left of the fold line is the wrong shape. Option B is ruled out because the figure has broken apart along the fold line. Option C is ruled out because the fold line has moved.

10. B
The left block in B is at the front of the figure on the right-hand side. The block at the bottom right in B is at the front of the figure on the left-hand side. The cube in B goes behind it.

11. D
The top block in D is at the back of the figure. The other two blocks in D are arranged in front of it.

12. C
The top block in C is at the back of the figure. The front left block in C is on the front left of the figure, and the cube in C is on the front right of the figure.

13. B
The block at the top left in B is at the back of the figure. The block at the bottom left in B is below it. The other two blocks in B are arranged at the front.

Test 33 — pages 114-116

1. B
The third cube view is the second cube view rotated 90 degrees right-to-left. So the triangle is on the top.

2. A
The third cube view is the first cube view rotated 90 degrees right-to-left, then 90 degrees clockwise in the plane of the page. So the trapezium is on the top.

3. B
The third cube view is the first cube view rotated 90 degrees towards you, top-to-bottom. So the circle with the cross is on the right.

4. B
The second cube view is the first cube view rotated 90 degrees clockwise in the plane of the page, then 90 degrees right-to-left. So the face with the four circles is on the left.
The third cube view is the second cube view rotated 180 degrees left-to-right. So the grey cross is on top.

5. D
There should only be one block at the front of the figure, which rules out options A and B. There should be a block two cubes tall at the back of the figure on the right-hand side, which rules out option C.

6. C
There should be a single cube on the left-hand side of the figure, which rules out option A. This cube should be at the back of the figure, which rules out option D. There should be a blue block at the bottom of the figure on the right-hand side, which rules out option B.

7. A
There should be a block two cubes tall at the back of the figure on the right-hand side, which rules out option B. There should be a single cube at the back of the figure on the left-hand side, which rules out option C. There should be a block two cubes long lying on its side at the front of the figure, which rules out option D.

8. B
There should be a single cube on the left-hand side of the figure, which rules out option A. This cube should not be at the back of the figure, which rules out option D. There should not be a cube at the front of the figure, which rules out option C.

9. C
There should be a block two cubes long going into the page on the right-hand side, which rules out option A. There should be a cube on the left-hand side at the back of the figure, which rules out option B. There should be a block two cubes tall at the back of the figure, which rules out option D.

10. B
Option B fits on the left-hand side of the figure.

11. C
Option C rotates 90 degrees clockwise in the plane of the page. It then fits at the back of the figure.

12. D
Option D rotates 180 degrees in the plane of the page. It then fits on the right-hand side of the figure at the back.

13. A
Option A rotates 90 degrees anticlockwise in the plane of the page. It then fits on the front of the figure.

Puzzles 10 — page 117

All for Nought (and Crosses)

Lily

Origami Animals

C

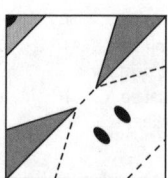